EMPLOYMENT LAW AND BUSINESS TRANSFERS: A PRACTICAL GUIDE

AUSTRALIA AND NEW ZEALAND
The Law Book Company Ltd.
Sydney : Melbourne : Perth

CANADA
The Carswell Company Ltd.
Agincourt, Ontario

INDIA
N.M. Tripathi Private Ltd.
Bombay
and
Eastern Law House Private Ltd.
M.P.P. House
Bangalore

ISRAEL
Steimatzky's Agency Ltd.
Jerusalem : Tel Aviv : Haifa

PAKISTAN
Pakistan Law House
Karachi

Property of
Group Legal

Group Legal + Admin
Royal Bank of Scotland
4th Floor
42 St. Andrew Sq.
Edinburgh.

EMPLOYMENT LAW AND BUSINESS TRANSFERS: A PRACTICAL GUIDE

FRASER R. YOUNSON, M.A. (Oxon)
Solicitor with Baker & McKenzie

LONDON SWEET & MAXWELL 1989

Published in 1989 by
Sweet & Maxwell Limited
South Quay Plaza,
183 Marsh Wall, London
Computerset by MFK Graphics,
Hitchin, Herts
Printed by Butler & Tanner,
Frome, Somerset

British Library Cataloguing in Publication Data
Employment law & business transfers: a practical guide.
1. Great Britain. Business firms. Personnel. Rights
344.104' 12596

ISBN 0-421 40530-9

ACKNOWLEDGEMENTS

The task of writing a book whilst practising as a busy employment lawyer, is not one to be taken lightly. It makes unreasonable demands on others who may have to take some of the strain. The author is therefore indebted to his colleagues in Baker & McKenzie's employment and pensions departments for their comments and suggestions, and in particular to Melanie Tether (also an employment lawyer) for her very helpful suggestions on style and content.

The author also wishes to thank (again) the legal researchers from IDS Brief and Industrial Relations Legal Information Bulletin for their continued accurate and fast reporting of cases, and HMSO for its permission to reproduce various extracts of legislation contained in Appendix C. Thanks is also due to the publishers for their patience and suggestions during the editing and production stages of this book.

Finally, but not least, I thank my wife, Gilly, for her support, patience and understanding during the preparation of this book.

F.R.Y.

PREFACE

In most companies, the workforce is one of its most important assets. So where its control or business is transferred to a third party, it is bound to have widespread repercussions for employees. Prior to 1982, the law provided them with little by way of employment protection. Most certainly there was no obligation upon the transferee of the business to offer them employment or to maintain their existing terms and conditions. However, the EEC "Business Transfer" Directive required the United Kingdom Government to implement its provisions; and this was put into effect by the Transfer of Undertakings (Protection of Employment) Regulations 1981.

The effect of these Regulations has been to introduce into the commercial equation, that makes up a business disposal or acquisition, an employment cost or liability in respect of the vendor's employees. The principle behind the Regulations is to place the purchaser into the vendor's shoes in respect of employment matters—*i.e.* the vendor's employees automatically transfer into the purchaser's employment together with their terms and conditions of employment. The result is a need for the purchaser to recognise the costs and liabilities that it will inherit from the vendor and make provision for the imminent and contingent liabilities that the Regulations create. There are also pitfalls for the vendor—especially where the purchaser requires the vendor to effect changes prior to the completion of the transaction (*e.g.* to make redundancies).

This book is, therefore, a practical guide to the employment law matters which need to be borne in mind in the context of business and share transfers. The first half explains the legal ramifications; and the second half is a practical approach (including sample documentation) indicating how to deal with those employment law problems. This book will therefore be of assistance to vendors and purchasers of companies and businesses, and their legal and financial advisors. It will also be very helpful to senior personnel advisers by pointing them in the direction of potential pitfalls.

It is important to note that this book deals with the employment law issues not only arising out of business transfers but also in respect of share transfers. The former concerns the transfer of business assets in the nature of a "going concern" and the latter with a change of ownership in the controlling shares of a company. Although the employment law ramifications in respect of the former are more pronounced, it should not be forgotten that some of them appear in respect of share transfers. However, this book does not deal with pensions schemes in the context of business or share transfer, except as these form part of employment law rights.

Throughout this book, the terms "vendor" and "purchaser" have been used to represent the transferor and the transferee of a business. This has been done to make the text more readable and because, in most cases, business transfers will be conducted between vendors and purchasers. However, it is important to note that the principles applied to vendors and purchasers, apply equally to other transferors and transferees. For example, it is now clear that the employment law implications of the Transfer Regulations (*sic*) also apply on the grant and surrender of certain business tenancies or licences, concessions, franchises and the provision of services. In this context, the licensor or landlord may on the surrender of a business franchise or licence be treated as the transferee of the business operated under that licence or franchise.

The Transfer Regulations are not drafted in the simplest of legal language and are designed to be superimposed on existing employment protection and the common law. Whilst the author has tried to deal with some of the more technical and academic issues thrown up by the wording of the Regulations, this book is primarily a practical one. It highlights the problem areas and makes suggestions on how these might be tackled; and in this respect he has drawn on the practical experiences of his own and his colleagues in Baker & McKenzie's employment department. The law is correct as at March 1989.

Fraser Younson

Baker & McKenzie
Aldwych House
Aldwych
London WC 2
March 1989

CONTENTS

ABBREVIATIONS

All E.R.	All England Law Reports
C.A.	Court of Appeal
Ch.D.	Chancery Division Law Reports
C.M.L.R.	Common Market Law Reports
C.R.E.	Commission for Racial Equality
C.S.	Court of Session
E.A.T.	Employment Appeal Tribunal
E.C.J.	European Court of Justice
E.O.C.	Equal Opportunities Commission
E.P.A.	Employment Protection Act 1975 (as amended)
E.P.C.A.	Employment Protection (Consolidation) Act 1978
H.C.	High Court
H.L.	House of Lords
I.C.R.	Industrial Cases Reports
I.R.L.R.	Industrial Relations Law Reports
I.T.R.	Industrial Tribunal Reports
K.I.R.	Knights Industrial Reports
N.I.R.C.	National Industrial Relations Court
Q.B.	Queens Bench Law Reports
Transfer Regulations	Transfer of Undertakings (Protection of Employment) Regulations 1981
T.U.L.R.A.	Trade Union and Labour Relations Act 1974
W.L.R.	Weekly Law Reports

TABLE OF CASES

TABLE OF STATUTES

TABLE OF RULES

TABLE OF EEC DIRECTIVES

1 SETTING THE SCENE

Types of transfer

The last five years have seen a dramatic increase in the level of activity involving the buying and selling of businesses or business interests. These have normally been by way of:

1. the purchase of a controlling interest in the shares of the business (a "share transfer"); or
2. the purchase of the assets of a business to continue to run it either as a business in its own right or as part of a much larger business (a "business transfer"); or
3. the purchase of some of the physical assets of a business for use in another quite separate business enterprise (an "asset transfer"); or
4. the surrender of leases, licences or franchises with an immediate grant to another person (a "licence transfer").

All of the above events will, to a greater or lesser degree, have an impact on the position of employees working in the business. The new owner of the business may want to make changes to staffing levels, or to standard terms and conditions of employment, or to working methods or practices, or to collective bargaining arrangements, or to the organisation of work at particular workplaces (*e.g.* by changing hours of work or relocating departments to other sites). Even where the takeover of a business is by way of share acquisition, the new owner of the controlling share interest (often a parent company) may want to integrate its new acquisition into its other group activities and conditions of service—*e.g.* so that all employees of the newly acquired company will be members of its pension scheme.

For the top management a share or business transfer will, to some extent, impinge on their responsibilities and decision-making powers. For example, it may be a consequence of a share or business transfer that certain members of the Board of the acquired company are removed as directors, or they have to report to a Group Director. Such changes will affect their status within the company. For all of these reasons (and many others) share, business, asset or licence transfers are bound to affect employees' rights in some way. Their employers will, as a result, probably face employment and/or company law liabilities.

Common law position

Common law implications of a transfer for the employee

A distinction needs to be made between takeovers or acquisitions effected by a transfer of the controlling shares in a company (*i.e.* a "share transfer") and the other three usual forms of disposing of business interests—*i.e.* business, or asset or licence transfers. The key lies in what happens to the legal identity of the employer.

"Share transfers"

The legal identity of the employer remains the same—all that has happened is ownership of the controlling interest in its issued share capital has changed. The employees are still employed under their existing contracts of employment by the same employer (*e.g.* X Ltd.); but the owner of some or all of the shares in X Ltd. has changed. This produces a simple analysis of the common law position in respect of persons employed by X Ltd.—there is no change! The mere fact of a change in ownership of the shares does not, of itself, constitute a breach of employment contracts. However it should be noted that various organisational and other changes made by the new owners subsequent to their acquisition of the controlling interest in the shares of X Ltd. may result in a breach of contract—depending on the nature and effect of those changes.

"Business transfers"

Since a contract of employment is one involving the performance of services by an employee personally, it cannot be assigned or transferred to another employer without the consent of both the employee and the prospective new employer. This means that an employee has no common law right to insist on transferring across with the business to a new employer; and likewise the purchaser of the business has no common law obligation to offer him employment on his existing contract terms, or at all. The purchaser employer has no obligation to the vendor's employees at common law, unless it has created some legal right upon which the employee can rely—*e.g.* by offering him employment.

Where the purchaser offers employment to some or all of the vendor's employees, the legal identity of their employer will change for those employees who take up the offer. For example, X Ltd. may decide to sell its entire business to Y Ltd., but retain its corporate identity for tax or other reasons. In practice X Ltd. will sell to Y Ltd. all or some of the following assets to enable Y Ltd. to carry on that business as a "going concern": machinery and equipment, customer lists, inventory, premises, goodwill, work in progress, existing contracts, cash, trade-marks other intellectual property etc. In effect, X Ltd. will be putting itself in a position where it cannot continue to employ its employees under their existing contracts of employment. Therefore X Ltd. will be repudiating the employment contracts of its employees—see *Nokes* v. *Doncaster Amalgamated Colleries Ltd.* [1940] A.C. 1014.

The same principle applies where X Ltd. decides to sell one of its divisions as a going concern. If, by doing so, X Ltd. puts it out of its power to continue to employ its employees in that division under their existing employment contracts, it will likewise be in breach of those contracts.

The *Nokes* case is not authority for the proposition that a "business transfer" of itself terminates the employment contracts—it is only authority for the proposition that a contract of employment cannot be assigned by the vendor of a business to the purchaser, without the employee's consent—see p. 48 for fuller discussion on the proper interpretation of the *Nokes* case.

It is important to note that, in the cases of those business transfers which are governed by the Transfer of Undertakings (Protection of Employment) Regulations 1981 [the "Transfer Regulations"]—with which this book is primarily concerned—the common law position is overridden. Those Regulations provide, amongst other things, that business transfer does not terminate employment contracts [see p. 6 below] and there is therefore no dismissal of employees by repudiatory breach of contract by the employer.

"Asset transfers"

This terminology is often used to embrace business transfers as well as the transfer of physical or intangible assets. Some commercial lawyers use it when distinquishing them from a share transfer. However this can be very confusing, and it is important to note the crucial distinction between business transfers and pure asset transfers. The former involves the disposal and acquisition of such a collection of a company's assets that what is being transferred is a business in the nature of a going concern. For example, the same business (*e.g.* making widgets) is being carried on after the transfer by another legal entity—*i.e.* by Y Ltd. instead of X Ltd.

In contrast, a transaction will be a pure "asset transfer" (not a business transfer) where the assets transferred do not, in fact, constitute a "going concern." For example an asset transfer might comprise of the sale of a particular factory or certain equipment or the remainder of a business lease on particular premises. The employer might remain in business, operating with other machinery or from new premises. The distinction between business transfers and asset transfers is an important one, and the dividing line can sometimes be rather blurred. Chapter 2 deals with this in some detail. At this stage it should be noted that neither the Transfer Regulations nor certain employment protection provisions apply to asset sales [see Chap. 3].

In many cases, an asset transfer may not involve a breach of the employment contract at common law. The employer may simply be selling old machinery because it is to purchase new equipment or has decided to stop manufacturing certain products. Alternatively the employer may be disposing of its business premises because it has decided to relocate to other premises. Again, the mere sale of the assets does not, of itself, put the employer in breach of the employment contracts of those of its employees affected by the sale. The key point is whether, by disposing of those assets, the employer has put itself into a position whereby it will be in breach of those employment contracts. This, in turn depends, on how those contracts are written.

For example, an employee's contractual job title might state that he is a "production operative." His employers may decide to shutdown a particular product line (*e.g.* making metal nuts and bolts) and sell the machinery used to manufacture that product. They might also decide to start up a new production line (*e.g.* making synthetic nuts and bolts), which involves new machinery. In such circumstances, the employers still have it within their power to retain the employee carrying out his contractual job duties as a "production operative"—he will simply be making another product. There will be no breach of contract by the employers. However, if the employee's contractual job title was more narrowly described as a "metal production operative," the employers would be in breach of his employment contract if they did not redeploy him in production work on metal products. Of course, if the employment contract gave the employers the right to redeploy the employee to other work, then again there would be no breach of contract provided the change of his job duties fell within the scope of the contractual right.

The same principle applies in respect of a disposal of business premises. Many employment contracts state an employee's workplace to be a particular factory or office. If they are silent on the matter, then the common law may imply particular premises to be his contractual place of work. Unless there is an express or implied right in the employment contract entitling the employer to change the employee's workplace, the disposal of the premises at which he works will put his employers into a position whereby they will inevitably breach his employment contract.

In the event of such a breach of contract, the employee has an option at common law. He can either acquiesce his employer's breach of contract and agree to his employment continuing under the changed terms, or accept the repudiatory breach and treat his contract as at an end. In the latter case, he will have a claim for damages for wrongful dismissal. These damages will be normally comprised of the net salary and other benefits of employment that he would have enjoyed had he been given his full notice entitlement. In such circumstances, he may also have claims for compensation for unfair dismissal and/or statutory redundancy pay [see Appendix A] if he has two years continuous service on the effective date of termination. Such claims will arise because the employee will be able to claim he has been "constructively dismissed." This is a statutory concept that enables an employee to launch unfair dismissal/redundancy pay claims, by treating himself as having been dismissed even though he has brought his employment to an end by resigning. It has been established that the test for constructive dismissal is: whether his employer has committed a repudiatory or significant breach of his employment contract?—*Western Excavating (ECC) Ltd.* v. *Sharp* [1978] I.C.R. 221. Thus it will be seen that, in some cases, a breach of contract at common law will give rise to the ability to pursue various statutory employment protection rights.

"Licence transfers"

This category covers those circumstances where the holder of a business licence, franchise, business tenancy decides to surrender it to the licensor, who then subsequently grants a new licence, franchise or tenancy to a third party, who then carries on much the same business activity as his predecessor. For example, it may cover small business enterprises such as pub tenancies, petrol station tenancies, franchises either within larger shops or on separate premises, or the sub-contracting out of self-contained business activities such as staff catering, office cleaning or product transport.

In these circumstances the question is whether the surrender and grant of a licence/tenancy/franchise, etc., can constitute a transfer of business between the outgoing and incoming licencees? Where it does so, the common law position will be exactly the same as for "business transfers" [see p. 21]. Where it does not, the common law position will be the same as for "asset transfers." In the latter case, the outgoing licencee is merely giving up an asset of its business (*i.e.* a licence or right to sell certain products or perform certain services at a particular location), with the consequential effects on employment contracts similar to the disposal of any other business asset [see above]. The distinction between these two circumstances is often blurred and is dealt with in detail on p. 21 below.

Any claim for damages for wrongful dismissal will lie against the vendor employer, not against the purchaser. This is because, under the common law, the employee has no contract with the purchaser upon which to found a claim.

Employment protection legislation

Statutory implications of transfers for employees

There are no special employment protection measures applicable to share transfers because the change in ownership of the shares of a company does not affect employment protection rights—employees remain employed by the same legal entity on their existing terms and conditions.

However, it will have been noticed that in the event of a business transfer or licence transfer, the common law provides employees with little employment protection, apart from their rights to be given due notice of termination of employment and redundancy pay. A purchaser of a business has no obligation to take on the vendor's existing employees. Even if the purchaser does offer them employment, under the common law it can do so under any terms and conditions it chooses (*e.g.* in a changed job, and on lesser salary and benefits). The purchaser can also be as selective as it chooses when offering employment to the vendor's employees, provided it does not discriminate on grounds of sex or race.

Under the common law, employments with two successive employers carrying on the same business enterprise are regarded as separate and distinct employments. This would mean that employees who had accumulated sufficient continuous service to claim various employment protection rights (*e.g.* unfair dismissal, redundancy pay or maternity rights) would immediately have to start from scratch re-qualifying for those rights. This is significant in the case of unfair dismissal, redundancy pay and maternity "job-back" rights all of which require two years qualifying service. Employment protection legislation therefore seeks to go some way towards protecting the position of employees in the the event of a business transfer.

Transfer of employment

The Regulations: background

The apparent unfairness of this situation has long been recognised. In 1977 the EEC "Business Transfer" Directive No. 77/187 came into force with the objectives of ensuring that:

1. union representatives of employees affected by the business transfer are informed and consulted by their respective employers; and
2. The employment contracts of those persons employed in the business to be transferred are automatically transferred to the purchaser along with the rest of the business; and
3. Employees are safeguarded against being dismissed in connection with a business transfer.

It was not until 1981 that Parliament passed the Transfer of Undertakings (Protection of Employment) Regulations 1981 which seeks to put an English interpretation of the Business Transfer Directive into effect in the United Kingdom. When steering the Regulations through Parliament Mr David Waddington (for the Government) said that he recommended them "with a remarkable lack of enthusiasm"! (Hansard 7.12.81 at col.680). For ease of reference these regulations are referred to as the "Transfer Regulations." This book deals mainly with their effect, which go a large measure of the way towards protecting employees' rights in the event of a business transfer. Their impact is substantial in respect of business transfers and some licence transfers; but they do not apply to share or pure asset transfers. Put simply, the Transfer Regulations have the following effect, *i.e.* they:

1. stop the common law rule operating by preventing the business transfer from constituting a dismissal—this means the employees automatically transfer across to the purchaser together with their existing terms and conditions (except pensions);
2. make the purchaser responsible for anything done by the vendor in connection with those transferring employees;
3. automatically transfer existing collective agreements and recognition rights in respect of the transferring employees;
4. provide that any dismissal connected with a business transfer is automatically unfair, unless the reason for the dismissal is a technical, organisational or economic reason entailing changes in the workforce;
5. require employers to inform and consult with trade unions they recognise for their employees affected by the business transfer.

It will be seen that the Transfer Regulations substantially change the common law position. The purchaser is forced to take on those persons who are the vendor's employees at the time of the transfer, and they in turn are automatically transferred across into the purchaser's employment regardless of their wishes. The purchaser must also continue to honour the terms and conditions of employment that they enjoyed with the vendor.

Continuity of employment

Effect on employees in a business transfer

Where employees are taken into the employment of the purchaser, they would lose their accrued statutory rights (*e.g.* protection against unfair dismissal, or entitlement to redundancy pay) if they had to re-qualify for those rights by accumulating a further two years continuous service. The unfairness of this position has been rectified by a provision in the statutory rules governing the calculation of periods of continuous service. Schedule 13 paragraph 17(2) of the Employment Protection (Consolidation) Act (E.P.C.A.) provides that, if a trade or business or undertaking is transferred, an employee's period of employment prior to the transfer counts as a period of employment with the transferee. However this rule only applies to those employees of the transferor at the time of the transfer. A fuller explanation of paragraph 17(2) and similar rules is on p. 137.

However paragraph 17(2) only applies to business transfers. It does not apply to either share or pure asset transfers. It is for this reason that the important distinction between business and pure asset transfers must be considered—see Chapter 2.

Redundancy pay

Forfeiture of redundancy pay

The operation of the common law rule meant that a business transfer would trigger a situation where an employee could claim that he had been dismissed. Since the vendor employer no longer had need for his services, he would be redundant within the statutory definition of redundancy [see p. 165] and eligible for redundancy pay. However, if the employee was promptly offered suitable alternative employment by the purchaser, he would get a windfall by remaining in employment, but still receiving his statutory redundancy pay. This would obviously be unfair on the vendor of the business and the redundancy pay costs would often be reflected in the purchase price paid by the purchaser.

To obviate this anomaly, E.P.C.A., s.94 provides that, where the transferee offers such an employee suitable alternative employment, that employee will forfeit his statutory redundancy pay if he unreasonably refuses that offer or unreasonably terminates the statutory one month trial period [see p. 141 for a fuller explanation of s.94].

EEC "business transfer" directive

Inconsistency between EEC acquired rights directive and the transfer regulations

The Transfer Regulations seek to implement the EEC Business Transfer Directive and, although they do in the most part achieve that objective, there are nonetheless differences between the two. These include the following areas:

1. The exclusion of business transfers not in the nature of a commercial venture from the ambit of the Transfer

Regulations, when there is no such limitation in the Directive [see p. 41]. It may be arguable that the Transfer Regulations should have adopted the existing statutory definition of the word "business" in section 153(1) E.P.C.A. which is widely defined to cover " . . . any trade, profession or other activity . . . " and contains no requirement that it must be in the nature of a commercial venture. In the case of *Wendleboe* v. *L.J. Music ApS* [1985] C.M.L.R. 496, the E.C.J. commented that the words of the Directive should be given their normal meaning under existing laws of Member States.

2. The obligation on the employer to give specified information to recognised trade unions about the business transfer refers to "long enough before the transfer to enable consultations to take place" in the Transfer Regulations whereas such information must be given "in good time before the transfer is carried out" under the Directive [see p. 119].
3. Under the Transfer Regulations the principle of the automatic transfer of employment is partially watered down where the business is being hived down by liquidators; yet there is no similar provision in the Directive [see p. 82].
4. The exclusion of employees' pension rights from automatic transfer to the employment by the purchaser is less far-reaching under the Directive than under the Transfer Regulations [see p. 71].
5. There may be strong arguments for saying that the literal application of the automatic transfer principle in the Transfer Regulations means that employees lose their common law right to refuse to transfer to the purchaser—unless they fall within the ambit of regulation 5(5)—see p. 77. Yet in the case of *E.C. Commission* v. *Belgium* [1986] 1988 2 C.M.L.R. 265, the E.C.J. said that the implementation of the Business Transfer Directive should not diminish employees' existing rights in any way.

These differences do not have any importance unless the EEC Directive is in some way enforceable by complainants in their Member States. Its significance as co-existing alongside the Transfer Regulations lies in two facets of its potential use:

1. as a cause of action in its own right and
2. as a tool for guidance by tribunals and courts when seeking to interpret those parts of the Transfer Regulations that are ambiguous.

However, the importance of a separate claim under the Business Transfer Directive may be relevant where it is felt that the Transfer Regulations, in fact, do not implement it properly. For example, it is now clear that the implementing legislation of the Member States must not cut down or limit any rights which employees already have—see *E.C. Commission* v. *Belgium* [1986] 2 C.M.L.R. 865, where the Belgian equivalent of the Transfer Regulations sought to exclude from its ambit protection against dismissal for probationary or student workers and those employees nearing retirement. The E.C.J. held that this was contrary to the Business Transfer Directive since these groups of workers had limited protection against unfair dismissal under existing Belgian employment protection law. It seems that a similar argument may arise in respect of the Transfer Regulations which, in effect, stop employees from objecting to the identity of their new employer on the transfer of their employment (except in very limited circumstances—see p. 77). By comparison, West Germany has interpreted the Business Transfer Directive as not diminishing, in any way, employees' existing employment rights and has therefore preserved employees' right to refuse to transfer to the new employer.

Direct enforceability

Enforceability of EEC directives

As a general principle, EEC Directives will be directly applicable in domestic courts where they are clear, self-contained and unconditional and their nature and wording are capable of being directly applied in domestic courts of EEC Member States—*Van Duyn* v. *Home Office* [1975] Ch.D. 358. However it has been established that EEC Directives are only directly enforceable against the State or organs of the State (such as area health authorities or Government Departments)—*Marshall* v. *Southampton & S.W. Hampshire Area Health Authority* [1986] I.R.L.R. 140. The Business Transfer Directive is not directly enforceable against other employers such as companies, charities, or other business entities or organisations. For example in *Foster* v. *British Gas plc.* [1988] I.R.L.R. 52, the Court of Appeal upheld the tribunal's conclusion that British Gas was not an organ or agent of the State prior to its privatisation. The Court commented that British Gas had not been administered directly by the Government but was a separate legal entity with its own governing authority—even though it was a nationalised industry. Similarly in *Rolls Royce* v. *Doughty* [1987] I.R.L.R. 447, the E.A.T. held that Rolls Royce plc was not an organ of the State, even though 100 per cent. of its shares were held by the State.

Jurisdiction of courts to hear action based on EEC directive

It is unclear whether the industrial tribunals or the ordinary courts are the proper forum for hearing claims based on EEC Directives. In the *Marshall* (see above) case the industrial tribunal applied the EEC "Equal Treatment" Directive, and in *Macarthys Ltd.* v. *Smith (No. 2)* [1980] I.R.L.R. 209, the Court of Appeal hinted that the industrial tribunal was the proper forum. However such decisions are open to question, since industrial tribunals are created by statute and have power to hear only those claims prescribed by statute. It is suggested that the proper forum for hearing cases under the EEC Business Transfer Directive is the High Court who has an inherent jurisdiction.

Resolving ambiguities

Conflict between EEC directives and English law

In *Duke* v. *G.E.C. Reliance Ltd.* [1988] I.R.L.R. 118; H.L. the House of Lords held that it was up to the domestic courts and tribunals to construe the meaning of a statute and that it was wrong for them to rely on an EEC Directive to construe a statutory provision, enacted prior to the promulgation of the Directive in question, to give effect to it. In other words, where

English law is in conflict with an EEC Directive which post dates it, the courts and tribunals cannot seek to give effect to the Directive by to construe the relevant provision of English law so that it conforms with the EEC Directive. This is a quite distinct issue from the direct enforceability of an EEC Directive. The *Duke* case concerned the "Equal Treatment" Directive which was being relied upon by the employee to establish a way round the provisions of the Sex Discrimination Act 1975 which excluded from its ambit sex discrimination claims based on different compulsory retirement ages for men and women. The House of Lords, in disallowing reliance on that Directive, placed some emphasis on the fact that the Sex Discrimination Act 1975 had not been enacted to give effect to the "Equal Treatment" Directive and therefore overrode the Directive where the latter was not directly applicable against the respondent (*i.e.* a company in the private sector).

However, where English statute or regulations have been enacted specifically to give effect to an EEC Directive, then courts and tribunals can interpret that statute or regulation in conformity with the EEC Directive. For example in *Pickstone and Others* v. *Freemans plc.* [1988] I.R.L.R. 357; the appellants sought to overturn the Court of Appeal's ruling that they could not bring their equal pay claim based on "equal value" because the wording of the implementing legislation (the Equal Pay (Amendment) Regulations 1983) appeared to stop them doing so where there was a man employed in the same job as them. There was no such limitation in the EEC "Equal Pay" Directive. The House of Lords gave effect to the Directive by importing into the relevant equal pay legislation words which made it consistent with the Directive. The House of Lords said such an importation was necessary to give effect to Parliament's intention—*i.e.* to implement the "Equal Pay" Directive.

Since the Transfer Regulations were specifically enacted to implement the "Business Transfer" Directive, there seems no reason why the courts and tribunals should not adopt a similar approach. The unresolved issue is whether the courts and tribunals will do so where the domestic legislation is absolutely unequivocal and unambiguous. Most certainly, where domestic legislation is ambiguous, the tribunals and courts will not be slow to construe it in accordance with the EEC Directive it purports to implement. At present it is unclear whether the House of Lords' ruling in the *Pickstone* case has changed the traditional view—*i.e.* that EEC Directives can be used to interpret those parts of domestic legislation which are ambiguous (*Robert Seligman Corporation* v. *Baker* [1983] I.C.R. 770), but not to determine the meaning of provisions which are unambiguous and unequivocal (*Meikle* v. *McPhail* [1983] I.R.L.R. 351). Both of these cases concerned attempts to construe the Transfer Regulations in accordance with the "Business Transfer" Directive.

Indeed the House of Lords adopted such a "purposive" approach in *Litster* v. *Forth Estuary Engineering Ltd.* [1989] (H.L. 16.3.89). In that case, the question arose over whether the Transfer Regulations adequately safeguarded the position of employees dismissed before a business transfer took place. Article 4(1) of the Business Transfer Directive provides that a business transfer itself cannot constitute grounds for dismissal except where the dismissal is for an "economic, technical or organisational reason entailing changes in the workforce". Whilst such a provision was incorporated into regulation 8 of the Transfer Regulations [see p. 93 below], it was possible for the automatic transfer principle enshrined in the Directive and the Regulations to be circumvented where the transferor dismissed employees before the transfer (for a reason other than an economic, technical or organisational one entailing changes in the workforce), so that liabilities in respect of them would not pass to the transferee. This obviously had serious consequences for employees where the transferor was insolvent and therefore had no money to settle claims of the dismissed employees (for unfair or wrongful dismissal for example). In such cases employees were left without an effective remedy.

The problem arose from the drafting of the Transfer Regulations which provided in regulation 5(3) that the automatic transfer principle only "bite" on the employment contracts of those persons still employed by the transferor "immediately before the transfer". When considering this dilemma in the *Litster* case [see above], Lord Templeman said that:

> "the courts of the United Kingdom are under a duty to follow the practice of the European Court of Justice by giving a purposive construction to Directives and to regulations issues for the purpose of complying with Directives."

He added that:

> "such a purposive construction will be applied even though, perhaps, it may involve some departure from the strict and literal departure from the strict and literal application of the words which the legislature has enacted to use."

Adopting the same approach, Lord Oliver (who gave the main speech of the House of Lords) said that after the words "immediately before the transfer" in regulation 5(3) there should be implied the following additional words: "or would have been so employed if he had not been unfairly dismissed in the circumstances described in regulation 8(1)." In other words, the House of Lords wrote into regulation 5(3) of the Transfer Regulations such additional words as were necessary to give effect to the purpose of the Directive, which the Transfer Regulations were intended to implement.

European Court of Justice

E.C.J. Approach In the few cases that have reached the E.C.J. from other EEC member states, the Court has tended to refer the matter back to the domestic courts to apply their normal rules of construction in respect of particular words contained in the Business Transfer Directive—*e.g.* the meaning of "employee" and "transfer of undertaking"—see *Wendelboe* v. *L.J. Music* [1985] E.C.R. 457 and *Mikkelsen* v. *Danmols Inventar A/S* [1986] 1 C.M.L.R. 316.

2 WHAT IS A BUSINESS TRANSFER?

Introduction: the significance of a business transfer

This issue is of great significance because the special rules applicable to employees on the takeover or transfer of a business only apply where the transaction constitutes a "business transfer." If it is a share transfer or pure asset transfer, the Transfer Regulations have no applicability, and the special protective measures which apply in relation to continuity of employment in E.P.C.A., Sched. 13, para. 17(2), (see p. 137) or to redundancy pay in E.P.C.A., s.94 (see p. 140) do not operate. Fortunately although these three provisions relate to different aspects of employment law and use slightly different terminology to describe a business transfer, tribunals and higher courts are happy to construe the concept in a uniform way. This means that the case law on the meaning of "change in ownership of a business" in section 94(2) is adopted for the meaning of a transfer of a "trade or business" under the Transfer Regulations and for a transfer of a "trade, business or undertaking" under the continuity rules of paragraph 17(2), Schedule 13, E.P.C.A. and vice-versa—see *Premier Motors (Medway) Ltd.* v. *Total Oil Great Britain Ltd. & Others* [1983] I.R.L.R. 471. In *Dabell* v. *Vale Industrial Services* [1988] I.R.L.R. 439, the Court of Appeal proceeded on a similar basis, but reserved its position on whether it was correct to do so.

General approach

Has there been a business transfer?

The question whether or not there has been a transfer of a business is the key to the operation of the Transfer Regulations or the application of the special rules relating to continuity of employment and forfeiture of redundancy pay. It involves asking the following questions:

1. has anything been transferred?
2. if so, what has been transferred?
3. is what has been transferred a "relevant transfer" for the purposes of the Transfer Regulations?

The first two questions must be asked in all cases where the law impinges in the context of business dispositions. The third question is only relevant if one is considering whether the Transfer Regulations apply to the particular disposition (which will be the vast majority of cases). This is because the business transfer has to satisfy additional criteria before the Transfer Regulations apply (see p. 40 below). It is important to note that, unless tribunals apply this method of approach, their decisions will contain errors of law—*Cook* v. *Kingston-upon-Hull City Council* (unreported E.A.T. 660/83).

In most cases it is not in dispute that some disposition has taken place or that shares or assets or rights have been transferred from one person to another. The central question is: exactly what has been transferred? Where there has been a sale of shares, there is usually little dispute that a business transfer has not occurred. However the position is considerably more blurred when trying to distinguish an asset transfer from a business transfer. This confusion arises from the fact that most business transfers include a disposal or sale of assets as part of the deal. It can be even more confusing when the main asset transferred is a licence to undertake some kind of business activity.

Definition of a business

The starting point is the scope of what constitutes a business? Regulation 2(1) of the Transfer Regulations defines an "undertaking" as "any trade or business . . . " (in the nature of a commercial venture). Paragraph 17(2), Schedule 13 E.P.C.A. refers to a transfer of a "business" and section 94 refers to a "change in ownership of a business." There is no definition of the word "business" for the purposes of the Transfer Regulations, but it is clear from the E.A.T.'s decision in the *Premier Motors* case that its meaning should be consistent with that for paragraph 17(2) and section 94 E.P.C.A. Section 153 defines this as including "*any activity carried on by a body of persons. . . .* " The only difference between a business for the purposes of the Transfer Regulations and its meaning for other purposes is that in the former case the business (or part thereof) must be in the nature of a commercial venture (see p. 41).

Principal test

The "going concern" test

It is now well-established that the test for deciding whether it is a business that has been transferred (as compared to physical or legal assets) is to ask the question: has there been the transfer of a going concern? This test was formulated by the High Court in *Kenmir Ltd.* v. *Frizzell & Others* [1968] 1 All E.R. 414, and has been followed ever since. Lord Widgery J. (at p. 418) said:

> "In deciding whether a transaction amounted to the transfer of a business regard must be had to its substance rather than its form, and consideration must be given to the whole of the circumstances, weighing the factors which point in one direction against those which point in another. In the end the vital consideration is whether the effect of the transaction was to put the transferee in possession of a going concern the activities of which he could carry on without interruption. Many factors may be relevant though few will be conclusive in themselves. Thus, if the new employer carries on business in the same manner as before, this will point to the existence of a transfer, but the converse is not necessarily true because a transfer may be complete even though the transferee does not choose to avail himself of all the rights he acquires thereunder. Similarly an express assignment of goodwill is strong evidence of a transfer of the business but the absence of such an assignment is not conclusive if the transferor has effectively deprived himself of the power to compete. The absence of the assignment of premises, stock-in-trade or

outstanding contracts will likewise not be conclusive if the particular circumstances of the transferee nevertheless enable him to carry on substantially the same business as before."

This definitive statement of the test was approved by the Court of Appeal in *Lloyd* v. *Brassey* [1969] 1 All E.R. 382, where Lord Denning (at p. 384) summarised the test even more concisely as:

> " . . . the new owner takes over the business as a going concern—so that the business remains the same business but in different hands. . . . "

The European Court of Justice has adopted a similar test when interpreting the Acquired Rights Directive. In *Spijkers* v. *Gebroeders Benedik Abattoir CV* [1986] 2 C.M.L.R. 296, the E.C.J. confirmed that all the factors must be looked at including goodwill, who is servicing the vendor's customers, stock-in-trade, buildings and other tangible assets, the value of the vendor's intangible assets, the activities carried on before and after the transfer, the extent of any disruption in those activities, the use of the employees by the purchaser, etc. The E.C.J. said:

> "it is necessary to determine whether what has been sold is an economic entity which is still in existence, and this will be apparent from the fact that its operation is actually being continued or has been taken over by the new employer, with the same economic or similar activities."

Substance of the transaction

Applying the "going concern" test

When applying this "going concern" test, the tribunals and courts look at the substance of the transaction, not its form (see the *Kenmir* case above). For example in *H.A. Rencoule (Joiners & Shopfitters) Ltd.* v. *Hunt* the High Court held that, although the parties described their transaction as a transfer of assets, it was in substance a business transfer; and the court went on to apply the law accordingly. Similarly, in *Martin* v. *Bond & White Ltd.* the E.A.T. held that the intentions of the parties to the commercial contract, although a factor, was far from being conclusive on whether the transaction in question was a business transfer.

Even if the commercial contract between the vendor and purchaser expressly states that their transaction is a sale of physical assets and so the Transfer Regulations do not apply, this can be overridden by section 140(1) of the Employment Protection (Consolidation) Act and regulation 12 of the Transfer Regulations. Section 140(1) states that:

> "any provision in an agreement (whether a contract of employment or not) shall be void in so far as it purports: (a) to exclude or limit the operation of any provision of this Act or, (b) to preclude any person from presenting a complaint to . . . an industrial tribunal."

Similarly regulation 12 provides:

> "Any provision of any agreement (whether a contract of employment or not) shall be void in so far as it purports to

exclude or limit the operation of Regulations 5, 8 or 10 above or to preclude any person from presenting a complaint to an industrial tribunal. . . . "

Although there is no case deciding the point, it is likely that these two provisions would operate to prevent the vendor and purchaser from expressing their commercial transaction as an assets transfer when, in law, it is a business transfer; and thus attempting to deprive employees of the employment protection given under the Transfer Regulations in respect of business transfers.

Care should be taken when applying the "going concern" test, since it is merely judicial shorthand for the test fully enunciated in the *Kenmir* case. In particular, the words "going concern" should not taken to imply that the profitability of the business is a relevant factor, since it matters not whether the business is profitable or about to become insolvent. In *Teeside Times Ltd.* v. *Drury* [1980] I.R.L.R. 72, the Court of Appeal rejected the argument that a business could not be a "going concern" if it was about to become insolvent. This view has received support from the E.C.J. in *Mikkelsen* v. *Danmols Inventar*. The concept of a "going concern" is used by the courts and tribunals as shorthand to describe a business activity having its own identity, as compared to a collection of physical assets.

Relevant factors

It is clear that to determine whether or not a particular transaction constitutes a business transfer requires an assessment of all of its factors and, in particular, exactly what was transferred from the vendor to the purchaser. This is a question of fact and degree in each case—*Melon* v. *Hector Powell Ltd.* [1980] I.R.L.R. 477. It is a matter for industrial tribunals to decide and, as such, it is quite possible for two different tribunals to come to opposite decisions on the same facts, yet both be right in law!—see the *Melon* case. As the *Kenmir* case indicates, no single factor is likely to be conclusive on this question, although some (such as a transfer of goodwill) do apparently carry more weight than others. Most business transfers will involve the transfer of some or all of the following business assets: premises, equipment, vehicles, stock of raw materials, inventory, work-in-progress, existing contracts, trade marks/brand names, intellectual property (*e.g.* patents, registered designs or copyright), goodwill, customer lists, intangible assets such as debtors and (possibly) tax losses, etc. In addition the commercial contract may contain clauses which are indicative that a business (rather than assets) is to be transferred—for example there may be restrictive covenants preventing the vendor from competing with the purchaser within a specified geographical radius for a stated period of time.

Use of assets by purchaser

The sale of physical assets can be construed as either the disposal by the vendor of equipment or premises he no longer requires for his business, or it may be evidence of the sale of the business itself. Much depends on how the purchaser utilises those assets once he has acquired them. If he uses them to manufacture the same articles, or to provide the same services, as were manufactured or provided by the vendor prior to their sale, then this is likely to be indicative of the transaction being, in substance, a business transfer, not a mere asset transfer. This will be especially the case where customer lists and work-in-progress are transferred with the physical assets. Conversely, if those assets are used by the purchaser for different purposes, then the strong inference will be that there has been no business transfer. Tribunals therefore look at the use to which those assets are put by the purchaser and ask themselves the question whether he is, in substance, carrying on the business of the vendor in respect of those assets transferred.

For example, in *Melon* v. *Hector Powell Ltd.* (see above), the vendor manufactured men's made-to-measure suits. Their factory at Dagenham produced the cloth which was used by that factory and another at Blantyre to make up the suits. The head office was based at the Dagenham factory. The vendor then decided to sell the Blantyre factory to the purchaser, which involved the assignment of the lease to the premises, the sale of the equipment in that factory, and the work-in-progress. In the commercial agreement, the purchaser also undertook to employ all of the vendor's employees working at the Blantyre factory and to ensure that 70 per cent. of the factory's production for the first six months only would be used to supply the vendor with made-to-measure suits, and the remainder of its production capacity was to manufacture ready-to-wear suits (which was the purchaser's particular line of business). After the six months was up, the purchaser could use its production capacity at its Blantyre factory for its own purposes—*i.e.* ready-to-wear suits. The House of Lords upheld the tribunal's decision that the transaction constituted an asset transfer, and not a business transfer (although they added that the opposite conclusion was also equally tenable on the particular facts of the case!). The tribunal had placed emphasis on the fact that the purchaser's business was the manufacture of ready-to-wear suits, whereas the vendor's business concerned made-to-measure suits. The temporary continuation of the production of made-to-measure suits by the purchaser solely for the vendor for a limited period of time was regarded by the tribunal as merely temporary assistance by the purchaser to the vendor to help the latter in its loss of production capacity consequent upon the sale of its Blantyre factory. The purchaser was not treated as continuing the vendor's business of manufacturing made-to-measure suits. No doubt, if the vendor had not been the sole customer of the purchaser for made-to-measure suits under a single contract manufacturing agreement, the inference placed upon the purchaser continuing with the manufacture of such suits would have been very different.

The use to which business assets are put by the purchaser is an important factor in ascertaining whether the transaction is a business transfer. It emphasises the need to examine closely what has been transferred, because it can often be misleading to look simply at the physical assets transferred without also looking at the use to which they are put. The key point is that those assets might be used for a different, although similar, type of business enterprise. For example in *Applebee* v. *Joseph Allnatt Centres* (unreported, E.A.T. 292/80), the St. Albans Hotel was sold to new owners. The vendor operated the hotel as a traditional family hotel, whereas the purchaser intended to run it as a holiday centre for sporting and educational activities mainly for children. However, as part of the commercial contract, the purchasers agreed to honour the guests' bookings made with the vendor until the end of the "season." Thereafter it would be transformed into one of the purchaser's holiday centres. The E.A.T. held that the transaction did not amount to a business transfer because the St. Albans Hotel was being run as a very different sort of establishment and for a different sort of clientele. Again, the honouring of existing bookings was regarded as a transitional requirement of the transaction.

As the House of Lords commented in the *Melon* case (see above), whether or not a particular transaction is a business transfer is one of fact and degree. No doubt the mere upgrading of a hotel from two-star to five-star by a purchaser, on his acquisition of the premises, would not be regarded as sufficient to make the use of that asset for a different business enterprise—even though the purchaser would hope to attract a different class of guest.

Similarly in *Duffen* v. *Fuzzard and Another* (unreported E.A.T. 352/83), there was no business transfer when a school was sold. The vendor had run it as a Catholic junior school for girls, whereas the purchasers ran it as a unisex school for all religious denominations.

However, there are sometimes circumstances where tribunals look not only at the kind of activity to be carried out by the purchaser, but also the market at which it is addressed. For example in *Crompton* v. *Truly Fair (International) Ltd.* [1975] I.C.R. 859, there was no business transfer when the purchaser of a factory, previously used for making children's clothes, utilised the premises, equipment and employees for making adults' trousers.

Where a vendor manufactures a range of items and, subsequent to the sale of a factory, the purchaser decides to manufacture some but not all of those items, it is likely a tribunal will consider that the purchaser is nonetheless carrying on the same business activity as the vendor. For example in *Modiwear Ltd.* v. *Wallis Fashion Group Ltd.* (unreported E.A.T. 535/80), the vendor made ladies' dresses and blouses, and after the sale of one of its factories to the purchaser, the latter made blouses for the vendor for a limited period, and thereafter concentrated on making dresses. The E.A.T. held that the transaction was a business transfer, and one of the key factors was the purchaser had continued to make dresses.

Transfer of premises

Very often the transfer of premises (usually by the assignment of a business lease) is a strong indicator that a business has been transferred. However it is by no means conclusive. Much depends on the extent to which the operation of the vendor's business is inextricably linked to the occupation of those premises. For example, in *Lloyd* v. *Brassey* [1969] 1 All E.R. 382, the vendor sold his farm to the purchaser. The sale in effect comprised the sale of the land and some farm machinery and there was no payment for goodwill. The Court of Appeal upheld the tribunal's decision that the sale amounted to a business transfer. The purchaser continued to farm as the vendor had done—*i.e.* the business of farming that land was carried on as a going concern by the purchaser. In effect the "goodwill" of the business was inherently linked to the land itself. The same approach has been adopted in respect of the assignment of pub leases between publicans (*Young* v. *Daniel Thwaites & Co. Ltd.* [1977] I.C.R. 877—see p. 26 below), and the change of persons running petrol stations (*Norris* v. *Bedwell & Bond*, unreported E.A.T. 788/83). In the latter case, the outgoing licensee who surrendered his licence to sell Chevron petrol was held to have transferred his business of running the Little Brickhills Petrol Station to the incoming licensee. The E.A.T. placed a large measure of emphasis on the fact that the activity carried on by the incoming licensee at that site was exactly the same as that carried on by the outgoing licensee prior to the surrender of his licence, and that the goodwill of the business was attributable to the site of the petrol station. It made no difference that there was, in fact, no transaction directly between the incoming and outgoing licensees (see p. 34 below).

Both of these cases have in common the continuation of the same business activity at the same site to which goodwill is inherently linked. No doubt if an incoming farmer uses the land for a different type of farming (changing from dairy farming to wheat production), it could not be said that he is carrying on the same business as his predecessor.

There are sometimes occasions where the business is so inherently linked to the premises, that the "business" is more properly described by reference to the premises rather than the person actually performing it. For example in *Robert Seligman Corporation* v. *Baker & Another* [1983] I.C.R. 770, the vendor sold various items of equipment to the purchaser when it surrendered its licence to operate the ladies' hair salon located in a Debenham's store. The E.A.T. held that there was no business transfer between the vendor and purchaser, because the vendor had no business to transfer. The "business" as such belonged to Debenhams because any customer goodwill attached to the ladies having their hair cut at that Debenham's store, not by the outgoing licensee. In other words, the business attached to the premises in the particular circumstances of that case.

It is sometimes the case that, from an employee's perspective, not much changes in his working environment. He may feel that he is performing much the same job functions as before, but for a different employer. However this is by no means an indicator that there has been a business transfer. For example in *Woodhouse* v. *Peter Brotherhood Ltd.* [1972] I.C.R. 186, the vendor manufactured diesel engines at its factory at Sandiacre. That site was sold to the purchaser together with some but not all of the equipment located there. The purchaser was an engineering firm concerned with the manufacture of spinning machines and steam turbines. As part of the commercial contract, the purchaser agreed to finish off some work-in-progress relating to diesel engines. The applicant was offered (and accepted) a job with the purchaser and was engaged in completing that work-in-progress. In effect he carried on doing exactly the same work after the transfer as he had done beforehand. When the work-in-progress was completed he was made redundant and he sought to claim his redundancy pay based on his combined service with the vendor and purchaser.

The Court of Appeal held that the transaction was not a business transfer, but an asset transfer since the purchaser's business was different from that of the vendor and the temporary completion of the vendor's work-in-progress by the purchaser was not indicative that the purchaser had decided to carry on the business of the manufacture of diesel engines.

Goodwill

This is probably one of the most important indicators of the difference between a business and an asset transfer. In the *Kenmir* case (see above) the High Court said that it was a strong, but not conclusive, factor; and in *Lloyd* v. *Brassey* [1969] 1 All E.R. 382, the Court of Appeal indicated that the transfer of goodwill was not a prerequisite to there being a business transfer. However some more recent decisions have put great emphasis on it. For example in the *Robert Seligman Corporation* case, [1983] I.C.R. 770, the E.A.T., in effect, decided the issue on the basis that the outgoing licensee had no goodwill in the hair salon in the Debenham's store and, therefore, had no business to transfer to the incoming licensee who was to take over the running of the salon. Similarly, in the *Modiwear* case (unreported E.A.T. 585/80) the E.A.T. indicated in clear terms the importance of goodwill:

> "although in the absence of any reference to goodwill is not decisive in showing that a business is not being transferred, no case has been cited to us in which goodwill has been assigned but it was held that no business has been transferred."

Since the transfer of goodwill is clearly an important indicator, it is necessary to consider what it is. In most cases it is simply an intangible asset of the business which embodies customer, employee and supplier loyalty. As the E.A.T. said in the *Modiwear* case it is:

> "the value of the business relationship with customers, suppliers, staff, etc., or the amount by which the open market value of a business as a going concern exceeds the value of the tangible assets employed in such a business."

For example certain customers may be happy with the quality of goods or services supplied by a particular company and therefore be more inclined to put repeat business its way. Similarly a firm may have a particular reputation in its field and will therefore be more capable of attracting the best staff, or suppliers may be prepared to give preference to a particular company when raw materials are in short supply or to furnish information to a company on an exclusive basis.

Goodwill may be transferred either expressly by a clause in the commercial contract between vendor and purchaser, or by implication from either the nature of the transaction or other obligations in the commercial contract. Where there is an express assignment of goodwill, tribunals will normally accept it at face value without examining whether it really has been assigned (see the *Modiwear* case).

The absence of an express assignment of goodwill does not necessarily mean than none has been transferred—see *Jeetle* v. *Elster* [1985] I.R.L.R. 227. Goodwill can also be impliedly assigned by the nature of the transaction. This is particularly the case where the transaction relates to the sale/assignment of premises which inherently embodies the goodwill. For example in *McLellan* v. *Cody & Cody* (unreported E.A.T. 14/86), a tenancy of a pub was transferred from one publican to another, and the E.A.T. held that the goodwill in the business of running the pub was transferred to the incoming publican when the tenancy was assigned to him. Similarly in the case of *Norris* v. *Bedwell & Bond* (unreported E.A.T. 738/83), although there was no express assignment of goodwill, nor any sum paid in respect of it, the goodwill was inherent in the site of the Little Brickhills Service Station which sold petrol.

There are other ways in which the assignment of goodwill can be implied:

1. the transfer of work-in-progress and existing contracts placed by customers of the vendor—see *H.A. Rencoule (Joiners and Shopfitters) Ltd.* v. *Hunt* [1967] I.T.R. 475;
2. the existence of a restrictive covenant restraining the vendor from engaging in a competing business—see *G.D. Ault (Isle of Wight) Ltd.* v. *Gregory* [1967] I.T.R. 301; where on the sale of its premises and all engagements, the vendor estate agent covenanted not to be concerned in any business which competed with that of the purchaser;
3. the transfer of the brand names and trade marks of the business, or its trading name—see *Thomsons Soft Drinks Ltd.* v. *Quayle* (unreported E.A.T. 12/81);
4. the transfer of the vendor's customers/clients—see *Atkin* v. *Ward & Haines Watts* [1983] I.R.L.R. 285; where the vendor (an accountant) sold a block of clients to the purchaser (also accountants). This transfer took place with the clients' consent and the only physical asset transferred was the collection of files for those clients.

It is important to note that the totality of the transaction must be examined—it can be highly misleading to look to see whether any of the above has been transferred to the purchaser as part of the transaction, and thus assume that goodwill has been transferred. For example in *Chapman* v. *Wilkinson* [1968] I.T.R. 39, the High Court held that the mere fact that the purchaser had acquired the vendor's clients did not, of itself, mean there had been a business transfer.

Just as a business can be a "going concern" even if it is on the verge of insolvency, so a business can have goodwill in such circumstances. Indeed in very many cases the only reason why liquidators can sell a business for more than its tangible assets is because of the goodwill which that business has in the marketplace—see *Thomsons Soft Drinks Ltd.* v. *Quayle* (see above) where there was a business transfer even though the sale was effected by the liquidator of the business. Further in *Litster* v. *Forth Estuary Engineering* [1989] (H.L. 16.3.89), Lord Templeman commented that, a business had been transferred even though the company was in receivership and the purchaser had declined to take goodwill expressly.

Transfer of workforce

Where the purchaser takes on all or most of the vendor's workforce and engages them on the same duties as they performed prior to the sale, this may be one factor indicative that there has been a business transfer. However it is by no means conclusive. In the *B.I.F.U.* v. *Barclays Bank* [1987] I.C.R. 495, case the only "asset" transferred was the provision of the services of a workforce, yet the E.A.T. held there was no business transfer. In contrast in *Secretary of State for Employment* v. *Spence* [1986] I.C.R. 651, the Court of Appeal held that a business could be transferred even though it had no workforce because they had all been dismissed shortly before the business transfer had taken place.

In *P. Bork International A/S* v. *Foreningen AF Arbejdsledere I Danmark and others* [1989] I.R.L.R. 41, the E.C.J. took a similar view. The E.C.J. said:

> "the fact that the undertaking in question was, at the time of the transfer, temporarily closed and did not have any employees certainly constitutes a factor to be taken into consideration for the purposes of determining whether an economic entity still in existence has been transferred. However, the temporary closure of the undertaking and the consequential absence of staff at the time of the transfer are not in themselves alone sufficient to preclude the existence of a transfer of an undertaking within the meaning of Article 1(1) of the Directive. This conclusion is inescapable particularly in the situation . . . in which the undertaking ceased its operations only for a short period and also coincided with the end of the year holidays."

Much depends on whether the vendor's business is one which comprises the provision to clients of "intellectual" capacity or brain-power of the vendor's employees. In such a case, if the vendor sells various assets, but does not transfer its employees, the core of its "business" cannot be said to have been transferred. In other words, the purchaser of the assets would not acquire the key asset which makes up the vendor's business—*i.e.* its employees. By comparison, many enterprises can be said to be businesses where they are sold without any employees. This is often done when liquidators seek to sell insolvent companies as "going concerns" to obtain a higher price, by hiving down its assets away from its employees.

Transfer of stock and contracts

The transfer of stock or work-in-progress is often an indicator that there has been a business transfer—see *G.D. Ault (Isle of Wight) Ltd.* v. *Gregory* [1967] I.T.R. 301, where the existing contracts of an estate development company were sold to the purchaser and *H.A. Rencoule (Joiners & Shopfitters) Ltd.* v. *Hunt* [1967] I.T.R. 475, where the stock-in-trade was sold and for the payment of an additional £1,100 the vendor agreed to assist in completing the vendor's work-in-progress and to introduce the purchasers to his existing customers. However where the purchaser agrees to complete work-in-progress merely as an interim measure to assist the vendor honouring its obligations to its customers, then it is unlikely to be a business transfer, especially if the purchaser intends to manufacture different products—see the *Melon* case (above).

Transfer of name

The transfer of a business name, trade marks or brand names is also indicative of a business transfer. For example in the *Kenmir* case, [1968] 1 All E.R. 414, the High Court said that trade marks for certain types of furniture sold to the purchaser together with other assets were indicative of a business transfer.

Similarly, in the *Robert Seligman* case (see above) one of the key factors which led the E.A.T. to conclude there had been no business transfer was the absence of a transfer of trading name from the outgoing to the incoming hairdressing concessionaire.

Transfer of employer running the business

Although, traditionally, Industrial Tribunals and the E.A.T. have tended to ask themselves the question whether the *ownership* of a business has been transferred, it appears that, for the purposes of the Business Transfer Directive, this approach is incorrect. In *Landsorganisationen I Danmark* v. *Ny Molle Kro* [1989] I.R.L.R. 37 the E.C.J. said that it was more appropriate to look at whether there had been a change of the legal person responsible for the *running* of the business. In that case the E.C.J. said:

> "the Directive applies . . . whenever as a result of a legal transfer or merger there is a change in the natural or legal person responsible for the running of the undertaking and who, because of this, enters into contractual obligations as an employer towards the employees working in the undertaking. It is of no importance to know whether the ownership of the undertaking has been transferred. In fact, the employees of an undertaking that changes its employer without a transfer of ownership are in a comparable situation to that of the employees of an undertaking which has been sold and therefore need equivalent protection. It follows that, insofar as the managing lessee acquires the capacity under the lease of employer within the above meaning, the transfer must be considered as a transfer of an undertaking to another employer as a result of a legal transfer within the meaning of Article 1(1) of the Directive."

The E.C.J. in the *P. Bork International AS* case took a similar view:

> "the Directive therefore applies whenever within the framework of contractual relations there is a change of a natural or legal person responsible for operating the undertaking who enters into contractual obligations as an employer with the employees of the undertaking."

Licences, concessions, franchises, etc.

Transfer of licences

Many commercial activities operate under licence from a third party—*e.g.* a petrol station, a franchise for selling brand name goods on certain premises, concessions to run businesses within a large enterprise, etc. For ease of reference, these are referred to as "licences"—because their existence depends on a third party agreeing to them operating in the first place. For example, a manufacturer of a certain brand of sportswear may have secured the agreement of various major department stores to allow them to operate a "store-within-a-store." The manufacturer will then find someone to run that unit—often someone who is in business on his own behalf. Alternatively a department store may not have the expertise to run a particular operation within its precincts (*e.g.* a hairdressing salon, or a restaurant) and so it contracts this out to a third party. Yet again, a hotel may wish to provide a particular service for its guests (*e.g.* a hair salon or a gift shop) and grants a concession to a third party to provide that service.

Whether the licensor's or licensee's business

The key question is: whose business is the licence/franchise/concession—the party granting the licence or the person operating under it (the licensee)? This is important when the licensee decides he no longer wishes to operate under the licence, or the licensor determines that someone else could run the franchise better than the existing licensee. When licensees change, is there a business transfer between the outgoing and incoming licensee? If the business belongs to the licensor (*e.g.* the manufacturer of the goods sold, or the department store or the hotel) the outgoing licensee clearly has no business to transfer. Thus on the assignment of a licence, or its surrender by the outgoing licensee followed by a grant of a new licence to the incoming licensee (it does not make much difference for reasons explained on p. 36 below), it has to be determined what has been transferred—assets or a business?

The starting point is to look at the nature of the activity being operated under the licence and the contractual terms under which the licensee operates. For example in *Robert Seligman Corporation* v. *Baker Ltd.* [1983] I.C.R. 770, the Seligman Corporation operated a concession to run a ladies' hairdressing salon within a Debenham's department store. Under the concession agreement the corporation was required to install the shop-fittings, but Debenhams were obliged to reimburse the costs of fixtures and equipment when the concession agreement came to an end. In addition the corporation was required to pay over to Debenhams a proportion of its profits earned in the concession. The corporation then decided to surrender the concession and Roband took it over. The same fixtures and fittings were used by Roband. The E.A.T. held that there was no business transfer between the Seligman Corporation and Roband when the latter took over the concession. There was no goodwill which belonged to the corporation which could be transferred. The goodwill belonged to Debenhams because the ladies who went to the hair salon did so because it was in Debenhams, not because it was run by the corporation. They were under the impression that their hair was being cut by Debenhams, not by the Seligman Corporation.

The *Robert Seligman Corporation* case should be compared with the E.A.T.'s decision in *Journey's Friend Ltd.* v. *Hayes & Another* (unreported E.A.T. 707/84), where the vendor ran a gift shop in a hotel under licence from the hotel. He was responsible for his own stock and carried the risk of losses as well as keeping all profits. The vendor ran into financial difficulties and the hotel agreed that the purchaser should run the shop in his stead. The vendor sold to the purchaser his existing stock. The E.A.T. rejected the argument that the business of selling gifts belonged to the hotel, and held that the goodwill in that business belonged to the vendor. Therefore when he relinquished his concession and sold his stock to the purchaser (who then proceeded to run the concession in his place), the transaction was a business transfer. The *Robert Seligman Corporation* case can be distinguished on the grounds that:

1. the vendor in the *Journey's Friend* case took the risk of making losses as well as profits,
2. he had no obligation to pay over some of the profits to the hotel, who merely received a rent for his shop space and
3. the customer goodwill was not inherently bound up with the hotel.

This distinction seems to be supported by the tribunal's decision in *Frazer* v. *Munroe (Teeside) Ltd.* (unreported S.C.O.I.T. 6809/85), where it was held that the surrender of a butcher's concession in a supermarket was not a business transfer to the supermarket in which it was housed. A material factor which led the tribunal to reach this conclusion was that the customer had no reason to think that the butcher was carrying out his own business in the supermarket. He had no trading name advertised and the customer buying meat from the butcher's stall did not pay him, but the supermarket at the check-out tills with the rest of her groceries. Thus, the customer had no way of knowing that the butcher's stall was not run by the supermarket. In other words, the butcher had no business in the supermarket to transfer—as in the *Seligman* case.

However, in the light of the E.C.J.'s decisions in the *P. Bork International AS* and *Ny Molle Kro* cases, it is now possible that the Robert Seligman case was wrongly decided. Since the E.C.J. have put emphasis on who *runs* the business, rather than who owns it, the importance of the goodwill appears to be diminished. Nonetheless, it is important to draw a distinction between the situation of a licensee operating a business on behalf of its owner, and one where the licensee merely provides a contract for services to the person who both owns and, in effect, runs the business. For example, in the *Fraser* v. *Monroe* case (see above) it could be argued that the butcher was not running part of the business of the supermarket in the true sense (*e.g.* he was taking no cash) and the butcher's section within the supermarket was really part of the overall operations run directly by the supermarket. In such a case, it might be a more correct view to consider that the butcher was merely providing services to the supermarket whereby it would supply meat and cut it up for customers on the supermarket's premises. In such circumstances, it could not properly be said that the butcher was running a part of the supermarket's business *in the place of the supermarket.*

However, such a distinction is a fine one and it is likely that there may be cases where different Industrial Tribunals come to different conclusions on very similar facts. It is important to note, however, that it would be erroneous for a Tribunal simply to look at whether a "licensee" is merely carrying out an activity on behalf of the "licensor." The E.C.J. cases all refer to an "economic activity or enterprise" and it is important to distinguish these from the provision of services to the "licensor." Put concisely, therefore, the distinction is between the provision of services for the benefit of someone else's business, and the operating of that business on their behalf.

In *Norris* v. *Bedwell & Bond* (unreported E.A.T. 738/83), Mr. Bedwell ran a petrol filling station at the Little Brickhills Service Station. He was required by his licence agreement with

Chevron only to sell its petrol and oils which he was required to purchase at the specified prices. There were stringent controls in the licence agreement controlling the nature and contents of advertising he could undertake. In addition the service station bore a large sign indicating it sold Chevron petrol. By way of sideline, Mr. Bedwell also sold sweets and soft drinks, etc. He decided to retire and asked Chevron to release him from the licence. Chevron was happy to do so and found Mr. Norris as a replacement. Under the terms of the licence, Mr. Bedwell could not assign or transfer it to a third party, so Mr. Norris took over the licence by the mechanism of the surrender by Mr. Bedwell of his licence, and the grant of a new licence to Mr. Norris by Chevron. The E.A.T. upheld the tribunal's conclusion that the transaction was a business transfer, and rejected the argument (raised by the author who appeared on behalf of Mr. Norris!) that the business and goodwill of selling Chevron's petrol belonged to Chevron (not Mr. Bedwell) and service stations were merely commercial outlets for that business. The E.A.T. held that the selling of Chevron's petrol and oils at the Little Brickhills Service Station was a business in its own right with the goodwill attached to that site. Therefore Mr. Bedwell has a business to transfer to Mr. Norris, albeit that there was no express assignment of goodwill, and the only direct transaction between the two men was the sale of some cutlery, miscellaneous garage equipment and some sweets, for about £300. This case followed the E.A.T.'s decision in the *Premier Motors* case, which concerned similar facts and which reached the same conclusion.

Since the effect of a tribunal finding that there has been no business transfer results in the employees affected being deprived of the protection of the Transfer Regulations, there is a tendency for tribunals to look hard to find that the "business" is vested in the licensee. It is really a matter of approach. One can either take the view that such concessions are merely outlets for selling the manufacturer's goods, or that such an activity (*i.e.* selling those goods) is a business in its own right. The latter is the preferable approach especially where the goodwill is impliedly attached to the site concerned—as with petrol stations. In such cases, the customer probably buys his petrol from a specific service station, not because of the particular brand of petrol sold there, but because of the price of petrol and the convenience of that petrol station to his home or route. However where the petrol company fixes the price at which its petrol must be sold (as compared to setting minimum petrol prices) and organises promotions which attract customers to service stations selling its petrol, this increases the likelihood of the licensee not having a business of his own.

In these types of cases tribunals place some emphasis on the extent to which the licensor controls the activities of the licensee and, in particular, the extent to which the licensor dictates how the franchise/concession should be run. However even the existence of quite a heavy measure of control by the licensor will be outweighed by a provision in the transaction between outgoing and incoming licensee referring to the assignment of goodwill. For example in *Hardy* v. *Jirjis* (unreported C.O.I.T. 1569/158), Mr. W. was the franchisee of a Wimpy Bar run under licence from Wimpy. The franchise agreement stipulated that:

1. Wimpy would fix the menu,
2. he was only allowed to sell Wimpy's foods supplied by Wimpy,
3. Wimpy's name had to be used,
4. Wimpy laid down guidelines on prices to be charged (although these were not mandatory).

Mr. W. kept the profits after paying a sum for the right to operate the franchise. Mr. W. agreed to sell the lease of the site, the fixtures and fittings and current stock to Mr. J. The commercial agreement between the two men expressly attributed part of the purchase price to the assignment of goodwill. However, the transfer could not take place without the agreement of Wimpy that Mr. J. could take over the franchise (which was granted). The tribunal held that the transaction did constitute a business transfer and rejected the argument that the business belonged to Wimpy. The tribunal placed some measure of emphasis on the fact that the transaction expressly assigned goodwill from Mr. W. to Mr. J., and the tribunal were not prepared to look behind that statement to see if there was any goodwill to transfer. It seems most probable that there may be other cases involving very similar types of franchise where the franchisor exercises such a degree of control that the franchisee has few, if any, commercial decisions to make except those within tightly-controlled guidelines. In the absence of an express assignment of goodwill, other tribunals may well conclude that a change of franchisee does not amount to a business transfer.

Where the concession or licence relates to the carrying on of an activity outside the licensor's mainline business, this substantially increases the likelihood of the licence being a business in its own right—even though there is some broader connection. For example in *Wood* v. *McNulty* (unreported C.O.I.T. 1700/179), a brewery company granted franchises to its pub managers to run their own catering business from the pub premises. A tribunal held that these were businesses in their own right which could be transferred between successive managers. The same conclusion was reached by the E.A.T. in *Cartwright* v. *Norton* (unreported E.A.T. 91/82).

Business tenancies

The position of tenants of a business activity linked to the occupation of land is similar to that of licensees (see above). This usually arises in respect of licensees of a pub who are not employed by the landlord brewery. The licensee's activities are greatly controlled by the brewery, including restrictions on his use of the premises for other business sidelines (for example, selling food), a prohibition on him assigning the tenancy, and a requirement that he purchases minimum quantities of beer and liquor from the brewery and does not sell drinks purchased from any other source. The brewery may often require that the general ambience and state of decoration of the premises matches its standards. In *Young* v. *Daniel Thwaites* [1977] I.C.R. 877, the tenant licensee of a pub surrendered his tenancy to run the pub and the brewery landlord decided not to grant a new tenancy but to install its own manager there. The E.A.T. held that the transaction constituted a business transfer from the outgoing tenant to the landlord brewery. The E.A.T. considered that the business in question was the running of that particular pub on those premises, and it made no difference that the landlord brewery controlled the tenancy at all times. The E.A.T. commented that, from the perspective of the pub's customers, the same business was being carried on (*i.e.* serving them drinks) but in different hands. This decision has been followed more recently by another division of the E.A.T. in *McLellan* v. *Cody & Cody* (unreported E.A.T. 14/86) which concerned the direct assignment of a tenancy from the outgoing to the incoming tenant.

Sub-contracting exclusive contracts

Contracting out activities to a third party

An important variant to a change of licensee, franchisee or concessionaire is the situation where a company decides to contract out a particular activity to a third party—for example contract catering, maintenance or cleaning. When the contractor company decides to award the contract to another firm, or to do the job itself, has there been a business transfer? To answer this, recourse must be had to the test laid down in the *Kenmir* case (see above) to determine whether such a change can properly be described as the continuation of the same business as a going concern, but in different hands. In many cases, the fact that the contract provides for the supply of a service to a single company may mitigate against the provision of that service being a business in its own right. When that contract is not re-awarded to the sub-contractor, it will then be regarded by tribunals as merely the loss of a valuable contract by the sub-contractor.

Maintenance contracts

In *Port Talbot Engineering* v. *Passmore & Evans* [1975] I.C.R. 235, P. & E. won the maintenance contract for a particular company, who had put it out to tender every year. In the past there had been a series of sub-contractors who had provided those maintenance services to that company and on each occasion the employees who actually did the maintenance work were engaged by the new sub-contractors. When P.T.E. Ltd. won the maintenance contract from P. & E. and subsequently made some of the employees redundant, the redundant employees argued that the maintenance contract was a business in its own right and therefore their continuity of service was transferred with them on each change of sub-contractor. The High Court rejected that contention on the grounds that the performance of the maintenance contract was not a business in the nature of a going concern. Nothing was transferred from the outgoing to the incoming sub-contractor, and the reason why the employees were habitually taken on by the incoming sub-contractor was merely one of convenience. The management of the maintenance work, the premises, the supply of materials, etc., was supplied by each separate sub-contractor.

Contract catering

In contrast, in *Rastill* v. *Automatic Refreshment Services Ltd.* (1978) I.C.R. 289, a company operated a canteen for its employees. In 1974 it contracted out this operation to outside caterers (A.R.S.). The agreement between the company and A.R.S. provided that:

1. A.R.S. had exclusive licence to sell food on its premises,

2. A.R.S. would take over the running of the kitchen,
3. the company would supply all the equipment,
4. the company maintained tight control over the prices charged by A.R.S.,
5. A.R.S. took the risk on making profits and losses, and
6. A.R.S. took over all the existing canteen staff.

After a few years, the company decided to terminate that arrangement and run the canteen "in-house" again. The E.A.T. held that both the contracting-out and the contracting-in of the canteen did constitute a business transfer.

This case can be compared with the more recent decision in *Hadden* v. *University of Dundee Students' Association* [1985] I.R.L.R. 449, where the students' union contracted out the management of its catering facilities to contract caterers. The students' union continued to employ the staff (except the manager and supervisors) and to provide the premises, equipment and insurance. The contract caterers were paid a management fee together with only a percentage of the profits. Most important, the contract caterers bore no risk in the event that the catering operation ran at a loss. This last factor was a key element to the E.A.T.'s decision that, on the cancellation of that contract, there was no business transfer. In addition the E.A.T. also placed some weight on the fact that the contract caterers had little overall control over the running of the catering facility, apart from its general management. From these two cases it appears that a vital element in a tribunal's deliberations on whether a contracting-out arrangement can constitute a business in its own right is the sub-contractor's risk as to making losses.

Contract cleaning

The same principles have been applied to contract cleaning. However a distinction needs to be drawn between those activities which can be operated as separate units and, as such, are identifiable parts of a large business enterprise, and those which cannot properly be severed from the main business. This latter question involves a consideration of what that larger business is. For example in *Johnstone* v. *Sketchley Contract Cleaning Services Ltd.* (unreported C.O.I.T. 1674/151), the tribunal held there was no business transfer when the Manpower Services Commission decided to contract out its cleaning and orderly work for its hostels to outside contract cleaners. The tribunal placed great emphasis on the fact that a fixed fee was paid for the provision of that service and that it could not be regarded as a severable enterprise from the hostel's general operations. The tribunal distinguished the *Rastill* case on the basis that the Manpower Services Commission's hostel could not function without bed-making and cleaning, whereas a factory could still continue without a works canteen.

Transport contracts

Some companies, who have their own fleet of lorries (to distribute products manufactured by them), decide it is more economical to contract out this function to be undertaken by a third party. Whether the contracting-out of such a function constitutes a transfer of a business (or part of one) will vary from case to case. Much depends on exactly what is transferred from the company to the outside contractor. For example, it is clearly not a business transfer for a company to close down its own transport department and then sign a contract with a haulage firm that the latter will distribute its products for an agreed fee as and when required by the company.

However the position may be very different where the haulage firm buys the company's fleet of lorries and ancillary equipment, and the contract gives the haulage firm the exclusive right to distribute the company's products for its duration. There is some authority to support the contention that the right to act as the company's exclusive distributor may, of itself, constitute a business as a "going concern." It might be possible to argue that there is an element of goodwill in the exclusivity of the right to distribute the company's products. To satisfy the "going concern" test, it seems that the haulage firm would have to bear some risk of making a loss under the contract as well as a profit. However in such cases companies do not normally run their transport departments as separate "businesses," but as an integral part of their overall operations. Therefore the tribunals will only be prepared to treat such transport activities as capable of being a "going concern" if it can properly be regarded as a severable and identifiable part of a large enterprise (see p. 31 below). This is more likely to be the case where the transport activity is run as a separate division.

For example in *McLeod* v. *John Rostron & Sons Ltd.* [1972] I.T.R. 144, J.R. Ltd. ran a fleet of 80 vehicles for the sole purpose of servicing its paper business—*i.e.* it had no external customers. The fleet operated as a separate division which kept its own accounts and had a manager in charge of its operations. Nonetheless there was a degree of integration between the transport division and the main part of J.R. Ltd.'s business. J.R. Ltd. then decided to sell its transport division to B.R.S. Ltd.; and under the contract of sale, B.R.S. acquired the fleet of 80 vehicles, agreed to take on all the staff working in the division, and continued to provide J.R. Ltd. with exactly the same service as the division had provided prior to the sale. The N.I.R.C. held that, since the transport division was a separate and self-contained part of a larger business enterprise, it could properly be described as part of a business itself in the nature of a going concern. The fact that there was a degree of integration between the division and the larger business enterprise was inevitable in a business of this nature, but the extent of such integration was not so great as to prevent it from being an identifiable self-contained unit.

Management contracts

The same principles apply to contracts for the administration or management of a particular activity. The key is whether that activity can properly be regarded as a self-contained identifiable unit in the nature of a going concern (see p. 31 below). For example in *Lumley Insurance Consultants* v. *Pruddah & T.S.B. Trust Co. Ltd.* (unreported E.A.T. 150/83), a firm of insurance brokers (L.I.C.) administered a credit insurance scheme to the T.S.B., using one of its branch offices exclusively for this purpose. T.S.B. subsequently decided they wanted to run this themselves and, with L.I.C.'s agreement, took over the responsibility of running the credit insurance scheme. T.S.B. also took over the lease for the computer used by L.I.C. and paid a licence fee for the use of the software that L.I.C. had developed for that work. T.S.B. also took on some of

L.I.C.'s staff who had been involved in that work. The E.A.T. held that the definition of "business" in section 153(1) of the Employment Protection (Consolidation) Act included " . . . any activity carried on by a body of persons, whether corporate or unincorporated." The E.A.T. said it was necessary to look at the nature of the activity carried on rather than solely the means by which it is carried on. The E.A.T. concluded that the nature of the activity in this case was the provision of credit insurance to T.S.B. borrowers; and in those circumstances a business as a going concern had been transferred to T.S.B. when T.S.B. decided to purchase L.I.C.'s tangible assets for that activity and carry it on in-house.

Similarly in *Mannin Management Services Ltd.* v. *Ward* (unreported E.A.T. 253/87) a shopping centre was owned by M. Ltd., but it had contracted out its day-to-day management to a husband and wife partnership who traded as M.M.S. After 10 years, M. Ltd. decided to take charge of the management of the Shopping Centre and it withdrew the management contract from M.M.S. M. Ltd. then set up a new company "M.M.S. Ltd." to run the Shopping Centre for M. Ltd. On the date this took effect, M. Ltd. put in two new managers who carried on the same activities as had been performed by M.M.S. They continued to use the same bank account as M.M.S. had been using, and all of M.M.S.'s staff carried on working for M.M.S. Ltd. The E.A.T. and the Court of Appeal upheld the tribunal's decision that the transaction did constitute a business transfer.

Supply of labour

As a general rule, the supply of labour from one company to another will not be regarded as a separate business where the supplier of the staff is part of the same group of companies as the user and it does not supply staff to organisations outside that group of companies. This will especially be the case where the supply function is separate from assets and goodwill of the business to which the staff are supplied. It is quite common for large groups of companies to employ certain staff in a "service company" and require those staff to undertake their employment duties by giving their services to one or more companies within the group (for example the personnel, accounting and administration functions).

For example in *B.I.F.U.* v. *Barclays Bank plc. & Others* Barclays Bank decided to establish a new investment bank—B.Z.W. This was formed from a merger of its merchant bank (B.M.B.) and other firms of stockbrokers in which Barclays had a controlling interest. Prior to this change, the staff engaged to work at B.M.B. were actually employees of Barclays and were seconded to B.M.B. under an inter-group labour supply arrangement. Barclays decided that the new investment bank B.Z.W. would be staffed from a new company it would set up for that purpose as well as to provide other services for B.Z.W. All the staff at B.M.B. consented to transferring across to this new service company called B.Z.W.-S. Barclays then transferred its labour supply arrangements to B.Z.W.-S, and then transferred B.M.B.'s business to B.Z.W. The banking union (B.I.F.U.) claimed that it should have been informed and consulted about these changes under regulation 10 of the Transfer Regulations (see p. 118). However B.I.F.U. had no such legal right to be consulted unless it could establish that the supply of labour function from Barclays to B.M.B. constituted a business in the nature of a going concern (or an identifiable part of one), and therefore when the labour supply arrangement was transferred from Barclays to B.Z.W.-S., this transaction was a business transfer. B.I.F.U. argued that it was such a transaction because assets and goodwill had been transferred from Barclays to B.Z.W.-S.—*i.e.* the assets were the pool of staff and the goodwill was the guaranteed "custom" of the various companies within the Barclays group of companies. The E.A.T. upheld the tribunal's conclusion that the labour supply function was not a business in which any goodwill or assets were engaged, nor was it an identifiable self-contained part of a larger business.

Parts of businesses

Transferring parts of businesses as a going concern

All of the above considerations apply equally to those cases where a part of a business is transferred as a going concern. Paragraph 17(2), Schedule 13 E.P.C.A. (continuity of employment), section 94 E.P.C.A. and the Transfer Regulations all apply equally to transfers of part of a business. However that part so transferred must still be capable of satisfying the "going concern" test set out in the *Kenmir* case (see p. 13 above). To do so, it must also be a separate, self-contained and identifiable part of the larger business which it is leaving—see *Green* v. *Wavertree Heating & Plumbing Co. Ltd.* [1978] I.C.R. 928. This will be easier to establish where the part transferred is run as a separate division or has its own accounts and management. It is not fatal that there is a degree of integration with the larger business enterprise provided the part can be so separated and identified—see *McLeod* v. *John Rostron* [1972] I.T.R. 144.

Separation and self-containment of business

In the *Green* case P. Ltd. carried out gas fitting and plumbing contracts. It subsequently sold the gas fitting side to W.H.P. Ltd. The E.A.T. held that this was a transfer of a going concern. The E.A.T. added (at p. 932):

> " . . . it is not really necessary to be able to show that the transferred part had prior to the transfer been carried on separately and in a self-contained manner. It is sufficient if it can be seen that the part transferred, which then is self-contained and separate, is a recognisable part of the whole business out of which it is separated."

On the facts of that case, the gas fitting part was regarded as separate although it used common administrative resources with the plumbing part. Similarly in the *McLeod* case (p. 29) and the *Rastill* case the transport and catering sections of a larger business were regarded as severable and identifiable self-contained parts.

Establishing self-containment

It is a question of fact and degree whether the relevant part of the business is sufficiently separate and severable. In the *Melon* case, [1981] I.C.R. 43 (at p. 50) Lord Fraser said:

> "a change in ownership of a part of a business will . . . seldom occur except when that part is to some extent separate and severable from the rest of the business, either geographically or by reference to the products or in some other way."

Thus in *Edgar* v. *Robert Elliott Ltd.* (unreported E.A.T. 581/85), the sale of one of three factories was regarded as a sufficiently severable and separate part of the business to constitute a business transfer. Similarly in *Atkin* v. *Ward & Haines Watts* [1983] I.C.R. 231, the sale by an accountant of a block of clients in the Nottingham area to another firm of accountants was a business transfer, even though the vendor kept on his clients he operated from his London office; and in *G.D. Ault (Isle of Wight) Ltd.* v. *Gregory* [1967] I.T.R. 301, the sale of an estate developer's Isle of Wight office and contracts was a sufficiently severable and separate part of the vendor's business which included other offices.

In contrast, the surrender of a particular contract by a company engaged in performing numerous contracts is most unlikely to amount to a business transfer. For example in *Newlin Oil Co. Ltd.* v. *Tratford* [1974] I.R.L.R. 205, Newlin acted as distributors for Shell and B.P. They subsequently gave up their B.P. distributorship and concentrated solely on Shell products. The N.I.R.C. held that the B.P. distributorship was not an identifiable and separate business, but was merely one contract carried on by the existing business of distributing oils/petrol. Newlin's business carried on as before, the only difference was that its supplier had changed.

The distinction is easier to draw where the part transferred is already operating as a separate division or deals wholly with a particular product line (for example where a factory producing only one of the company's many products is sold). It is more difficult where the "unit" being transferred is merely a department within a closely integrated larger organisation. Even there, self-contained identifiable parts can still be found—see the *Rastill* case (p. 27) where the catering activity was regarded as sufficiently self-contained and separate. However in the *B.I.F.U.* v. *Barclays* case [1987] I.C.R. 495, an inter-group labour supply arrangement was held by the E.A.T. not to be a sufficiently identifiable part of the business. In contrast in *Dishman* v. *Mansfield Engineering Ltd. & Paterplan Ltd.* (unreported; C.O.I.T. 1399/70) a tribunal held that a contract between M.E. Ltd. and British Gas, whereby the former supplied personnel and draughting services to British Gas, was a separate and severable part of M.E. Ltd.'s business.

In *Dallow Industrial Properties* v. *Else* [1967] I.T.R. 304, the High Court held that the maintenance and security departments of a factory which manufactured stoves were not severable and separate parts of the business. The High Court said that the word "activity" in the definition of "business" did not include each constituent department concerned in the running of an enterprise, unless it was truly self-contained and severable from that enterprise.

Transfers of contract manufacturing agreements

Contract manufacturing agreements are more problematic. In some business transfers, the purchaser acquires the trade marks, brand names, existing contracts and goodwill of one of the vendor's products. As such there will be a business transfer when those assets are sold. However, the commercial contract may provide that the vendor will retain its manufacturing capacity for those products (for example, its factory, machinery, raw materials and staff) and the vendor enters into a contract manufacturing agreement with the purchaser to supply an agreed quantity of the products for a specified period of time at an agreed price. For important reasons which will be made clear when the Transfer Regulations are dealt with later in this book (see p. 52), the manufacturing employees of the vendor will probably not transfer across with the business into the employment of the purchaser, but will remain with the vendor. What therefore happens when the contract manufacturing agreement comes to an end and the agreement is either awarded to another manufacturer or the work is done by the purchaser? Can the activity of providing the purchaser with certain brand products be regarded as a separate and identifiable part of the vendor's business?

There are two possible scenarios. First, the commercial transaction may provide for the vendor's business (including its manufacturing rights) to be transferred to the purchaser, who then immediately licenses them to the vendor for a limited period under a contract manufacturing agreement. Secondly, the purchaser may only acquire the exclusive distributorship and brand names of certain products, but not the means of manufacturing those products. However until the purchaser can build his own factory, the vendor agrees to continue to supply the purchaser with those products. In the first case, it may well be arguable that the exclusive licence to manufacture certain products for the purchase is a business in its own right in common with other trading licences (see p. 24). Therefore when the vendor surrenders the licence on the expiry of the contract manufacturing agreement, it could be argued that there is a separate (part) business transfer of the business. In the second case, the manufacturing of the purchaser's products is unlikely to be a business in its own right. This distinction seems to be supported by the tribunal in *Evans & Gardiner* v. *Tri-R. Ltd.* (unreported [1984] C.O.I.T. 1550/57) where C. Ltd. manufactured and sold parts for the motor and caravan industries. C. Ltd. then decided to contract out the manufacture of two particular parts to T. Ltd. The commercial contract between C. Ltd. and T. Ltd. consisted of a leasing agreement whereby 75 per cent. of C. Ltd.'s equipment was leased to T. Ltd., an undertaking by C. Ltd. to purchase T. Ltd.'s goods, and an undertaking by T. Ltd. to supply C. Ltd. with those two parts on an exclusive basis. The tribunal held that the transaction did involve a sufficiently separate and identifiable part to C. Ltd.'s business to constitute the sale of part of a business in the nature of a going concern. The tribunal placed emphasis on the fact that the two products were the same, as was the machinery used to produce it and the market to which it was supplied.

In the first scenario, whether or not there has been a single transfer or two transfers depends on how the initial transaction between the purchaser and vendor has been structured. In some cases, the purchaser may not immediately acquire the manufacturing rights, but may subsequently do so on the exercise of an option. In such a case a tribunal may consider the exercise of the option by the purchaser as merely one of several steps in the same overall transaction. The E.C.J.'s views in the *Ny Molle Kro* case [1989] I.R.L.R. 37 suggest that a contract manufacturing agreement may well amount to the operating of an identifiable part of the purchaser's business.

Has there been a transfer?

Establishing a transfer of assets

It is normally clear whether or not tangible or intangible assets have been transferred from the vendor to the purchaser—there will almost always be some contractual document containing the terms of the transaction. However the absence of a formal legal document does not exclude the possibility that assets have been transferred—the only written evidence of an assets sale might be a bill of sale or receipt. Indeed in *Cartwright* v. *Norton* (unreported E.A.T. 91/82) the E.A.T. suggested that there need be no direct legal relationship between two persons for there to have been a transfer of a business if the nature of the business is inherently and necessarily bound up with the occupation of certain premises (such as a hotel or pub).

De facto transfers

In *Dabell* v. *Vale Industrial Services (Nottingham) Ltd.* [1988] I.R.L.R. 439, the Court of Appeal held that a transfer could take place even though there was no formal agreement between the parties. It was sufficient that there had been a *de facto* transfer of the business to the transferee. In that case, by the date of the applicant's dismissal, the transferor had closed its premises and handed over to the transferee its equipment, customers, goodwill, existing contracts and employees—even though the formalities of a business transfer had not been completed. The Court of Appeal held that a business transfer could take place, even though there was a possibility that it might be transferred back to the vendor if negotiations fell through—*i.e.* a transfer could take place even though it was not final and conclusive. The *Dabell* case has obvious implications for parties to a business transfer who arrange for transfer of assets to the purchaser in the period between exchange of contracts and completion. If, at the relevant time, the extent of the assets transferred, and the purchaser's involvement with the business to be transferred, can be regarded as a business in the nature of a going concern (as compared to merely a collection of assets), then there is a real risk that a tribunal may conclude that the moment of transfer has taken place at a date earlier than completion.

No direct transaction between parties

Tri-partite transactions

As has been explained above (see p. 23), it is possible for a business to be transferred between two parties even though there is no direct transaction between them. This may occur, for example, where a pub tenancy or franchise or petrol station licence changes hands. The tribunals have concluded that transfers have taken place, although they have differed on how that result was achieved. For example:

Possible methods of transfer

1. In the *Premier Motors* case, [1983] I.R.L.R. 471, the

E.A.T. held that on the change of licensee of a petrol station, there was one transfer of business on the surrender of the licence to the petrol company (*i.e.* the licensor) and another business transfer from the licensor to the incoming licensee when the new licence was immediately granted to him. The E.A.T. said that the petrol company was owner of the business of selling its petrol at a particular petrol station for a split second before granting a new licence to the incoming licensee.

2. In the *Norris* case (unreported E.A.T. 738/83), the E.A.T. held that there was a direct transfer of the licence to run the Little Brickhills Service Station from Mr. Bedwell to Mr. Norris, even though (a) there was no direct assignment of the licence between the two, (b) the transfer was achieved by the petrol company accepting the surrender of Mr. Bedwell's licence and then immediately granting a new licence to Mr. Norris, and (c) the only assets transferred between Mr. Bedwell and Mr. Norris were some miscellaneous equipment for which Mr. Norris paid about £300. The E.A.T. considered that the surrender of the licence and the grant of a new one was merely a formality which was necessary to put Mr. Norris in ownership of Mr. Bedwell's business.

These two "routes" to effect a transfer of a business between two persons or companies do not, of course, need to be relied on where the outgoing licensee obtains the licensor's consent to assign the licence, tenancy or franchise. It is suggested that the approach adopted by the E.A.T. in the *Premier* case is preferable because the E.A.T.'s reasoning in the *Norris* case is, with respect, rather artificial where the licensor both finds the new licensee and has the power to stop the outgoing licensee from transferring his business to someone of his own choice or at all. The fact that surrender of a lease to the lessor and the grant of a new lease to a new lessee can effect a business transfer has been confirmed by the European Court in *Foreningen AF Arbejdsledere I Danmark* v. *Daddy's Dance Hall A/S* [1988] I.R.L.R. 315. In that case Mr. Tellerup was a manager of one of a series of bars and restaurants run by Irma Catering under a non-transferable lease with the landlord Palads Teatret. Irma Catering surrendered its interest in the lease to Palads Teatret, and the latter then granted a new lease to Daddy's Dance Hall A/S who then ran the restaurants and bars in the stead of Irma Catering. The European Court held that this was a business transfer within the scope of the Business Transfer Directive and that it did not matter that the transfer was effected in two stages. However, the court did not say whether it was a single transfer directly between the two lessees, or two separate transfers (each involving the lessor). In two subsequent cases (the *P. Bork International AS* and *Ny Molle Kro* cases) the E.C.J. adopted a similar view without, again, saying whether such surrender of a lease/licence and its re-grant to an incoming licensee was a single or a double transfer. In the *Ny Molle Kro* case, the E.C.J. said:

"It follows that insofar as the managing lessee acquires the capacity under the lease of employer within the above

> meaning, the transfer must be considered as a transfer of an undertaking to another employer as a result of a legal transfer within the meaning of Article 1(1) of the Directive. Similar considerations apply in the event that the owner takes back the running of the leased undertaking following a breach of the lease by the managing lessee. Such a resumption also takes place on the basis of the lease. Consequently, insofar as its effect is that the managing lessee loses its capacity as employer which capacity is re-acquired by the owner, it should be considered as a transfer of undertaking to another employer as a result of a legal transfer within the meaning of Article 1(1) . . .".

In the *P. Bork International AS* case, the E.C.J. said:

> "when the lessee in its capacity as employer loses this capacity at the end of the lease and the third party subsequently acquires this capacity under a contract of sale included with the owner, the resulting transaction could fall within the scope of the Directive, as defined in Article 1(1). The fact that, in such a case, a transfer takes place in two stages in as much as the undertaking is initially re-transferred by the lessee to the owner, who then transfers it to the new owner, does not preclude the application of the Directive, providing that the undertaking in question retained its identity . . .".

It will be seen that, in both cases, the E.C.J. merely stated that the Directive applied, and did not say whether the transaction was a single or a double transfer. However, that the inference from the quotation in the *P. Bork International* case tends to favour the former view.

Types of dispositions

Thus the above cases show that a transfer of a business can take place by a variety of routes:

1. a simple contract of sale or other disposition of a business (stated to be such);
2. the sale or gift of a collection of assets which, in the circumstances, constitute a business in the nature of a going concern;
3. the assignment of a tenancy, licence or franchise (usually requiring the licensor's consent);
4. the surrender of a licence, etc., and the grant of a new one;
5. the contracting-out of a severable and separate activity previously carried on "in-house" (*e.g.* catering and cleaning);
6. the end of a contract manufacturing agreement (in some circumstances);
7. the termination of a contract for certain services previously provided by an outside contractor—see the *Hadden* case (above p. 27).

Series of transactions

Tribunals look at the totality of a particular transaction when deciding whether on not a transfer has taken place and between whom. However the Transfer Regulations expressly allow for regard to be had to a series of transactions between the same parties. Regulation 3(4) provides:

> " . . . a transfer of an undertaking or part of one may be effected by a series of two or more transactions between the same parties, but in determining whether or not such a series constitutes a single transfer regard shall be had to the extent to which the undertaking or part was controlled by the transferor and transferee respectively before the last transaction, to the lapse of time between each of the transactions, to the intention of the parties and to all the other circumstances."

This provision is obviously necessary to stop vendors and purchasers from circumventing the dramatic effect of the Transfer Regulations (see p. 6 for a brief summary) by arranging for the business being transferred in small units so that the assets are transferred separately from the employees. This would have the effect of defeating the prime objective of the Transfer Regulations—*i.e.* that the employees should transfer along with the business with their existing terms and conditions of employment intact. However, it is unclear whether regulation 3(4) requires that all the transactions must be between the same parties, or whether the word "may" is merely permissive in its effect. This point has not been finally resolved by the tribunals; but it is thought that the use of the word "may" attaches to the possibility that a relevant transfer may be effected by a series of transactions rather than to the identity of the parties to those transactions. Thus, it is submitted, the proper construction of regulation 3(4) does require all the transactions to be between the same parties. This would not have the effect of defeating the objective of the Transfer Regulations since, in most cases, the eventual transferee would inherit the relevant employees under the Transfer Regulations by means of a "double transfer," as in the *Premier Motors* case. However, unfortunately, the E.A.T. has not always adopted a common view on this issue.

In the *Norris* case (see above) the E.A.T. said that the surrender by Mr. Bedwell of the licence (to run a petrol station) to the petrol company and the grant of a new licence to the incoming licensee (Mr. Norris) and a sale of a few miscellaneous pieces of equipment between Messrs Bedwell and Norris was, in effect, a series of transactions between the transferor (Mr. Bedwell) and the transferee (Mr. Norris). The E.A.T. placed emphasis on the fact that the various transactions occurred at about the same time and that the intention of the parties was to put Mr. Norris in possession of the running of the business of selling Chevron's petrol and oils from that filling station. They considered that the involvement of the petrol company was merely a vehicle to give effect to this. With respect to the E.A.T. in this case, they did not take account of the key fact that at the moment of the last transaction (*i.e.* the grant of Mr. Bedwell's surrendered licence to Mr. Norris), Mr. Norris had no control over that last stage. Theoretically the petrol company could have decided not to grant the licence to Mr. Norris. It is for this reason that the approach adopted in the *Premier Motors* case is preferable—*i.e.* to treat the facts as two consecutive business transfers. However the E.A.T. in Scotland adopted a similar approach to regulation 3(4) in *Forth Estuary Engineering*

Ltd. v. *Litster* [1986] I.R.L.R. 59, where it indicated that it did not matter that all the transactions were not between the same parties so long as they were all part of the same general scheme of transactions. Whilst this may certainly comply with the spirit of the Transfer Regulations, it must be doubted whether it really is the correct interpretation of the wording of regulation 3(4). Similarly, in *Sibbard* v. *Fraser* (unreported E.A.T 298/87), the E.A.T. held the transfer of a licence for a pub from H. to B., followed by a similar grant from B. to the new licensee S. was a single transaction. The E.A.T. seemed to put some emphasis that an eventual grant of the licence to B.'s nominee (*i.e.* S.) was expressly provided for in the agreement between H. and B.

In *Litster* v. *Forth Estuary Engineering Ltd.* [1989] (H.L. 16.3.89) Lord Oliver approved the approach adopted by the E.A.T. earlier in the case. He said (*obiter*)

> "What is said is that regulation 3(4), which declares . . . that a transfer may be effected by a series of two or more transactions between the same parties, rules out, by implication, as a relevant element in the transfer, a transaction between one of the parties and a third party . . . I do not, for a start, consider that any such implication can be legitimately drawn from the wording of the Regulation, but in any event, regulation 3(4) does not purport to be anything more than declaratory and cannot be properly construed as in any sense an exclusive definition of what can constitute a transfer."

Some commentators have suggested that the E.C.J.'s ruling in *Foreningen AF Arbejdsledere I Danmark* v. *Daddy's Dance Hall A/S* (see above) is authority to support the view that the surrender of a lease by the outgoing lessee and the grant of a new lease to an incoming lessee constitutes a single business transfer. It is submitted that this interpretation of the E.C.J.'s ruling is not correct. It is true that the E.C.J. said that the Acquired Rights Directive applied to such a tripartite transaction and had the result of putting the incoming lessee into the shoes of the outgoing lessee. But the E.C.J. did not say whether this result had been achieved by one or two business transfers. This issue may be one of semantics since under both views, the eventual licensee will inherit the relevant liabilities for the employees. But the difference may be of importance where there are dismissals between the surrender of one licence and the grant of another.

Contract manufacturing agreements

Can a contract manufacturing agreement be a business?

As already discussed (on p. 33), it is a moot point whether a contract manufacturing agreement can properly be said to be a business in its own right. The answer depends on the facts of each case. However such agreements do also throw up a second question: on the expiry of the agreement, is there a transfer to the purchaser and, if so, of what? The answer depends on how the contract manufacturing agreement fits into the overall structure of the commercial transaction between the vendor and purchaser.

If the exclusive manufacturing rights had been transferred

to the purchaser with the rest of the assets acquired from the vendor, then it seems that the expiry of the contract manufacturing agreement has the effect of reverting that right to the purchaser. In such circumstances it is at least arguable that this reversion is merely the last in a series of transactions between the same parties, and so regulation 3(4) applies accordingly.

In contrast, where the commercial transaction between the vendor and purchaser left the manufacturing rights with the vendor, but gave the purchaser an option to acquire them, it may be arguable that there is a second business transfer—*i.e.* of the manufacturing rights (if these can properly be said to be a business in their own right). Alternatively, there is a possibility that, as in the *Sibbard* case, where the tribunal put great weight on the fact that the possibility of transfer had been foreseen in the main agreement, and therefore the exercise of the option by the purchaser was merely the last in a series of transactions.

3 WHEN DO THE TRANSFER REGULATIONS APPLY?

Introduction: significance of the regulations

It is only if there has been a business transfer that the Transfer Regulations apply to protect various employment rights of employees and recognised trade unions [see p. 12 above]. However, although the E.A.T. has made it clear that the words "transfer of undertaking" (in the Transfer Regulations), "transfer of trade, undertaking or business" (in E.P.C.A., para. 17(2) Sched. 13, continuity of employment) and "change in ownership of a business" (in E.P.C.A. s.94, forfeiture of redundancy pay) should be construed to have the same meaning, employees and their trade unions will not have the protection afforded by the Transfer Regulations unless certain additional criteria are satisfied. This means that, in some business transfers, employees will qualify for the fuller protection afforded by the Transfer Regulations, whilst in others only their period of continuous service will be protected (E.P.C.A., para. 17(2), Sched. 13), and they may run the risk of losing their statutory redundancy pay (E.P.C.A., s.94). See p. 140 for a summary of the position where the Transfer Regulations do not apply to business transfers.

Conditions for transfer regulations to apply

The Transfer Regulations apply where the following conditions have been satisfied:—

Transfer must be of an undertaking situated in the United Kingdom

The Regulations only apply to a: "transfer from one person to another of an undertaking situated immediately before the transfer in the United Kingdom or a part of one which is so situated" regulation 3(1). This means that there must have been a business transfer [see p. 12 above] and that the business or part of it so transferred is situated in the United Kingdom. Therefore the Regulations will also apply to United Kingdom subsidiary companies and United Kingdom branches of overseas multinational companies. The time for ascertaining where the undertaking is situated is "immediately before the transfer." This has been interpreted as meaning the moment before the transfer takes place—see *Secretary of State for Employment* v. *Spence* [1986] I.R.L.R. 248; but see p. 54.

How the transfer is effected: regulation 3(2)

The Regulations are drafted very widely to cover any business transfer whether it: "is effected by sale or by some other disposition or by operation of law"—regulation 3(2). See p. 54 above for the wide range of methods by which the transfer might be effected. The Regulations refer to the "transferor" and "transferee," and it is clear that they apply to cases other than a simple sale of a business. However, for ease of reference this book uses the terms "vendor" to cover the "transferor" and "purchaser" to cover the "transferee"—in practice most business transfers will be straight sales. But it should be noted that the words "some other disposition" clearly cover any method by which a business changes hands—*e.g.* by surrender and grant of a licence or franchise. There need also be no money or other consideration transferred between the two owners—see *Brooks* v. *The Grays Co-operative Society* [1967] I.T.R. 345.

It should also be noted that, by virtue of regulation 3(4), the Transfer Regulations do apply to business transfers effected by a series of transfers between the same parties—see p. 36 above.

The "commercial venture" requirement: regulation 2(1)

The business transferred must be in the nature of a commercial venture. Regulation 2(1) defines an "undertaking" including: "any trade or business but does not include any undertaking or part of an undertaking which is not in the nature of a commercial venture." This is the main distinction between business transfers covered by the Transfer Regulations and those which are not. The Regulations do not state what is meant by a "commercial venture," but it is generally assumed to mean an activity run with a view to making a profit and taking the risk as to losses. Unfortunately the cases have not been particularly helpful. In *Woodcock* v. *Committee of Friends School, Wigton and Another* [1987] I.R.L.R. 98. May L.J. said in the Court of Appeal:

Case law on regulation 2(1)

> " . . . as a general guide I think the fact that a venture is entered into with a view to making a profit is a consideration in deciding whether or not it is in the nature of a commercial one, that is only a guide and I prefer the first impression approach of the E.A.T. to the particular question in issue. I think that it is impossible to cover every particular set of circumstances."

May L.J. went on to say that he knew a commercial venture when he saw one and left that issue to be decided by industrial tribunals. The effect of such a test is to leave in the hands of industrial tribunals the assessment of whether a particular activity is in the nature of a commercial venture. This will obviously lead to some uncertainty of approach by tribunals and make it very difficult to appeal against their conclusions on this issue.

In the *Woodcock* case [see above], the tribunal had found that a fee-paying school run under a charitable trust was not in the nature of a commercial venture since its aim was merely to break-even and apply any surplus funds for the school. Interestingly, the tribunal had accepted that the school was a business.

The profit-motive loomed large in *Hadden* v. *University of Dundee Students' Association* [1985] I.R.L.R. 449, where the students union contracted out its catering operation to A.R.A. Services Ltd. It was to be run on a break-even basis with A.R.A. Services taking a percentage of any profit made and a fixed management fee. The E.A.T. upheld the tribunal's conclusion that the catering operation was not in the nature of a commercial venture, principally because it took no risk on the losses. However the E.A.T. did comment that the term "commercial venture" is wide in scope and could cover situations where a venture is deliberately run at a loss.

The importance of profit and loss has been consistently applied in other cases where the commercial nature of a business has been in doubt:

Specific types of transfer: are they within regulation 2(1)?

Council projects. In *Loughran* v. *Coseley Community Services* [1984] unreported (C.O.I.T. 1487/134), the tribunal held that the training scheme run by the Council for young people was not in the nature of a commercial venture since there was no intention to make profits or risk of suffering a loss. Similarly in *Ferretti* v. *Southwark & Lambeth Archeological Projects Ltd.* [1984] unreported (C.O.I.T. 1479/222), the activity of supervising archeological excavations funded by various other organisations was not a commercial venture because there was no possibility of making a profit; and in *McDonough* v. *Wigan Metropolitan Borough Council* [1983] unreported (C.O.I.T. 1417/196); I.T., a community project financed by the M.S.C. for training was similarly not a commercial venture. However in *Craggs* v. *Sutherland Training & Trading Ltd.* [1983] unreported (C.O.I.T. 1420/84); I.T., the tribunal held that a council project set up to train young people in the commercial work and which sold products to other Council departments, was in the nature of a commercial venture. The tribunal placed particular emphasis on the facts that:

1. the word "trading" appeared in its title,
2. the company was formed by the Council to widen its market and to operate from a commercial perspective,
3. its prime activity was selling which (the tribunal thought) is a distinctive feature of a commercial venture and
4. the company's aim was to break even and it bore the risk of running at a deficit.

Inter-group transfers. In many cases a change in the identity of the company providing services to other companies within the same group of companies will not be a business transfer in the nature of a commercial venture—see *B.I.F.U.* v. *Barclays Bank plc* [1987] I.C.R. 495, where an internal group arrangement for the supply of staff was held not to be a venture of a commercial nature.

Privatisation. There has been little caselaw on the question whether the privatisation of a community activity such as rubbish collection or street cleaning is a business in the nature of a commercial venture. In the *Craggs* case [see above] the tribunal commented that the privatisation of the NCB or British Steel would be. It is suggested that there is no reason why the rubbish collection department or the street cleaning departments of local councils cannot be regarded as a severable and identifiable part of a larger enterprise (the local council) and for it to be run as a commercial enterprise after its privatisation—see the cases on transfers of parts of business on p. 31 above.

Time at which undertaking must be a commercial venture

Unfortunately the Regulations are not clear on whether it is also necessary that the business is in the nature of a commercial venture *prior* to its transfer. A literal reading of the words of the Regulations, suggests that it is. Regulation 3(1) says the Regulations apply to: "... a transfer ... of an undertaking. ..." Regulation 2(1) excludes from the definition of undertaking "any undertaking or part ... which is not in the nature of a commercial venture." If these two references are read together, they suggest that the Regulations do not "bite" on a transfer of anything but an "undertaking" as defined in regulation 2(1). Yet such an undertaking must be in the nature of a commercial venture in order for the Regulations to apply to it. It therefore follows that if the venture or activity in question is not one which falls within the Regulations' definition of an "undertaking" (*i.e.* one of a commercial nature) *at the moment of the transfer* there is no undertaking upon which the Regulations can attach themselves; and thus they will not apply. This raises the key question: is a public service (which is run with no intent of making a profit) suddenly metamorphised into a commercial venture merely by the completion of the transfer agreement? It is rather a "chicken and egg" exercise. If it is the transfer itself which creates the transformation from a non-commercial to a commercial venture, then the Regulations cannot apply to it since the transfer would have taken place a split second *before* the venture changes its character. But, if it is the intention of the transferee which is the key factor, then it does not matter that, technically, the transfer has to precede the transformation. One problem in the way of this approach is the suggestion in the *Woodcock* case [1987] I.R.L.R. 98, that it is the vendor's intention that is relevant, not the purchaser's. However if the latter interpretation is correct, the way may then be clear for tribunals to conclude that the transfer took place of a venture which *at the same moment in time* changed from one of a non-commercial nature to one of a commercial nature. It is suggested that, although the former view is probably correct from a purely legal perspective, the latter view may be adopted by tribunals since it follows the spirit of the Business Transfer Directive and would stop many thousands of council employees from losing their protection when their departments are privatised. Some support for the view that the undertaking need not be operating as a commercial venture prior the date of transfer may be found in *Royal Ordinance plc* v. *Pilkington* [1988] I.C.R. 606, where the E.A.T. seemed to accept (without deciding the point) that the privatisation of the Royal Ordinance factories did fall within the scope of the Transfer Regulations. However this issue is highly contentious and caselaw guidance is urgently needed.

By way of contrast, where a nationalised industry was previously run with a profit motive (*e.g.* National Buses), it seems very likely that tribunals will conclude that the undertaking is in the nature of a commercial venture.

It does not matter whether or not the particular undertaking is operating at a loss at the time of the business transfer, provided it is *capable* of being run at a profit—see *Anderson* v. *Kluwer Publishing Ltd.* [1985] (unreported; C.O.I.T. 15068/85), where the activity of publishing of a magazine was held to be in the nature of a commercial venture, even though, at the time of the sale, it was running at a loss.

EEC law

It is open to debate whether the exclusion of non-commercial ventures from the scope of the Transfer Regulations is in contravention of the Business Transfer Directive. There is no express exclusion in the Directive although, it might be argued that the use of the word "business" connotes a commercial body. However, in the *European Commission* v. *Belgium* case [1988] 2 C.M.L.R. 865, the E.C.J. clearly stated that the implementing legislation of Member States should not diminish existing rights of employees. Prior to the implementation of the Transfer Regulations, employees working in non-commercial ventures had the same rights as all other employees; but the Transfer Regulations excludes that class of employee from its scope. This seems to be as much a breach of the Directive as in the *EC* v. *Belgium* case [see above], where the Belgian equivalent of the Transfer Regulations sought to exclude seasonal and student workers from it, and thus limiting their existing rights.

A further reason to suggest that the definition of an undertaking is in breach of the Directive lies in the dicta in the *Wendelboe* case [1985] 1 C.M.L.R. 476; E.C.J., to the effect that the interpretation of the words of the Directive should be the same as currently adopted by Member States in their existing law. The Directive uses the word "business" synonomously with "undertaking"; and under section 153(1) of the E.P.C.A. the word "business" is defined as including "any activity" and has no exclusion of non-commercial ventures. Further, the case law pre-dating the Transfer Regulations had not sought to put a "commercial gloss" on to that definition of "business." [See p. 8 above for how the Business Transfer Directive might be relied on.]

Transfers of parts of undertakings

Transfers of parts of undertakings must be transferred as a business. It is clear that the Transfer Regulations require that parts of undertakings transferred must satisfy two requirements:

1. the part must be identifiable and severable from the large business from which it is being separated [see p. 31 above]; and
2. it must also be "transferred as a business"—see regulation 2(2).

The second requirement is a little ambiguous. Does it mean that the part transferred must have been run as a business in its own right at the moment of transfer, or that it will be run as a business from the moment of transfer? Unfortunately there have been no cases yet on what these words mean. It is suggested that they merely confirm the existing case law authority that the part transferred must be a severable and identifiable business unit as at the moment of transfer. There is no definition of the word "business" in the Transfer Regulations, but since the E.A.T. in the *Premier Motors* case [1983] I.R.L.R. 471; E.A.T. suggests that the E.P.C.A. and Transfer Regulations should adopt uniform meanings of trade or business, it is possible to refer to E.P.C.A., s.153(1), which contains a definition of "business" as follows: "includes a trade or profession and includes *any activity carried on* by a body of persons. . . . " The words "any activity" seem wide enough to cover identifiable departments, product lines or divisions within a company or other organisation. It is submitted that they do not mean business in its commercial sense.

Scope of the transfer regulations

Foreign law governing the transfer: regulation 3(2)

The Regulations apply regardless of the law governing the business transfer (*e.g.* the sale or acquisition agreement between the vendor and purchaser)—regulation 3(2)(a). Therefore parties cannot preclude the operation of the Regulations by adopting the law of another country to be governing law of their contract.

As will be seen later, the Transfer Regulations apply to safeguard the rights of employees on a business transfer. They apply regardless whether the governing law of the person's employment contract is that of England, Scotland or any other country—regulation 3(2)(c); and they apply to protect the employment rights of any person employed in the undertaking situated in the United Kingdom, even though he ordinarily works outside the United Kingdom—regulation 3(2)(b). This later rule will apply, for example, where a senior executive is employed by a branch or company or other undertaking which is situated in the United Kingdom, even though he spends most of his time working outside it.

Transfers outside the scope of the regulations

The Transfer Regulations do not apply to share transfers or to pure asset transfers—only to business transfers which are in the nature of a commercial venture. Nor do they apply to a transfer of a ship by itself—regulation 2(2). However where a ship represents one of the assets of a shipping line which is sold or otherwise transferred, the Transfer Regulations will apply to that business transfer and will protect the employment rights of seamen on only those ships registered in the United Kingdom immediately before the transfer took place.

Meaning of contracts of employment/employee

Definition of employee: regulation 2(1)

Much of the Transfer Regulations refer to employees and their employment contracts. However it should be noted that the definition of an employee is wider than for normal employment protection purposes. Regulation 2(1) defines an employee as:

> "any individual who works for another person whether under a contract of service or apprenticeship or *otherwise* but does not include a contract for services. . . . "

This wording is wider than the statutory definition of an employee under the E.P.C.A., but it expressly excludes contractors such as self-employed contractors or consultants. However the definition does appear to cover persons such as casual workers or trainees on Government training schemes who do not satisfy the narrower E.P.C.A. definition of "employee."

The definition of employee is important because only employees'contracts of employment are automatically transferred by the business transfer from the vendor to the purchaser under regulation 5 [see p. 53 below]. The use of the words: "any individual who works for another . . . " is a little

Seconded workers

misleading. It is submitted that it does not cover persons who are assigned or seconded by *another* employer to work at the vendor's premises or to assist the vendor in its business. At first sight the words: " . . . whether under a contract of service, apprenticeship or otherwise . . . " should be construed "*eiusdem generis*"—*i.e.* that they refer to some kind of legal relationship between the individual person and a third party (his employer). This construction is consistent with the wording of regulation 5(1) which identifies the contract of employment as the legal concept on which the automatic transfer principle under the Transfer Regulations "bites."

Meaning of contract of employment

Regulation 2(1) defines a contract of employment as: "any *agreement* between an employee and his employer determining the terms and conditions of his employment" (the author's emphasis). It is therefore erroneous to look simply at the identity of the employer who is receiving the benefit of his services. That employer will not be the individual's own employer unless there is a legal relationship of some sort between them. Further, that legal relationship (whether oral or in writing) must cover the employee's terms and conditions (*e.g.* hours of work, pay, etc.). Therefore the automatic transfer principle enshrined in the Transfer Regulations does not operate on the contracts of employees of sub-contractors or associated employers (*e.g.* a parent company) who have assigned or seconded them to work for the vendor of a business transfer.

"Relevant transfer"

What is a "relevant transfer"?

The Regulations refer to the concept of a "relevant transfer." This is merely a term of art used to describe a business transfer to which the Transfer Regulations apply (reg. 2(1)—see above).

Contracting-out of the transfer regulations

Circumventing the regulations: regulation 12

It is not possible for the effect of the Transfer Regulations to be circumvented by any agreement which seeks to limit or exclude their operation. Regulation 12 provides that:

> "Any provision of any agreement (whether a contract of employment or not) shall be void in so far as it purports to exclude or limit the operation of regulation 5, 8 or 10 . . . or to preclude any person from bringing a complaint to an industrial tribunal under regulation 11. . . . "

This means that an employee cannot waive his rights under the Transfer Regulations and, if he does so, such waiver will be void and thus unenforceable. This restriction on contracting out applies to the following parts of the Regulations:

1. regulation 5, which embodies the automatic transfer of employment principle—see chapter 48 below;
2. regulation 8, which provides for automatically unfair dismissals in certain cases—see chapter 6;
3. regulation 10, which contains a right of recognised trade unions to be informed and consulted about a proposed business transfer—see chapter 8.

Provisions to which the limitation on contracting-out does not apply

The limitations on contracting out do not apply to

regulation 6 (*i.e.* transfer of collective agreements), regulation 7 (exclusion of pensions from the scope of regulations 5 & 6), and regulation 9 (transfer of union recognition). In practice, these omissions are of little importance, since collective agreements between unions and employers are not legally enforceable between those parties unless they have agreed to the contrary in writing in the collective agreement itself (T.U.L.R.A. 1974, s.18). Similarly union recognition is not legally enforceable. However, in so far as a collective agreement forms part of employees' contracts of employment (*i.e.* by incorporation of its terms), such terms are in any event protected by regulation 5.

The European Court of Justice's approach to waiver

Great emphasis is placed by the European Court on the Acquired Rights Directive applying to employees regardless of their wishes. Indeed in *Foreningen AF Arbejdsledere i Danmark* v. *Daddy's Dance Hall AS* [1988] I.R.L.R. 316, the European Court indicated that an employee cannot validly waive his rights under the Directive even, if by doing so, he is securing certain benefits which would leave him better off. This does not mean that, on a business transfer, an employee and the purchaser cannot agree revised terms and conditions provided that the employee's rights in respect of such an agreement are the same as if the there had been no business transfer.

4 THE TRANSFER REGULATIONS: EFFECT ON EMPLOYMENT CONTRACTS

Background: the aim of the regulations

The Transfer Regulations were introduced with the objective of safeguarding employees' rights when their employer transferred the business to a third party. As already stated, the common law and previous statutory position gave them little (if any) protection [see p. 1 above]. Regulation 5 therefore embodies the principle behind the Transfer Regulations—*i.e.* to transfer automatically the employees together with their terms and conditions into the employment of the purchaser. In other words, the new owner of the business steps into the shoes of the old owner and inherits his employees as if they had been his employees from the start. However the way the Regulations achieve this is a little confusing and it is therefore necessary to look more closely at the language used.

Transfer does not give rise to dismissal

Overcoming the common law position: regulation 5

The first objective behind the Regulations is to transfer the vendor's employees into the purchaser's employment. This means that the common law obstacle had to be overcome [see p. 49]—*i.e.* because the House of Lords in the *Nokes* [1940] A.C. 1014, case held that an employer cannot assign a contract of employment without the employee's consent. In the *Nokes* case [see above] Lord Atkin said that this could only be effected by statute. Hence regulation 5(1) which provides that:

> "A relevant transfer shall not operate so as to terminate the contract of employment of any person employed by the transferor in the undertaking or part transferred, but any such contract which would otherwise have been terminated by the transfer shall have effect after the transfer as if originally made between the person so employed and the transferee."

Effects or regulation 5(1)

Regulation 5(1) comprises of two parts. Balcombe L.J. in *Secretary of State for Employment* v. *Spence* [1986] I.R.L.R. 248, summarised the position concisely as follows:

> "So the paragraph has two effects: first, that a relevant transfer does not terminate a contract of employment; and the second effect, commencing with the word '*but*,' is that there is a statutory novation of the contract."

The first part of regulation 5(1) is quite clear—the relevant transfer will not terminate the employment contract. In other words, the employees of the vendor cannot refuse to transfer along with the business into the employment of the purchaser and there will be no dismissal if they refuse to do so. The second part of regulation 5(1) is more difficult to unravel. The confusion arises from the meaning of the words "any such contract which would otherwise have been terminated by the transfer. . . . "

It is necessary to examine the common law position to find out whether such employment contracts would otherwise have been terminated by the business transfer. This exercise is important because, without it, it is difficult to ascertain those employees whose employment contracts are automatically transferred to the purchaser and those whose contracts are not.

The common law position

Nokes v. Doncaster Amalgamated Colleries Ltd.

The leading case on the effect, at common law, of a business transfer on employment contracts is *Nokes* v. *Doncaster Amalgamated Colleries Ltd.* [1940] A.C. 1014. The case turned on rather unusual facts and, in particular, on whether a certain provision in the Companies Act 1929 had the effect of transferring employees from one employer to another. The House of Lords held that the common law position was that employment contracts could not be assigned by one employer to another without the employee's consent, and that the relevant provision in the Companies Act 1929 did not alter that.

It is important to note that nowhere in the Lords' speeches is there dicta to the effect that a business transfer *automatically* terminates employment contracts, but only references to the fact that employees so affected will have claims for damages for wrongful dismissal. It has been from this that some judges and several legal commentators have deduced that a business transfer *of itself* terminates an employment contract. For example in *Bullard* v. *Marchant* [1986] I.C.R. 389, the E.A.T. commented that business transfers automatically terminate employment contracts at common law, and this view was reiterated by Balcombe L.J. in the *Spence* case. However in both cases, both judges were merely summarising, by way of background, what appears to be their view of the common law, as enunciated by the *Nokes* case [see above]. In particular there is no analysis of the common law position in either case. It is interesting to note that the wording of the first part of regulation 5(1) also appears to proceed on the same basis—*i.e.* because it says that a relevant transfer shall not operate to terminate the employment contract.

It is respectfully submitted that this is not the correct interpretation of the common law position. Using basic principles of contract law, an employment contract can be terminated by a variety of ways including a direct dismissal by an employer, a resignation by an employee, by death or by operation of law. In the latter case, the employment contract terminates by operation of law on the happening of a specified event—*e.g.* frustration. However, in such cases there is no breach of contract by either party and thus no claim by the employee for damages for wrongful dismissal. Yet it will be recalled that in the *Nokes* case [1940] A.C. 1014, the House of Lords said that in the event of a business transfer there is a claim for damages for wrongful dismissal. So, the *Nokes* case [see above] cannot be regarded as authority for the proposition that business transfers automatically terminate employment contracts *by operation of law*, in its normally accepted sense.

How does termination arise?

It is difficult to see how a business transfer can properly be seen as a direct employer termination, since such requires an intention on the part of the employer to end the employment relationship. For example V. may manufacture and sell fountain pens and pencils. Each product is manufactured by a separate division. V. decides to sell its fountain pens division to P., and thus transfers all its assets used for this purpose to P. But V. wants to start a new division manufacturing biros and he needs to retain his employees to work in that same division. In such circumstances, does V. want to dismiss his employees in the pens division? Is the mere fact of the business transfer, *of itself*, to be treated as a termination of the employment contracts of those employees in the pens division. It is submitted that the answer to both of these questions is "no."

It is submitted that the proper common law position is that it is not the *mere fact* of a business transfer which terminates the employment contract, but the *consequence* of the business transfer which does so. A business transfer may or may not constitute a repudiatory breach of contract by the employer; and, if it is such a breach, the employee has a choice whether or not to accept the breach and treat the contract as at an end, or to waive the breach and work under the new contract terms. For example, where the V. sells the whole of his business, he will put himself in the position where he cannot perform his obligations to the employee under the employment contract. In practice, the employee will have no realistic choice but to accept the breach and terminate his employment contract. However where V. sells part of his business and the terms of its employment contracts with employees allows it to assign them to other work or other premises, the transfer of that part will not automatically terminate the employment contracts of those employees working in it, if V. still has it in his power to continue to engage them without being in breach of contract. If V. decides that he does not need all or some of them, then their employment contracts will be terminated by V. If V. wants to use those employees in another area or factory, but has not the contractual right to require employees to move, then V. will be in breach of contract and the employees have their choice (see above). If the employees refuse to move, they can resign and claim constructive dismissal (and thus claim damages for wrongful dismissal). But if they choose to go along with the move, they merely accept the variation in their contracts and there is no termination of their contracts.

This approach (*i.e.* that the test is whether there has been a repudiatory breach of contract) has been confirmed by the House of Lords in *Litster* v. *Forth Estuary Engineering Ltd.* [1989] (H.L. 16.3.89). Lord Oliver said:

> "The reason why a contract of employment is said to 'terminate' on a transfer of the employer's business is

simply that such a transfer operates as a unilateral repudiation by the employer of his obligations under the contract and thus as a dismissal of the employee from his service. Because the relationship between employer and employee is an essentially personal nature, the repudiation severs the factual relationship resulting from the contract, since the primary obligations on both sides are no longer capable of being performed. The contract itself, however, is not, strictly speaking, terminated but remains in being and undischarged so far as the enforcement of secondary obligations are concerned."

How the common law position fits in with regulation 5(1)

Regulation 5(1)

It is hoped that the above explanation of the common law position puts into context the words " . . . any such contract which would otherwise have been terminated . . . " in regulation 5(1).

In the *Litster* case [see above], Lord Oliver said:

> "The necessary assumption in para (1) of the regulation is that the contract of employment to which the consequence stated in the paragraph is to attach, is one which, apart from the transfer, would have continued in force and that what 'terminates' it, or would, apart from the Regulations, have terminated it, is the repudiatory breach constituted by the transfer. That paragraph can, therefore, only operate on a subsisting contract."

Unfortunately, the draftsman of regulation 5(1) does not appear to have addressed his mind to the possibilities of the vendor wanting to retain employees, or of the employees being willing to accept a change in job rather than transfer to the purchaser. As will be seen below, there are many situations where a business is sold, but employment contracts with the vendor would not be terminated—*e.g.* where either the employer has the contractual right to assign the employee to another site or other work, or where the employee is happy to be so assigned and thus agrees to a variation in his contract. In both these cases the employee's contract would not "otherwise have been terminated by the transfer."

Employees to be retained by vendor

One of the problems behind regulation 5(1) is that it appears to have been drafted on the basis that a business transfer is automatically a dismissal of those employees engaged in the business to be transferred. It does not really address itself either to the common occurrence that the vendor may be transferring only part of its business, or the possibility that the vendor and certain employees might agree between themselves that they do not transfer across to the purchaser will the part of the business sold.

Where a business transfer does constitute a repudiatory breach of contract, whether a particular employee's contract "would otherwise have been terminated by the transfer" depends on whether or not he accepts that repudiatory breach of his employment contract. In some cases the answer to this will not be known until after the moment of transfer has occurred.

The problem only really arises where the vendor sells only part of its business. It raises a classic "chicken and egg" dilemma. The following practical analysis is suggested:

1. Where the vendor does not offer the employee an alternative job in its retained business, the employee would have no real choice but to accept the repudiatory breach. Therefore his contract would otherwise have been terminated by the transfer—*i.e.* he transfers across to the purchaser under regulation 5(1).
2. Where the vendor does make the employee a job offer in its retained business and the employee accepts that offer before the moment of transfer, his contract would not otherwise be terminated by the transfer—*i.e.* he does not transfer across under regulation 5(1).
3. Where the vendor makes a job offer to remain in its retained business to an employee, but the latter does not accept it by the moment of transfer, it seems that it is a question of fact in each case whether the employee would have accepted the repudiatory breach of contract. This is almost impossible to determine as at the moment of transfer—especially if the employee does nothing. It is likely that tribunals will presume that, in the absence of clear evidence that the employee has expressly or tacitly waived the repudiatory breach (*i.e.* by remaining working for the vendor in the new job), he would have accepted the repudiatory breach. Thus he transfers to the purchaser under regulation 5(1).

The third scenario above is not satisfactory from the operational viewpoint of either the vendor or the purchaser, because each will want to know on advance of the moment of transfer which employees are transferring to the purchaser. If the employees do not expressly accept the vendor's job offers prior to the moment of transfer, the parties will have to rely on circumstantial evidence to indicate whether a particular employee has transferred to the purchaser. It is for this reason that the vendor and purchaser are strongly advised to sort out, in advance, which employees are to transfer to the purchaser and those which are to remain with the vendor [see p. 127 below].

Which employees are caught by regulation 5(1)?

Conditions necessary for regulation 5 to apply

The Transfer Regulations need something upon which to "bite"; and regulation 5(1) says it is the "contract of employment of any person employed by the transferor in the undertaking or part." Regulation 5(3) goes on to explain that this is a reference: "... to a person so employed immediately before the transfer, including, where the transfer is effected by a series of two or more transactions, a person so employed immediately before any of those transactions."

Thus, for the automatic transfer of employment to operate in respect of a particular employee, it must be shown that:

1. he was employed under a contract of employment by the transferor (*e.g.* the vendor); and
2. he was so employed "immediately before" the transfer took place; and
3. his employment contract would not "otherwise have been terminated by the transfer" (see above).

Unless all three of these conditions are met the automatic transfer principle enshrined in regulation 5 will not operate in respect of the particular person's employment contract. Regulation 2(1) defines a contract of employment as "any agreement between an employee and his employer determining the terms and conditions of his employment."

Whether an employee of the transferor?

Regulation 2(1): who is an employee?

Regulation 2(1) defines an "employee" in slightly wider terms than is normally used for employment protection purposes. An employee covers:

> "any individual who works for another person whether under a contract of service or apprenticeship or otherwise, but does not include anyone who provides services under a contract for services."

This appears to cover certain types of casual or temporary workers or trainees under a Government training programme, but not self-employed independent contractors.

Independent contractor or casual worker?

On some occasions, the dividing line, between whether a consultant is an independent contractor or a casual worker, can be a little blurred. Purchasers should therefore ask for lists of regular employees, casual workers and "self-employed" consultants so that it will be aware of who potentially could be automatically transferred into its employment. The fact that the vendor has categorised certain persons as working under contracts for services is not, of course, conclusive of whether or not they are, as a matter of law, employees for the purposes of the Regulations.

Groups of companies

There are often occasions where a holding company or a management services company provides services to other operating companies or identifiable operating units within the same group of companies—*e.g.* a group personnel manager or a group financial controller. The automatic transfer principle of regulation 5 will only operate if he is employed in the business or part transferred. Thus if an employee providing those group services is employed in a different company than that which his being sold, the Transfer Regulations will not "bite" on his contract—because he is not employed by the business being transferred. One simply looks at the legal identity of the employer of the person in question. This means identifying the legal person with whom the employee has a contract of employment (as defined above). In most cases this will be the employer with whom he has an agreement dealing with his salary, benefits and other terms and conditions of employment.

Employees who are employed by a holding company

The same principle applies where the person is employed by a holding company, but is required to provide services exclusively to one of its subsidiary companies. Since his employment contract is not with the subsidiary company (whose business assets are to be sold as a going concern), his employment will not transfer with that business to the purchaser. However it may well be that the holding company thereby has nothing left for him to do, and therefore has to make him redundant or seek his agreement to vary his job duties. The important point is that the employee's remedies or causes of action (if any) remain with his existing employer (*i.e.* the holding company).

For example, in *B.I.F.U.* v. *Barclays Bank* [1987] I.C.R. 495, the employees were employed by Barclays who provided their labour to another company within the group (B.M.B.). When the B.M.B.'s business was transferred to B.Z.W., the employees actually working at B.M.B. did not transfer with the business to B.Z.W. since they had in the meantime voluntarily become employed by B.Z.W(s) (a service company to B.Z.W.).

The position is a little more difficult where the employee in question is employed by the *same* employer who subsequently sells part of its business. If he was providing services exclusively to the part transferred, he would be regarded as being employed in that part. But where he provides services to other parts of the business which are to remain with his employer, then the question whether he is transferred along with the part of the business sold off depends on whether his "contract would otherwise have been terminated by the transfer" [see p. 51 above and p. 61 below].

Where an employee has two employment contracts with different companies in the same group of companies, the position of each contract has to be considered separately. Where he has one contract with a company whose business is to be transferred (company A) and another employment contract with a company not affected by the transfer (company B), then the Transfers Regulations will "bite" on his employment contract with company A, but not on his contract with company B.

Employed by the transferor immediately before the transfer?

Was person employed immediately before transfer?

This question concerns not whether the person was employed by the transferor, but rather whether he was so employed up to immediately before the transfer. This involves two separate, but linked, issues:

1. how close to the moment of transfer must the employee be employed by the transferor?
2. when, exactly, does the transfer take place?

Judicial interpretation of "immediately before"

The words "immediately before the transfer" have given rise to a substantial amount of judicial debate. Initially the E.A.T., in *Apex Leisure Hire Ltd.* v. *Barratt* [1984] I.C.R. 452, took the view that the words were of a "flexible nature" and could cover a matter of days before the transfer took place. In that case the employees were dismissed on a Friday and the business was transferred the following Monday. The E.A.T. held that the employees had been employed by the vendor up to "immediately before the Transfer" to enable regulation 5(1) to transfer their contracts to the purchaser. However, this view has been overruled by the Court of Appeal in *Secretary of State for*

Employment v. *Spence* [1986] I.R.L.R. 248. In that case the employees were dismissed on grounds of redundancy at 11 a.m. and the business was transferred at 2 p.m. the same day. The Court of Appeal held that the words "immediately before" had their plain and literal meaning—*i.e.* the moment before. Therefore a gap of even a few hours between the dismissal of employees and a subsequent business transfer is not "immediately before the transfer," and is therefore sufficient to prevent regulation 5 operating in respect of the employment contracts of those concerned.

The *Spence* case [see above] has been recently approved by the House of Lords in *Litster* v. *Forth Estuary Engineering Ltd.* [1989] (H.L. 16.3.89). However Lord Oliver thought that a *de minimis* rule might apply to the "moment of transfer" test enunciated by the Court of Appeal in the *Spence* case. Indeed on the facts of the *Litster* case (where the gap between the dismissals and the business transfer was one hour) he considered that there were "respectable arguments" for saying that the dismissals and the business transfer took place at the same time. He went on to say:

> "Where, before the actual transfer takes place, the employment of an employee is terminated for a reason unconnected with the transfer, I agree that the question of whether he was employed immediately before the transfer cannot sensibly be said to depend on the degree of temporal proximity between the two events, except possibly in a case where they are so closely connected in point of time that it is, for practical purposes, impossible realistically to say that they are not practically contemporaneous. Either the contract of employment is subsisting at the moment of transfer or it is not . . . ."

However the House of Lords, in the *Litster* case, said that the *Spence* test (*i.e.* the "moment of transfer" test) only applied where the reason for the dismissal was either wholly unconnected with the business transfer, or if it was connected it was "an economic, technical or organisational reason entailing changes in the workforce" [see p. 95 below for the meaning of that expression].

The House of Lords went on to apply a different test where the dismissal is connected with a business transfer, but it was *not* an economic, technical or organisational one entailing changes in the workforce. They said that, in such cases, the words "immediately before the transfer" in regulation 5(3) should be qualified so that they read as follows:

> ". . . employed immediately before the transfer, *or would have been so employed if he had not been unfairly dismissed in the circumstances described in reg 8(1).*"

In other words, where a dismissal connected with a business transfer is not for an "economic, technical or organisational reason entailing changes in the workforce" (see p. 95), an employee dismissed before the moment of transfer, is deemed to have been still employed as at the moment of transfer for the purposes of the automatic transfer principle applying to him. As Lord Oliver said:

"It follows from the construction that I attach to regulation 5(3) that where an employee is dismissed before and by reason of the transfer, the employment is statutorily continued with the transferee by virtue of the Regulations."

He added later that:

"a dismissal effected before the transfer and solely because of the transfer of the business is, in effect, prohibited and is, for the purpose of considering the application of Article 3(1), required to be treated as ineffective."

Lord Keith took a similar view:

"... he is deemed to have been employed in the undertaking immediately before the transfer or any series of transactions whereby it was effected."

In adopting this purposive construction of regulation 5(3), the House of Lords followed the dicta of the E.C.J. in *P. Bork International AS* v. *Foreningen AF Arbejdsledere I Danmark* [1989] I.R.L.R. 41 where the E.C.J. said that a dismissal which contravened the mandatory requirements of article 4(1) of the Directive (*i.e.* one which was connected with a business transfer but not for an economic, technical or organisational reason entailing changes in the workforce) was an exception to the date/time of dismissal test. The E.C.J. went on to say:

"It follows that workers employed by the undertaking whose contract of employment or employment relationship has been terminated with effect from a date before that of the transfer, in breach of article 4(1) of the Directive, must be considered as still employed by the undertaking on the date of the transfer with the consequence, in particular, that the obligations of an employer towards them are fully transferred from the transferor or transferee, in accordance with article 3(1) of the Directive."

Given the application of the meaning of the words "immediately before the transfer", there still appears to be some divergence between the English courts' "moment of transfer" test (an enunciated by Court of Appeal in the *Spence* case and approved by the House of Lords in the *Litster* case), and the actual words used by article 3(1) of the Directive—"date of transfer". Lord Oliver noticed this point in the *Litster* case, but dispenses with it by saying that the two expressions were really the same. He referred to the French text which uses the words "au moment du transfert" which, he said, embraced "the notion that what has to be regarded is the status of the employee vis-a-vis his employer at the very instant at which the employer's business is transferred". Although it is certainly true that the E.C.J. have used the expressions interchangeably on occasions, the wording of article 3(1) of the Directive is clear and unequivocal—"date of transfer". Lord Oliver's rationale is, with respect, a little confusing and it is suggested that this issue still needs to be clarified by the E.C.J. If the E.C.J.'s purposive construction of the Directive is to be applied to the words "immediately before the transfer", that should be construed as if it read "immediately before the *date* of the transfer". Nonetheless, Lord Oliver's view must be regarded as the current statement of the law, unless and until it is disapproved.

Implications of *Spence* case

The interpretation by the Court of Appeal in the *Spence* case [see above] has far-reaching repercussions on the effectiveness of the Transfer Regulations to protect the employment rights of employees working in a business which is to be transferred. In effect, the vendor and purchaser could agree to dismiss employees a few hours before the moment the transfer takes place and therefore stop the Regulations applying to their employment contracts. However there are some dangers for both the vendor and purchaser where the purchaser seeks to offer employment to some of the dismissed employees on less favourable terms and conditions [see p. 36 below].

Date v. time of transfer?

Only partial assistance can be derived from the cases on the Acquired Rights Directive. In *Wendelboe* v. *L.J. Music ApS* [1985] 1 C.M.L.R., Slynn A.G. said in his opinion to the European Court:

> "Articles 3(2) and 4 of the Directive under consideration . . . seem to me to be clearly limited to existing employees at the time of the transfer."

> In its judgment, the E.C.J. said:

> "Those provisions relate only to employees in the service of the undertaking on the date of the transfer, to the exclusion of those who have already left the undertaking on that date."

It is uncertain whether the E.C.J. was adopting the same test as Slynn A.G. since the former adopted a "date of transfer" test and he adopted a "time of transfer" test. This distinction is important and would, for example, have produced a different result in the *Spence* case [1986] I.R.L.R. 248; C.A. It is, however, interesting to note that in the subsequent case of *Mikkelsen* v. *Danmols Inventar A/S* [1985] C.M.L.R. 316; E.C.J., Slynn A.G. interpreted the E.C.J.'s ruling in *Wendelboe* [see above] as meaning "that only persons employed by the transferor at the moment of transfer fall within the provision." Yet in its judgment in the *Mikkelsen* case, the E.C.J. again uses references to the "date of the transfer," but without commenting on the correctness of Slynn A.G.'s interpretation.

Therefore, to some extent, the E.C.J. has taken the view that the protection of the Acquired Rights Directive only applies to transfer across the employment contracts with the vendoer existing on the day of transfer. Whilst it is clear that the E.C.J. considers that an employment contract terminated the day before the business transfer would to be protected, it is unclear whether the E.C.J. agrees with Slynn A.G.'s further refinement of the "moment of transfer."

In *P. Bork International AS* v. *Foreningen AF Arbejdsledere I Danmark* [1989] I.R.L.R. 41, the E.C.J. said:

> "the only workers who may invoke the Directive are those who have a current employment relationship or a contract of employment at the *date of the transfer* (author's emphasis). The question whether or not a contract of employment or an employment relationship exists at that

date must be assessed under the national law, subject to the observance of the mandatory rules of the Directive concerning the protection of workers against dismissal by reason of the transfer."

When is the transfer?

Since the *Spence* case [see above] makes it clear that regulation 5 only operates on those employment contracts of employees still employed by the transferor *up and till just before the moment the transfer takes place*, (or are deemed to be so employed) the key question is: when, exactly, is the transfer? Most business transfers are effected into two stages: exchange of contracts and completion. This is especially the case where land is sold as part of the transaction or there are various conditions precedent which the vendor must comply with before completion. However it is not uncommon for exchange and completion to take place on the same day—especially where the business is in liquidation. Is the transfer on exchange of contracts or on completion?

Initially the E.A.T., in *Kestongate Ltd.* v. *Miller* [1986] I.C.R. 672, held that the transfer took place on exchange of contracts, not on completion. Such a conclusion (whilst certainly trying to keep within the spirit of the Regulations) caused commercial difficulties. For example, what if the transfer is never completed because one of the conditions precedent is not satisfied? However in *Wheeler* v. *Patel & J. Golding Group of Companies* [1987] I.R.L.R. 211, the E.A.T. held that the *Kestongate* case [see above] was wrongly decided and that the transfer took place at completion. In the *Wheeler* case [1987] I.R.L.R. 211, the employee was dismissed between exchange of contracts and completion, and therefore she was not employed by the vendor immediately before the transfer. The *Wheeler* case is supported by dicta in the Court of Appeal in the *Spence* case [see above], and later supported in *Secretary of State for Employment* v. *Galbraith & others* [1987] unreported (E.A.T. 82/87). However this issue has not yet been authoritatively decided, and a firm ruling by the Court of Appeal is awaited. In the meantime, the approach adopted by the E.A.T. in the *Wheeler* case [see above] is probably the preferred one, and has been supported by the E.A.T. in the *Brook Lane Finance* case 1988 I.R.L.R. 283.

Regulation 3(4): a series of transactions

It will be recalled that regulation 3(4) provides that a transfer effected by a series of transactions between the same parties may constitute a single transfer [see p. 36 for full text]. However, in the *Wheeler* case [see above], the E.A.T. firmly quashed the ingenious argument that an exchange of contracts and completion were two separate transactions between the same parties and therefore should be regarded as a single transfer. If this argument had been upheld, it would have meant that a person employed at the moment of exchange of contracts would be regarded as employed as at the moment of the transfer—since exchange and completion were to be treated as a single transfer by virtue of regulation 3(4).

There are two situations where the picture may appear a little blurred:

1. where there is a "double-transfer," and

2. where the purchaser takes over the *de facto* running of the business in the period between exchange and completion.

Double transfers

These might occur where, for example, a licence, tenancy or franchise is surrendered by the outgoing licensee to the licensor, and very shortly afterwards the licensor grants a new licence to the incoming licensee. As has already been stated, the E.A.T. has adopted two different approaches to this situation [see p. 35 above]. In the *Premier* case [1983] I.R.L.R. 471, the E.A.T. said that there was one business transfer from the outgoing licensee to the oil company, and a second business transfer very shortly afterwards between the oil company and the new licensee; and therefore for a brief moment the employees had been employed by the oil company. In contrast in the *Norris* case [1984] (unreported E.A.T. 731/83), the E.A.T. held that there was a straight business transfer between the outgoing and incoming licensees of the oil company's petrol station. The *Premier* approach is the preferable one. This distinction can make a difference where, before the business is actually transferred to the incoming licensee, there occurs an act which results in the dismissal of the employee in question. In those circumstances the licensor will be left with any liability arising from such dismissal—*e.g.* damages for wrongful dismissal, compensation for unfair dismissal or redundancy pay. See also p. 36 for the E.C.J.'s view on "double transfers" in the *Daddy's Dance Hall* case [1988] I.R.L.R. 315.

Purchaser in de facto control

In some cases (particularly in small transactions) the vendor may be prepared to allow the purchaser into the business to take *de facto* control of it before completion has occurred. This might happen between exchange of contracts and completion. For example in *Mohammed* v. *Delaney* [1986] (unreported E.A.T. 606/86), the purchaser made an offer for the vendor's business on October 23, 1985, which was accepted by the vendor with a qualification on October 30, 1985. The purchaser accepted the vendor's qualification on October 31, 1985. The contract provided for January 1, 1986 to be the completion date when the purchaser would be allowed entry into the premises. However the parties subsequently agreed that the purchaser should take over the day-to-day running of the vendor's business on November 4, 1985. In the meantime final negotiations over the transaction were being completed and on November 2, 1988 one of the employees was dismissed. The E.A.T. upheld the tribunal's view that there had been a *de facto* transfer on October 30, 1988 because the purchaser's manager had already started the day-to-day control of the premises (*e.g.* by supervising staff and handling the vendor's money). Therefore the employee had remained in the vendor's employment up to the moment of transfer. The *Mohammed* case [see above] conflicts with E.A.T.'s earlier dicta on the same subject in *S.I. (Systems & Instruments) Ltd.* v. *Grist & Riley* [1983] I.R.L.R. 397, that there was no transfer when a purchaser took over the day-to-day running of the vendor's business during negotiations over its sale. In that case the purchaser had been allowed in to help run the vendor's business and had withdrawn when the negotiations had broken down. There is clearly a conflict of authority here and much will depend on the basis upon which an intending purchaser is allowed to take charge of the day-to-day management of the vendor's business. If the effect of the early entry by the purchaser is, in effect, to bring forward the date of the practical completion of the deal (although various legal formalities have yet to be completed) there is a risk that a tribunal may conclude that there has been a *de facto* transfer—see also *Kennedy Brookes Hotel & Catering Ltd.* v. *Reilly & Cook* [1983] (unreported E.A.T. 563/83). Both of these cases highlight the importance of the parties to a business transfer clearly pinpointing when the business will be transferred.

No final agreement between the parties

Similarly in *Dabell* v. *Vale Industrial Services (Nottingham) Ltd.* [1988] I.R.L.R. 439, the Court of Appeal held that the moment of transfer can occur when there has been a *de facto* transfer of the business, even though no final agreement and documentation has been signed by the parties. The Court expressly rejected the argument that there could be no transfer if the business would be transferred back again to the transferor if negotiations broke down. In the *Dabell* case [see above], Vale Industrial Services had, during negotiations, closed its premises and transferred its equipment, goodwill, customer connections, existing contracts and staff to Nofotec and written to its customers telling them so. The Court of Appeal upheld the industrial tribunal's decision that this constituted a business transfer, notwithstanding that there was no formal agreement to that effect and there was a risk (as later occurred) that negotiations might break down.

Use of statutory continuity of employment rules. It has now been established that, employees cannot use any part of the E.P.C.A.'s rules (in Schedule 13 of the E.P.C.A.) for calculating continuity of service as a means of stretching their employment to the moment of completion, so that regulation 5(1) will operate on their employment contracts. For example in *Bannister & Others* v. *Brasway plc* [1983] (unreported C.O.I.T. 1377/49), the employees tried (unsuccessfully) to rely on paragraph 4 Schedule 13 of the E.P.C.A. to extend their employment from the date of dismissal on June 27 to the moment of transfer on June 30. They sought to argue that since, under the statutory continuity rules, a part of a week counts as a whole week, therefore their employments should be likewise deemed extended until the end of the week. The tribunal rejected that argument, holding that the Court of Appeal's dicta in *Teeside Times Ltd.* v. *Drury* [1980] I.R.L.R. 72, had no application to the question whether a person was still "employed" for the purposes of the Transfer Regulations.

Use of E.P.C.A., ss.55(5), 90(3)

Some commentators have suggested that employees might be able to rely on section 55(5) and section 90(3) of the E.P.C.A. which artificially extend the effective date of termination (again, for certain continuity purposes) by the amount of an employee's statutory notice to which he was entitled, but had not received. With respect, such an argument is untenable because both section 55(5) (which relates to unfair dismissal) and section 90(3) (which relates to redundancy pay) both only apply to extend artificially the deemed periods of continuous service for two purposes only:

1. to enable an employee to qualify for the relevant right with the requisite two years service, or
2. to calculate the amount of the basic award or redundancy pay.

Contract not otherwise terminated by the transfer

The reader is referred to p. 51 above for what is submitted to be the meaning of the words "not otherwise terminated by the transfer." To recap, it is not the business transfer which, *of itself*, terminates the employment contract, but the *consequences* of the transfer—*i.e.* if either the employee is directly dismissed by the vendor or he brings the contract to an end by accepting his employer's repudiatory breach of contract. In other words, *only those employment contracts which would, under the common law, be subject to a dismissal (whether direct or constructive)* are capable of being automatically transferred across by regulation 5(1). If there is no direct dismissal or the employee is happy to waive his employer's repudiatory breach, his contract does not transfer across to the purchaser.

Position where vendor sells whole of his business

Needless to say, where an employer directly dismisses an employee, if the dismissal takes effect before the moment of the transfer, regulation 5(1) cannot operate on that employment contract. But it can so operate where the dismissal takes effect at the moment of the transfer (it does not matter whether or not full notice of termination was given). However, in most cases where a vendor sells the *whole* of its business, it will put itself in the position where it will be unable to employ the employee in accordance with his employment contract—thus making the employee's acceptance of his repudiatory breach of contract inevitable. Such acceptance will terminate the employment contract. Yet there may be cases where the vendor decides to sell one business and to acquire or start up another, for which he needs his existing workforce. Alternatively, the vendor may sell a severable and identifiable part of its business, but wants to retain employees to work in the part which it is retaining. Whether or not those employees are transferred to the purchaser by regulation 5(1) depends, it is submitted, on whether the vendor commits a repudiatory breach of contract which is accepted by the employee. There are various possible scenarios which could prevent such employees from transferring to the purchaser.

Position where vendor selling part of his business or acquires a new one

Flexibility clauses

Flexibility clauses. The employment contract in question may be drafted in such terms so that the vendor has a job flexibility or location mobility clause covering the proposed changes in the employee's contract terms. Care should be taken to ensure that the flexibility clause does in fact cover all the various changes to the employee's contract. In most cases pay and conditions will stay the same, but job duties, workplace and hours of work may change. Employers should beware of assuming that a widely-worded clause giving them the right to change *any* of the employee's terms and conditions will be enforceable. In most cases such a clause will be void. Such flexibility clauses should be limited to duties, workplace and hours of work.

The same principle will apply where the employer has the

right to assign the employee to work for other companies within the group. In such cases, the employee has, by signing the employment contract, given his consent to the assignment of his contract or his services. However the vendor may not want to offer the employee another job, even though he has the contractual right to do so if he so chooses. In such cases, the vendor will be left with the choice of either dismissing the employee or committing a repudiatory breach of contract (which the employee has no real choice but to accept and terminate the contract).

Significance of wide job title

Wide job titles. This is a variation of the flexibility clause above—*i.e.* the employee's job title is expressed in sufficiently wide terms to cover the change in his contract caused by the business transfer. For example, V. Ltd. runs two divisions, one making sausages and the other making pies. V. Ltd. decides to sell its sausage business to P. Ltd., but wishes to retain its employees, premises and machinery to be devoted wholly for the pie division which is to be expanded. However there is clearly a business transfer because V. Ltd. is selling its goodwill, trade names and customers to P. Ltd. in respect of its sausage business. Joe is employed by V. Ltd. as a "production operative" and, after the business transfer his terms and conditions will not change apart from the fact that the product he is helping to make are pies rather than sausages. In such a case, it is submitted that there would be no repudiation of his employment contract and therefore his employment would not be caught by regulation 5(1) to transfer it to P. Ltd. The position would probably be different if his job title was "sausage production operative."

Vendor acquires new business immediately

The same principles might apply in the rare situation where a vendor disposes of one business in its entirety and then immediately acquires or starts up a totally different one. If an employee is employed by V. Ltd., for example, as an "accounts clerk," there appears to be no reason why there should be any breach of her employment contract where that legal entity (V. Ltd.) continues to observe all her terms and conditions of employment in respect of the new product or services now supplied by V. Ltd. However the change in the employee's duties must have taken place prior to the moment of transfer—*i.e.* he must have been re-deployed to the vendor's new business or product line before that time. It is submitted that the argument—to the effect that it is an implied term of the employment contract that she would only be engaged in respect of a particular product or service—is not correct—unless the contract expressly so states. If that argument were correct, it would mean that every time an employer added a new range of products or services to its business operations, it would be in breach of contract. It is submitted that such a position cannot be tenable in law, where the job titles/job descriptions are drafted in sufficiently wide terms.

Employee agreement to changes

Employee agrees to the contract changes. Even though the employer is in repudiatory breach of contract by selling its business or part of it, it may offer the employee continued employment on changed terms and conditions. If the employee agrees to those changes, there will have been no termination of his employment contract other than by the transfer. There may often be cases where the employee does not wish to transfer into the employment of the purchaser—*e.g.* because of the "company culture" of the purchaser, or because such a transfer will mean that he will not be able to participate in such a good pension scheme as he enjoys with the vendor (as will be seen later, the Transfer Regulations transfer all his employment package except pensions).

Case law

Although there is little case law dealing with this question, such authority as there is does support the views expressed above. For example in *Direct Radiators Ltd.* v. *Howse & Shepherd* [1986] (unreported E.A.T. 130/86), Mrs. Howse was employed by Mr. Shepherd as a book-keeper in his business. Mr. Shepherd agreed to sell his business to D. Ltd. who told him that they did not need Mrs. Howse's services. The business was sold on February 28, 1985 and Mr. Shepherd kept Mrs. Howse employed until April 5, 1985 to help collect debts and carry out remaining book-keeping and clerical work for him. She was dismissed by Mr. Shepherd when that work was completed on April 5, 1985, and claimed redundancy pay against D. Ltd., arguing that she had transferred into D. Ltd.'s employ by virtue of regulation 5(1). The E.A.T. held that if, Mrs. Howse had remained employed by Mr. Shepherd after the transfer date on February 28, 1985, then she did not transfer into the employment of D. Ltd. under regulation 5(1). The E.A.T. sent the case back to the tribunal to make the necessary findings of fact on that question. Similarly in *Daisley* v. *Leicester Light Transport Ltd.* [1986] (unreported C.O.I.T. 1405/53), L. Ltd. sold its transport business, but the purchaser had told L. Ltd. that they did not need Mr. Daisley. L. Ltd. therefore employed him at another of its garages, which Mr. Daisley agreed to. The tribunal held that his employment did not transfer to the purchasers by virtue of regulation 5(1), and therefore L. Ltd. was liable for redundancy pay when it made Mr. Daisley redundant shortly afterwards. Although, in both of these cases, the employee in question was dismissed by the vendor a little time after the transfer took place, this had no relevance to the question whether regulation 5 "bit" on their employment contracts to transfer them to the purchaser.

It is helpful to apply the above approach to different situations to see how it applies in practice.

Contract manufacturing agreements

(a) *Contract manufacturing agreements.* These are arrangements arising from a business transfer whereby the purchaser does not acquire from the vendor the means of manufacturing the products of the business. Thus the purchaser will acquire the goodwill, trade names/trade marks, customers, existing contracts and other assets of the vendor's business, except for the means of manufacture. The purchaser may not want the factory, or the vendor may not wish to sell it (*e.g.* because it manufactures other product lines which are not part of the vendor's deal with the purchaser). The purchaser and vendor may then enter into an agreement whereby the vendor undertakes to manufacture the relevant products for the purchaser. Such a contract manufacturing agreement is usually of limited duration of between six months and two years. It is submitted that, in such cases, regulation 5(1) will not operate to transfer the vendor's production staff since the vendor will want to retain them in order to comply with its obligations under the contract manufacturing agreement. Provided there is no breach of their employment contracts (as there should not be in such circumstances) regulation 5(1) will not transfer them into the employment of the purchaser. However, other staff (*e.g.* the salesforce engaged solely on the products lines sold to the purchaser) probably will transfer across.

This, then, raises the question whether those employees retained by the vendor will transfer across to the purchaser when the contract manufacturing agreement comes to an end and is not renewed. There are two possible approaches:

1. If the activity of manufacturing products for the purchaser is a separate and identifiable business (or part thereof) in its own right, therefore, at the end of the contract manufacturing agreement, there is a *second* business transfer from the vendor to the purchaser. Whether this is so depends on the nature and effect of the contract manufacturing agreement—see p. 32 above.
2. The end of the contract manufacturing agreement (*i.e.* the surrender of the right to manufacture the purchaser's products) is merely the last in a series of transactions under which the vendor's business of manufacturing *and* selling its products was transferred to the purchaser. In such circumstances, it may be arguable that regulation 3(4) applies to treat it as a *single* transfer. This is a question of fact for industrial tribunals to decide, and regulation 3(4) requires them to look at the control of the business prior to the last transaction, the parties' intentions, the timescale and all the surrounding circumstances. If the contract manufacturing agreement was made with the intent that the activity of manufacturing the relevant products would be eventually assumed by the purchaser (*e.g.* after it had acquired a site for its own factory), then there is a real risk that regulation 3(4) will apply to link the termination of the contract manufacturing agreement with the business transfer.

However, even if either of the two above scenarios are applicable, the retention by the vendor of its employees within the terms of their employment contracts will operate to stop regulation 5(1) transferring them to the purchaser.

Transfer reduces the scope of an employee's job

(b) *Loss of part of duties/reduction in scope of job.* The effect of the disposal by the vendor of part of its business may have the effect of reducing the scope of an employee's job where his duties cover *all* of the vendor's business. For example, Joe is employed by a hotel chain as its "Group Operations Director." Prior to the disposal of one of its hotels, he was responsible for a total of six hotels; and, as a result of the disposal, he will be responsible for five. Whether he transfers across with the hotel sold to the purchaser depends on whether his contract would otherwise have been terminated by the transfer.

If the above guiding principles are applied to these facts, there will be no transfer where the disposal of the single hotel does not constitute a repudiatory breach of his employment contract. It is submitted that, if his job title is "Group Operations Director" (without specific reference to particular hotels) then regulation 5(1) will not operate on his employment contract. In such a case his job duties cover operational responsibility for all the vendor's hotels (however many there may be in the group). If it was correct to imply into his contract a limitation on the number of hotels, then his employers would be in breach of his contract every time they sold or acquired a hotel; and that, plainly, cannot be correct in law. The position may be more blurred where an employee's contract (unwisely) refers to specific units of the vendor's business for which he is responsible. However, even here, regulation 5(1) will not operate where either the employee agrees to the reduced responsibility or the employer has the right to changes his duties in such a way.

Case law

The only English case on point is *Anderson* v. *Kluwer Publishing Ltd. & Buckley Press Ltd.* [1985] (unreported C.O.I.T. 15068/85), where the industrial tribunal applied a "proportionality test" when deciding whether or not regulation 5(1) operated on the employment contract of one of the vendor's employee's who lost 80 per cent. of his job as a result of a sale of one of the vendor's magazines. The tribunal held that, such was the high proportion of the loss of his responsibilities, that regulation 5(1) did apply to transfer him to the purchaser. With respect to the tribunal in that case, the proportionality of the change is only relevant to *when* there has been a breach of contract, not *whether* there has been a breach of contract in the first place. It appears that the tribunal did not examine whether the loss of 80 per cent. of his job was a breach of contract which would otherwise have terminated his contract of employment. Thus the *Anderson* case [see above] should be treated with caution.

Business Transfer Directive

Under the Directive, the automatic transfer principle applies to transfer to the purchaser only those employees of the vendor who are wholly engaged in the business (or part) transferred. Slynn A.G. commented in *Botzen* v. *Rotterdamsche Droogdok Maatschappij BV* [1986] 2 C.M.L.R. 50, that:

> "a basic working test . . . is to ask whether, if that part of the business had been separately owned before the transfer, the worker would have been employed by the owners of that part or by the owners of the remaining part. The only exception I would admit to the requirement that an employee must be 'wholly' engaged in that part of the business would be where an employee was required to perform other duties to an extent which could fairly be described as de minimis. On the other hand, if the worker is engaged in the activities of the whole business or in several parts, then he cannot be regarded for the purpose of the Directive as an employee 'of' the part of the business transferred."

The E.C.J. followed this distinction and held that the Directive does not require the transfer of those employees of the vendor either who are not engaged in the part of the vendor's business transferred but use its assets, or who work in one of the vendor's departments providing services to various parts of its business (including the part transferred).

Where an employee leaves the vendor's employment, on his own free will, with effect from the moment of the business transfer, it seems that none of the vendor's obligations to him transfer to the purchaser. In *Mikkelsen* v. *Danmols Inventar AS* [1986] 1 C.M.L.R. 316, the E.C.J. said:

> "Article 3(1) of . . . the Directive . . . must be interpreted to mean that it does not cover the transfer of the rights and obligations of persons who were employed by the transferor at the date of transfer but who, of their own free will, do not continue to occupy a position as an employee with the transferee".

What is transferred with the employees?

Regulation 5(2)

Although regulation 5(1) has the effect of reversing the common law position by providing that a transfer of business operates to transfer employment contracts from the transferor to the transferee, regulation 5(2) explains in more detail exactly what the transferee employer is taking on. It provides that:

> "Without prejudice to para. (1) above, on the completion of a relevant transfer
> (a) all the transferor's rights, powers, duties and liabilities under or in connection with any such contract, shall be transferred by virtue of this Regulation to the transferee; and
> (b) anything done before the transfer is completed by or in relation to the transferor in respect of that contract or a person employed in that undertaking or part shall be deemed to have been done by or in relation to the transferee."

It is clear that the references to "such contract" in regulation 5(2) refer back to those employment contracts automatically transferred across to the transferee by the relevant transfer under regulation 5(1)—see the *Spence* and *Litster* cases (above). In essence, the first leg of regulation 5(2) transfers to the transferee (*e.g.* a purchaser) all "rights, duties, powers and liabilities" which belonged to the transferor (*e.g.* the vendor). The second leg of regulation 5(2) makes the purchaser responsible for anything done (or not done) by the vendor in respect of such employment contracts transferred across by regulation 5(1). It is these twin provisions that really make the purchaser stand in the vendor's shoes in respect of the vendor's employees it has inherited. These are now examined in more detail below.

Transfer of rights, powers, duties & liabilities

What rights, duties and liabilities are transferred under regulation 5(2)?

It is clear that regulation 5(1) transfers to the purchaser all parts of the employment contract between the vendor and its employees transferred under regulation 5(1). This includes the employee's salary, remuneration package, contractual fringe benefits, flexibility/mobility obligations, and any contractual terms implied by custom and practice and particular undertakings given to or by the employees so transferred. The main exception is pensions (see p. 72 below). Other liabilities/ rights, etc., which transfer across include the following:

Continuity of employment

Continuity of employment. There is some debate whether regulation 5(2) transfers across an employee's accrued period of continuous employment. This is because regulation 5(2)(a) refers to the transfer of rights, duties, powers and liabilities: "under or in connection with any such contract, . . . " and, strictly speaking, the concept of continuity of employment is not connected with an employment contract. Continuity is a statutory concept and it should be noted that under Schedule 13 of the E.P.C.A. continuity may accrue even though there is no contract of employment in force [see para. 9 Sched. 13, E.P.C.A.]. The debate is really academic because continuity of employment (which is necessary to preserve statutory employment protection rights), will in any event be preserved by paragraph 17(2) of the E.P.C.A. 1978 and, in some cases, in more advantageous ways than if it had been transferred under the Transfer Regulations. [See p. 137 below]. However, it should be noted that in *Brook Lane Finance Co.* v. *Bradley* [1988] I.R.L.R. 283, the E.A.T. proceeded on the basis that regulation 5(2)(a) did operate to transfer continuity of service, but without deciding the point.

Restrictive covenants

Restrictive covenants. These are also transferred, although the effect of a transfer may affect the likelihood of their enforceability. For example, a restrictive covenant may be drafted to prevent the employee from soliciting his employer's customers for a specified period of time (*e.g.* one year). At the time that covenant was drafted such a restriction might be quite reasonable so far as that employee was concerned because the employer only sold one product and had a small number of customers. However if that employer sells its business to a much larger corporation with a very large number of customers and a diverse range of products, the reference to the "Company's customers" or its products will suddenly become far wider than is reasonably necessary to protect the corporation's legitimate business interests. It will restrict the employee from soliciting customers with whom he has had no dealings on his employer's products which he sold and will therefore be unenforceable.

Therefore purchasers should be aware that, although regulation 5(2) does transfer across the benefit of restrictive covenants, these will need to be reviewed to ensure that the effect of the transfer has not resulted in them becoming too wide

Confidentiality agreements

to be capable of enforcement. It is submitted that a separate "confidentiality agreement" (which contains restrictive covenants) will also transfer to the purchaser under regulation 5(2)(a) if such an agreement is "connected with" the employee's employment contract, as will usually be the case.

Profit-sharing schemes

Profit-sharing schemes. These are obviously connected with the contract of employment and will therefore transfer across under regulation 5(2)(a). However, some profit sharing/bonus schemes for top executives are constructed (in whole or part) on the profit performance of other companies within the group. For example, an executive's profit share might be split 50 per cent. in respect of the profits earned by his employing company and 50 per cent. in respect of group profits. If his employer then sells the business to a purchaser, then under regulation 5(2)(a) his profit sharing/bonus scheme transfers across with him. But, what if the business of his former employer is then merged by the purchaser with its existing operations, how can his bonus be calculated?

Clearly, it will not be possible to ascertain the profits of his former employer's business since separate accounts are no longer kept, and it would be a nonsense to pay him 50 per cent. bonus based on the profits of a group of companies of which he is no longer a part. In practice, the purchaser will have to offer the executive a new bonus scheme giving equivalent maximum bonus/profit share as he previously enjoyed and calculated in a broadly similar way. Failure to do so will entitle the executive to either sue his new employers for damages or to claim constructive dismissal. It is therefore important for purchasers to ask the vendor about such bonus/profit share schemes and to make provision for the payment of profit share or bonus in respect of the last financial year (if it has not already been paid) and for the current financial year.

Share options connected with employment contract

Share options. These will only transfer across if they are regarded as "connected with" the employee's employment contract. It seems that the mere fact that a person has to be an employee to obtain and exercise such options is not a sufficient connection, especially where the stock option scheme is "self-standing" and contained in separate documentation. For example in *Chapman & Elkin* v. *C.P.S. Computer Group Plc* [1987] I.R.L.R. 462, the plaintiff employees had rights under C.P.S.'s stock option scheme. However under the terms of that scheme they could not exercise their stock option rights earlier than three years from the date of grant unless they fell within certain specified exceptions which included where their employment ended on grounds of death, incapacity or redundancy. In such cases, the scheme provided a "window" during which the employees could exercise their stock option rights. Before three years has elapsed, C.P.S. sold the business in which the plaintiffs were employed to a purchaser, whereupon the plaintiffs sought to exercise their stock options early on the grounds that their employment with C.P.S. had ended by reason of redundancy (*i.e.* C.P.S. no longer needed them to carry out their duties for C.P.S.). C.P.S. sought to resist the claims on the grounds that, as the plaintiff's employments had been transferred to the purchaser together with their existing employment contracts, there was no dismissal for redundancy.

The Court of Appeal upheld the plaintiff's claims on the ground that the stock option agreement was not part of the plaintiffs' employment contracts, but was a separate collateral contract. It did not fall within regulation 5(2) and therefore was not transferred to the purchaser. Accordingly liability remained with C.P.S. In addition, although regulation 5(1) provided that there was no dismissal, this did not prevent the plaintiffs satisfying the activating requirements of C.P.S.'s stock option scheme—*i.e.* their employment with C.P.S. had ended and, as C.P.S. no longer needed their services, the reason for such termination was redundancy. It made no difference that, under employment protection legislation, the plaintiffs would not have been able to have claimed statutory redundancy pay.

This case turned on its own peculiar facts and upon the Court of Appeal's (perhaps surprising) finding that the stock option agreement was not "connected with" the plaintiffs' employment contracts. With respect to the Court, it is submitted that if the rules of a scheme are that an employee cannot benefit unless he is an employee and (as a general rule) can only exercise options whilst remaining an employee, this would seem to be sufficient connection with his employment contract [see p. 134 below on the practical implications of such schemes].

It is now clear that a court is unlikely to imply into employment contracts a term to the effect that the employer will do nothing (*e.g.* sell the business) which will have the effect of stopping an employee from exercising his stock options. In *Thompson* v. *ASDA MFI Group plc* [1988] I.R.L.R. 340; H.C., the plaintiff was an employee of a subsidiary company within the ASDA MFI group. He had two stock options for shares in ASDA MFI; and under the terms of that Inland Revenue approved stock option scheme he forfeited his right to exercise his options as soon as he ceased to be employed in the ASDA MFI group of companies. About one year later, the shares in his employer were sold to another company, outside the ASDA MFI group. He unsuccessfully sought to establish that he was nonetheless entitled to exercise his stock options when the time came due, even though he was no longer employed in the ASDA MFI group. The High Court rejected his claim on the ground that, under the terms of the stock option scheme he had ceased to be employed by a participating employer. The Court rejected his arguments that:

1. ASDA MFI should not be entitled to rely on a state of affairs brought about by its own deliberate act, and
2. there was an implied term in the rules of the scheme that ASDA MFI would no nothing (*i.e.* sell its shares in his employer) which would prevent him from exercising his stock options.

Liability for termination costs

An employee cannot claim unfair dismissal compensation, wrongful dismissal damages, or redundancy pay unless he has been dismissed (*e.g.* either directly or constructively). Where the dismissal takes effect *before* the moment of transfer, liability in respect of these legal actions are not the responsibility of the purchaser—subject of course, to the *Litster* case (see p. 99). However, the purchaser will be liable for the legal repercussions of a dismissal by the vendor, when such dismissal takes effect on or after the moment of dismissal. This applies where the vendor has given notice of dismissal well before the moment of transfer, but that notice expires on or after the moment of transfer—see *Fenton* v. *Stablegold Ltd.* [1986] I.R.L.R. 64; E.A.T. and *Apex Leisure Hire* v. *Barratt* [1984] I.C.R. 452; E.A.T.

Purchaser's liability for his own pre-transfer acts

In some cases, the purchaser will end up being liable for its own pre-transfer decisions and acts involving the vendor's employees. For example, in *Batchelor* v. *Premier Motors (Romford) Ltd. & Petropolis Ltd.* [1982] (unreported C.O.I.T. 1359/181), Premier agreed to sell its petrol station to Petropolis. Mr. Batchelor was the forecourt manager, and the purchasers offered him a revised contract of employment under which, although his basic salary was higher, he lost overtime pay and the use of a company car. This offer was made by the purchaser before the business transfer was completed and Mr. Batchelor resigned claiming constructive dismissal (based on anticipatory breach of contract by the purchaser). His resignation took effect on the moment of transfer. The industrial tribunal upheld his unfair dismissal claim against the purchaser.

Similarly in *Premier Motors (Medway) Ltd.* v. *Total Oil Marine, Lowe & Dyer* [1983] I.R.L.R. 471, Premier transferred its business of running a petrol station to Total Oil, who planned to run the business itself until it found suitable licensees to run it. Total Oil made it clear that it would not need the services of two particular employees after the sale was completed. After Premier ceased operations the two employees stopped working at the petrol station. The E.A.T. held that Total had, by indicating that it would not employ the two employees after the completion of the sale, repudiated their employment contracts and had thereby constructively dismissed them. The reason for their dismissal was redundancy, and the question was: who was responsible for making the redundancy payment to them? There were three possibilities:

1. Premier,
2. Total Oil, or
3. the caretaker licencees to whom Total Oil almost immediately put in to run the business.

The E.A.T. held that regulation 5(2)(a) transferred liability for the redundancy pay from Premier to Total Oil because the two employees had remained in Premier's employment at the moment of transfer to Total Oil. However, regulation 5(2)(a) did not operate again to shift liability on to the caretaker licensees because, as the E.A.T. found, the two employees had been dismissed by Total Oil when it told them it did not want to employ them. Thus, for a moment before Total Oil transferred the business on to the caretaker licensees, the two employees had moved into Total's employment and been dismissed before the second business transfer to the caretakers. The result was that Total ended up remaining liable for the redundancy payments due to the two employees.

In some cases the effect of the purchaser being responsible for dismissals initiated by the vendor can lead to surprising results. In *Fenton* v. *Staplegold Ltd.* [1986] I.R.L.R. 64; E.A.T., the vendor dismissed Mrs. Fenton at the purchaser's request; but since her dismissal took effect at the moment of transfer, regulation 5(2) operated to transfer liability for her dismissal to the purchaser. The following day she was offered employment by the purchaser and then dismissed for redundancy some six weeks later. She claimed compensation for unfair dismissal in respect of both dismissals. She succeeded and the E.A.T. held that the purchasers were responsible for both awards of compensation—*i.e.* they had to pay two unfair dismissal basic awards.

In such cases as these, employee applicants are strongly advised to join both the transferor and transferee as joint respondents in any employment protection litigation since, if they bring a claim against the wrong party they will not be able to rectify their mistake, unless the claim against the other employer is made within a three month period from the date their employment ends—see *Hansford* v. *Mumford Ltd. & Evans* [1983] (unreported C.O.I.T. 1476/49).

Redundancy, S.S.P. and S.M.P. rebates

As well as inheriting the burdens of the vendor's dismissals, the purchaser is entitled to claim its benefits—such as redundancy, S.S.P. or S.M.P. rebates in respect of employees they have inherited under regulation 5—see *Secretary of State for Employment* v. *Anchor Hotel (Kippford) Ltd.* [1985] I.R.L.R. 452.

Liability for torts or breach of statutory duties

It appears that the transferor's liability to his own employees in respect of torts or breaches of statutory duty may be likewise transferred by regulation 5(2)(a)—see *obiter dicta* in the *Spence* case [1986] I.R.L.R. 248. Such liabilities might arise in connection with claims for damages for accidents at work, or other health and safety issues. It would appear that vicarious liability of an employer for a negligence claim by one of its employees against another transfers over under regulation 5(2)(a), but not vicarious liability in respect of the negligent act of its employee against a third party (not being an employee). However this point has not yet been settled. Even if tortious claims (*e.g.* for personal injury at work) are not transferred to the purchaser, it may be that the employee may still have a claim under contract in respect of his injuries—*e.g.* a breach of the implied terms to provide a safe place and system of work.

What liabilities do not transfer over?

As a matter of statutory construction, only those liabilities, duties, powers and rights which are connected with or under employment contracts, transferred to the purchaser under regulation 5(1), are inherited by the purchaser. Thus nothing else is transferred—*e.g.* not PAYE liability or national insurance contributions. However the Transfer Regulations provide some additional areas which are excluded from the application of regulation 5(2)(a).

Criminal liability

Criminal Liability. By virtue of regulation 5(4), the liability of any person prosecuted for, or convicted of, or sentenced for any offence, are not transferred to the purchaser by regulation 5(2). It seems this covers criminal offences connected with employment—*e.g.* breaches of the Health & Safety at Work Act 1974 and similar legislation, or a prosecution under the Data Protection Act.

Regulation 7: pensions

Pensions. Under regulation 7, pensions are excluded from the transfer effect of regulation 5. It provides that:

> "Regulations 5 & 6 above shall not apply—
> (a) to so much of a contract of employment or collective agreement as relates to an occupational pension scheme within the meaning of the Social Security Pensions Act 1975 or the Social Security Pensions (Northern Ireland) Order 1975; or
> (b) to any rights, powers, duties or liabilities under or in connection with any such contract or subsisting by virtue of any such agreement and relating to such a scheme or otherwise arising in connection with that person's employment and relating to such a scheme."

What is an occupational pension scheme?

An occupational pension scheme under the Social Security Pensions Act 1975 means:

> "any scheme or arrangement which is comprised in or has one or more instruments or agreements and which has, or is capable of having, effect in relation to one or more descriptions or catagories of employments so as to provide benefits in the form of pensions *or otherwise*, payable on termination of service, or on death or retirement, to or in respect of earners with qualifying service in an employment of any such description or category" [S.S.P.A. 1975, s.66 (1)].

This definition is particularly wide. Read literally, it would seem to embrace any scheme or arrangement operated by an employer which provides benefits on the termination of employment or on retirement or death ; and such benefits can be in the form of pensions *or otherwise*. On its strict wording it would seem to cover enhanced redundancy schemes and self-standing life assurance schemes which are wholly unconnected with pensions. Therefore, since regulation 7 excludes from the automatic transfer principle all rights, powers, duties and liabilities relating to to an occupational pension scheme, all those benefits arising on termination of employment, death or retirement would similarly be excluded from the ambit of

Regulation 7 and the Directive

regulations 5 and 6. If the above literal meaning of an "occupational pension scheme" is correct, then it would appear that regulation 7 is in contravention of the Business Transfer Directive which exempts from its automatic transfer effect "employees' rights to old-age, invalidity or survivors' benefits *under* supplementary company or inter company *pension schemes* outside the statutory social security schemes in Member States" (Art. 3(3)). This exclusion is clearly a much narrower one than provided for in the Transfer Regulations and it links the specified benefits to the pension scheme operated by the employer. In the light of the House of Lords' "purposive construction" of the Transfer Regulations, to give effect to Article 3(3) of the Directive, it is submitted that an occupational pension scheme should be construed as only including "old-age, invalidity or survivor's benefits".

Almost all company pension schemes are likely to fall within the wide definition of an occupational pension scheme. It does not matter whether such schemes are contracted-out of SERPS, or are "top-up" schemes. It also makes no difference whether the schemes are contributory or non-contributory, and it covers both "money-purchase" and "defined benefits" schemes.

Other benefits attached to the pension scheme

It should also be noted that not only are rights, liabilities, duties or powers in respect of the pension part of the scheme excluded from transfer under regulation 5, but also other benefits which form part of the pension scheme and which arise on the member's death or retirement or on termination of service. These would seem to include life assurance cover, widows benefits and various concessionary benefits for retired employees (*e.g.* reduced travel or discounts). It is submitted that the definition of "occupational pension scheme" extracted from S.S.P.A. 1975, s.66 appears to become ambiguous when inserted into the context of regulation 7. It may be possible to argue that that the words "benefits payable on termination of service" should be construed in the context retirement or death of employees. Therefore those words are descriptive of *when* those benefits become payable and are not indicative of the *nature* of the benefits. Even if this more limited interpretation of the ambit of an occupational pension scheme is correct, it seems that those life assurance and other concessionary schemes which do not form part of the employers' pension scheme, are still excluded by regulation 7.

"Portable" pension schemes

It is becoming increasingly common for employees to have their own "portable" pension schemes. The employer's obligation is stated to be the payment of a fixed sum or percentage of salary per annum into the individual's personal pension scheme. It seems that such personal pension schemes do not fall within the scope of regulation 7. This is because they do not provide pensions: " . . . in relation *to one or more* descriptions or categories of employments. . . . " Such personal pension schemes subsist regardless of employment and who it is with. The importance of this distinction lies in the fact that if such schemes do not fall within the definition of an occupational pensions scheme in section 66 of the S.S.P.A. 1975, then the vendor's obligation to contribute the fixed sum or percentage per annum will be transferred across to the purchaser under regulation 5(2) along with other employment benefits.

Single-member company schemes

The statutory definition of an occupational pension scheme under S.S.P.A. 1975, s.66 refers to a: " . . . scheme . . . which has, or is capable of having, effect in relation to one or more descriptions or categories of employments. . . . " It is unclear whether a scheme of which only one person is a member can be said to fall within this definition. Strictly speaking, the words: "description . . . of employment . . . " suggest that they could be limited to a single person; yet the use of the word "earners" at the end of the definition suggests occupational pension schemes should cover more than one person. It is submitted that an employer-sponsored pension scheme will fall within the statutory definition of an occupational pension scheme even where it has one member; although this point awaits confirmation from the courts.

Significance of regulation 7

The importance of regulation 7 is that the purchaser is under no obligation to continue the vendor's pension scheme, or to provide the same level of benefits or to run any pension scheme at all. For any employees (especially those nearing retirement age) this is probably the most important aspect of their benefits package—yet it is not protected by the Transfer Regulations. This lack of protection is not in contravention of the Business Transfer Directive, since Article 3(3) provides that the automatic transfer principle enshrined in the Directive does not extend to "employees' rights to old-age, invalidity or survivors' benefits under supplementary company or inter-company pension schemes outside the social security schemes of Member States."

Employees' rights in respect of loss of pension scheme

What, then, are employees' rights in respect of occupational pension schemes when their employments are transferred to a new employer under the Transfer Regulations? The legal position can be summarised as follows:

Claim against purchaser

1. There can be no claim against the purchaser, because no pension obligations are transferred to it. However if the purchaser subsequently maintains the vendor's pension scheme or makes representations to the transferring employees regarding pensions, then *those* later acts may give rights to some form of claim in respect of pensions. The Transfer Regulations clearly do not.

Claim against vendor

2. At first sight, there can be no claim against the vendor, provided it honours its pensions obligations up to the moment of transfer. Some commentators have suggested that the transferring employees may have a cause of action against the transferor for breach of contract, on the grounds that there is some sort of implied term that the vendor will not sell its business with the result that employees will have lesser pensions benefits. That argument is, with respect, untenable (see also *Thompson* v. *ASDA MFI* [1988] I.R.L.R. 340). Most pension schemes have provisions for what happens to pension rights when a member leaves employment before pensionable age (*e.g.* return of contributions, transfer payments or return of contributions). The vendor is not in breach of contract merely by selling its business, and cannot be in breach when it honours its pension obligations up to the moment of transfer.
3. However, in most business transfers employees are not given due notice—usually because, if the Transfer Regulations apply, there is no need for the vendor to give notice of termination. Their employment contracts are transferred to the purchaser automatically. Although, due to regulation 5, the employments and a package of rights, duties, powers and liabilities are transferred to the purchaser, pensions are left behind. It *may* be possible for transferring employees to argue that the common law position still subsists in respect of pensions (*e.g.* a transfer

is a repudiatory breach of contract) even if regulation 5 overrides it for other employment benefits. This will mean that when the business transfer occurs, regulation 5 will operate to transfer the non-pension benefits, etc., to the purchaser, but, it will not operate on the pensions part of the employees' contracts of employment. Thus the business transfer will constitute a repudiatory breach of contract in respect of the vendor's obligations for pensions. It will be a breach which the employees have no choice but to accept. Their damages will be for wrongful dismissal and will be limited to the loss to their eventual pension benefits of not having been dismissed with full notice. This is normally calculated on an actuarial basis and may be more or less than the vendor's pension contributions for the notice period, depending on the circumstances. Of course, if the purchaser provides a similar pension scheme or promises continuity of pensionable service, the employees will probably have suffered no, or minimal, loss.

4. Liability for that breach of contract claim will not transfer to the purchaser because of the effect of regulation 7.
5. It is debatable whether the employees will have a constructive (unfair) dismissal claim against the vendor (there can be no claim against the purchaser). This point has not yet been decided.

Protective awards

Where an employer proposes to make redundancies from its workforce in respect of which it recognises a trade union, it has an obligation under E.P.A. 1975, s.99 to give that union certain information about the redundancies and to consult with that union [see p. 89 for a fuller explanation]. If an employer fails to comply with its statutory obligations under section 99, the recognised union concerned can apply to an industrial tribunal to make a protective award covering those employees affected. The award made by the tribunal will be an order that the employer pays to them a specified number of days' pay. If the employer fails to do so, then the employee can go to the tribunal for an order requiring his employer to pay him his protective award.

It seems that regulation 5(2)(a) does not transfer across to the purchaser liability in respect of such a protective award because, according to EAT in *Angus Jowett & Co.* v. *NUTGW* [1985] I.C.R. 646, E.A.T.:

> "the liabilities which lead to the making of a declaration and a protective award under the Act and arise in connection not with any contract with an individual employee, but by reason of a failure to consult recognised unions. . . . "

This ruling has been widely criticised but, since it is the only authoritative judicial pronouncement on the subject, it must be regarded as a statement of the current law. It also appears that an employer's liability for an award under regulation 11 of the Transfer Regulations for failure to inform or consult trade unions about the business transfer likewise does not transfer under regulation 5(2)(a). The *Angus Jowett* case [see above] has been criticised principally on the ground that, although it is the union who first initiates the claim under section 99 (or regulation 11), the compensation is payable to employees affected; and if the employer fails to comply with the tribunal's order, the employee can claim his share of the protective award directly.

Industrial training levy

This is, apparently not transferred under regulation 5(2)(a)—see *Plastics Processing ITB* v. *Norsk Hydro Polymers Ltd.* [1984] unreported.

Transfer of acts and omissions

Warnings for poor performance or misconduct

Employer's promises and misdeeds

Regulation 5(2)(b) states that anything done before the transfer by or to the transferor (*e.g.* the vendor) is treated as having been done by or to the transferee (*e.g.* the purchaser). This means that the purchaser steps into the vendor's shoes in its dealings with employees on all matters except pensions. For example, where an employee has been given warnings for poor performance or misconduct, he takes these with him into his employment with the purchaser. He can also carry across any representations or promises made to him by the vendor (*e.g.* permission to start work later due to domestic reasons). The purchaser will also inherit the vendor's misdeeds towards employees. These might include the following:

1. Acts of sex and race discrimination;
2. Action short of dismissal against trade union members (*e.g.* in breach of E.P.C.A., s.23);
3. Breach of contract claims (*e.g.* bonus and commission claims), equal pay claims;
4. Debts owed by the vendor to any transferring employees (*e.g.* arrears of pay, holiday pay, or overtime)—see the E.C.J.'s dicta in the *Abels* v. *Administrative Board* case [1987] 2 C.M.L.R. 405; E.C.J.;
5. A course of unreasonable conduct or harassment of an employee (which could give rise to constructive dismissal claims).

It is important to note that, this transfer of liability only applies in respect of those employees who have transferred to the purchaser by virtue of regulation 5(1).

Residual liabilities of the Vendor

The effect of regulation 5 is to transfer all liabilities (except for pensions) to the purchaser, in respect of those employees actually or deemed to be employed in the business transferred up to the moment of transfer. However this does leave the vendor with some residual liabilities in respect of them. These include the following:

1. liability for failing to inform and consult with recognised trade unions under E.P.A. 1975, s.99 (protective awards), or under regulation 10 (see p. 89 below);
2. PAYE and NI contributions up to the transfer date;
3. a possible claim in respect of pensions (see p. 72 above);
4. any vicarious liability in respect of a claim by a third party against an employee who has transferred to the purchaser under regulation 5(1)—*e.g.* for personal injuries;
5. criminal liability.

It is not possible for a transferring employee to bring a claim against the vendor in respect of a liability which the Transfer Regulations or the Directive have transferred to the purchaser—see *Berg* v. *Besselsen* [1988] (unreported; E.C.J. Case No 144/87) where the E.C.J. said that Article 3(1) (*i.e.* the automatic transfer principle:

> "must be interpreted as meaning that after the date of transfer, and by virtue of the transfer alone, the transferor is discharged from his obligations arising from the employment contract or the employment relationship, even if the workers employed in the undertaking do not consent or oppose that consequence. . . .".

The right to object to the new employer

The common law position

Prior to the implementation of regulation 5(1), the common law allowed employees to object to being employed by the purchaser because their employment contracts could not be assigned without their consent. Now that regulation 5(1) has provided for the automatic transfer of their employment to the purchaser, they would be left without any right to object to their new employer (however horrible!)—but some measure of relief is afforded by regulation 5(5). This provides that regulation 5(1) is:

Right to object under regulation 5(5)

> "without prejudice to any right of an employee arising apart from these Regulations to terminate his contract of employment without notice if a substantial change is made in his working conditions to his detriment. . . . "

Regulation 5(5) goes on to state that:

> " . . . no such right shall arise by reason only that, under [reg. 5(1)] the identity of his employer changes unless the employee shows that, in all the circumstances, the change is a significant change and is to his detriment."

Thus regulation 5(5) is in two parts and, although they form a single paragraph in the Regulations, they need to be considered separately.

Part 1: "Without prejudice to any right. . . . "

Interpretation

It is difficult to understand why this part has been included. It does not create any new right or purport to change the law. It simply confirms that the automatic transfer principle in regulation 5(1) does not prejudice any *existing* right of an employee to treat his contract as at an end by reason of his employer's unilateral changes in his working conditions—*i.e.* the right to resign and claim that he has been constructively dismissed. From such a base, the employee can then launch claims for damages for wrongful dismissal, compensation for unfair dismissal or redundancy pay. In the context of a business transfer, this right may arise where a purchaser seeks to change the remuneration package offered to the vendor's employees so that they may be on uniform terms and conditions with the purchaser's existing workforce. Alternatively the purchaser may seek to change an employee's place of work or job duties or working hours, without having the contractual right to do so. In both circumstances the employee may not wish to work under those changed conditions.

In other words, the first part of regulation 5(5) appears to do no more that preserve an employee's right to accept his employer's repudiatory breach of contract when the latter attempts to impose new working conditions. It is well-established that the common law test is: whether the employer has committed a fundamental or significant breach of contract—see *Western Excavating* v. *Sharp* [1978] I.C.R. 221; C.A.

Problems with regulation 5(5)

However the way regulation 5(5) seeks to preserve this right of the employee is a little puzzling on two counts:

1. The test in regulation 5(5) for exercising the existing right to claim constructive dismissal is stated to apply to "substantial changes . . . to his detriment" whereas the common law right to claim constructive dismissal arises upon the employer's repudiatory *breach of contract* test;
2. The regulation 5(5) test is limited to "working conditions" whereas the common law test covers *any* breach of contract (*i.e.* there can be changes to working conditions which are not breaches of contract).

At first sight both differences appear to change scope of the right to claim constructive dismissal in the normal way. First, the use of the words "substantial change" suggest variations to working conditions which need not be contractual nor repudiatory. This may indicate a lower standard for employees to meet when claiming constructive dismissal under regulation 5(5). Secondly, the use of the word "detriment" indicates that a right to claim constructive dismissal under regulation 5(5) may not be available to an employee where an employer changes a selection of terms and conditions which make him no worse off on a "swings and roundabouts" basis (under the common law employees can insist that their individual terms remain intact). Thirdly, the regulation 5(5) test refers to "changes in working conditions." Does this mean the employee's *physical* working conditions or all his terms and conditions of employment?

Unfortunately the effects of these three differences have not yet been decided by the courts and tribunals. Nonetheless, it is submitted that the first part of regulation 5(5) is unlikely to have been intended to create a new basis upon which employees can claim constructive dismissal. It is not expressed in words which indicate the creation of a new right. But is it intended to vary the existing common law right to claim constructive dismissal? As has been seen, in some parts the effect of the differences are in employees' favour and in other parts it is the converse. But the problem with that argument is that it is stated to be "without prejudice" to existing rights and a more restricted application would be contrary to the spirit of the Business Transfer Directive. It is submitted that the first part of regulation 5(5) is intended to do nothing more that preserve employees' existing rights to claim constructive dismissal.

Case law

This issue has yet to be determined by the courts and tribunals. The only case which has begun to approach it, is *Wright & Another* v. *A.W. Smith (Gosport) Ltd. & A. & J. Bull*

Ltd. where the purchaser sought to change the basis upon which the applicant was paid. Instead of receiving a flat rate wage (with bonus) of £125 p.w. for a 44 hour week, he was offered a basic rate of £102 for a 50 hour week with a considerable productivity bonus. A colleague who worked under the new conditions was able to double his pre-transfer pay. An industrial tribunal rejected the applicants' constructive dismissal claims. In so doing, the tribunal commented that the changes were not to the applicants' detriment, and added that, if the claim had not been dealt with under the Transfer Regulations, it would have succeeded. The correctness of the tribunal's decision is open to some doubt, especially in the light of the E.C.J.'s ruling in the *Foreningen* case [1988] I.R.L.R. 315.

Part 2: change of identity of employer

Since regulation 5(5) preserves an employee's right to claim constructive dismissal, the automatic transfer principle would be destroyed, if the employee can do so on account of the change of identity of his employer. One of the prime objectives behind regulation 5 is the transfer of employment regardless of the employee's wishes—unless, of course, he wants to leave on his own accord by resigning. However this could lead to some unfairness, especially where that change of employer means that the employee's working environment is very different. The second part of regulation 5(5) therefore tries to strike a balance. It provides that:

1. the mere fact of a change of identity of the employer will not of, itself, entitle a transferring employee to claim he has been constructively dismissed; but
2. it may do so, if the change in the identity of his employer is both significant and to the employee's detriment.

Interpretation

Again, the second part of regulation 5(5) does not create a new right to claim constructive dismissal on new basis. This is because the opening words of the second part ("but no such right shall arise . . . ") obviously refer back to the first part of regulation 5(5). It will be recalled that the first part does not create a new additional right to claim constructive dismissal, but merely confirms the existing right.

So a transferring employee cannot claim he has been constructively dismissed merely because his employer has changed by virtue of the operation of regulation 5(1). But he can do so, where *the change in his employer's identity* is also significant and detrimental to him. This means that such a significant and detrimental change must be in respect of his new employer. This appears to create a new basis upon which a constructive dismissal claim might be brought. The Regulations do not specify what those significant and detrimental changes might be; but when this regulation was being explained by Mr David Waddington (then Under-Secretary of State for Employment) as the Regulations were going through Parliament he said:

> "Regulation 5(5) provides that that does not affect the employee's right to resign, but he will have a remedy in law only where he resigns because of a substantial change in his working conditions. He will have no remedy if he resigns

only because the identity of his employer has changed unless he can show that the change in all the circumstances is a significant change to his detriment. It is somewhat difficult to find examples of where such a change could be significantly to the employee's detriment. When I asked those who advise me to give examples, the only ones they could think of were examples of new employer's running off with their employees' wives or murdering their fathers. We wish to close any possible gaps"!!!

It seems that the examples given by Mr Waddington are not particularly helpful, since such behaviour by an employer would undermine the implied term of trust and confidence and give rise to a constructive dismissal claim in the normal way. However, it seems that regulation 5(5) might conceivably include the following situations:

Possible detrimental changes

1. a change in identity means that the employee is part of a much larger corporation where his influence on policy-making or decision-making is much less (*e.g.* because the parent company exercises substantial control over its subsidiary companies or divisions);
2. promotion prospects are lessened or seniority adversely affected;
3. there is lesser job security with the purchaser;
4. the purchaser does not recognise unions or is strongly "anti-union."

If an employee can claim constructive dismissal on this basis, then this does appear to widen the basis of such claims from the existing law—questions of job security, extent of parent company control, loss of promotion opportunities and an employer's attitude to unions do not normally form part of a contract of employment (unless expressly made a term of the contract). Yet, as is well-established, the test under the existing law for constructive dismissal is directly linked to a repudiatory breach of contract, and the second part of regulation 5(5) expressly refers back to the "existing law." Some commentators have suggested that regulation 5(5) might entitle a transferred employee to object to the identity of his new employer where that new employer operates in a way which the individual employee personally finds objectionable—*e.g.* by trading in South Africa. It is submitted that such suggestions appear to be wrong.

Significance of regulation 5(5)

It is unlikely that the second part of regulation 5(5) is intended to cover significant changes in working conditions resulting from the change of identity of employer. This is because, if the contrary was true, the employee's position is already protected under the existing law, and therefore the second part of regulation 5(5) would be superfluous. In addition, the words "the change is a significant change and to his detriment," relate back to the reference to the change of identity of the employer.

However the overall effect of regulation 5(5) is confusing and is in urgent need of judicial interpretation. It is possible that this limited right to object to the change of identity of the employer may be in breach of the Business Transfer Directive, which the E.C.J. held in *European Commission* v. *Belgium* [1986]

2 C.M.L.R. 865; E.C.J., should not be implemented by Member States in any way which diminishes employees' existing rights. It might be argued that, prior to the enactment of the Transfer Regulations, employees in the United Kingdom had the common law right to object to the assignment of their employment contracts without their consent [see the *Nokes* case [1940] A.C. 1014, H.L.—p. 49]. Regulation 5, in effect takes away that right where an employee cannot show that the change in the identity of his employer is significant and to his detriment. For example West Germany has implemented the Business Transfer Directive by domestic legislation which preserved employees' existing right to refuse to transfer with the business.

It is also interesting to note that, to some extent employees' position under the Transfer Regulations has been worsened in respect of their right to claim redundancy pay. For example, prior to the Regulations employees would only lose their right to redundancy pay in the context of a business transfer if they unreasonably refused an offer of suitable alternative employment from the purchaser. In most cases such a refusal would be reasonable (or the offer would be unsuitable) if the purchaser failed to maintain an equivalent pension scheme as the employee enjoyed with the purchaser; and so he would not lose his right to redundancy pay. Yet, under the Transfer Regulations, employees no longer have to object on this basis since regulation 7 provides that regulation 5 does not apply to occupational pension schemes [see p. 72].

5 EFFECT OF THE TRANSFER REGULATIONS ON INSOLVENT EMPLOYERS

Selling an insolvent company

It has already been well-established that a business transfer can be effected by an insolvent company which, through a liquidator or receiver, sells its assets in order to pay its creditors—see for example the *Spence* case [1986] I.R.L.R. 248. Thus the Transfer Regulations apply where a liquidator sells off a company's business as a going concern. However, in some cases a potential purchaser might be put off from buying the company's assets in circumstances where it would mean taking on liability for all the company's employees. Nonetheless liquidators can usually obtain more money for the company's assets if they can be sold as a "going concern," since some goodwill will still attach to the business.

"Hiving-down": what is hiving-down?

How is "hiving-down" achieved?

To facilitate this possibility liquidators and receivers have developed a practice called "hiving-down." It involves splitting the assets of the business from the employees, so that the business will look a more attractive proposition for potential purchasers. The liquidator achieves this by taking or forming a wholly-owned subsidiary of company A., and then transferring to that subsidiary (company B.) all the assets of company A.'s business. The employees remain with company A. It represents a sort of internal group "asset-stripping" exercise. The liquidator/receiver then arranges for company A. to second its employees to provide services for company B. Finally, the liquidator/receiver offers company B. for sale as a going concern, and potential purchasers will be pleased to see that company B. has no employees on whose contracts of employment the Transfer Regulations can operate.

"Hiving-down": regulation 4

It is in everyone's interest that the liquidator/receiver is successful in finding a purchaser of company B. as a going concern, since this will raise more money for the creditors and it will increase the chances of the purchaser offering jobs to some of the employees of company A. working in that business. The Transfer Regulations preserve this hiving-down practice. However a measure of protection is needed to stop it being abused to circumvent the Regulations. Regulation 4 seeks to maintain such a balance. It applies:

> "where the receiver of the property or part of the property of a company [or an administrator of a company appointed under Part II of the Insolvency Act 1986], or, as in the case of a creditor's voluntary winding up, the liquidator of a

company, transfers the company's undertaking (the 'relevant undertaking') to a wholly owned subsidiary of the company. . . . "

When does regulation 4 apply?

Therefore regulation 4 only applies where a receiver, administrator (under the Insolvency Act 1986), or a liquidator (under a voluntary liquidation) has been appointed in respect of company A. which is insolvent. Regulation 4 apparently does not apply where the Court has appointed a liquidator. The receiver/administrator/liquidator must also have transferred some or all of company A.'s property to a wholly owned subsidiary (company B.). If both these conditions have been met, the operative part of regulation 4 will apply. It provides that in such an event:

> "the transfer shall for the purpose of these Regulations be deemed not to have been effected until immediately before:
> (a) the transferee company ceases (otherwise than by reason of being wound up) to be a wholly owned subsidiary of the transferor company; or
> (b) the relevant undertaking is transferred by the transferee company to another person;
> whichever occurs first, and, . . . the transfer of the relevant undertaking shall be taken to have been effected immediately before that date by one transaction only."

Paragraphs (a) and (b) above cover two very different situations.

Property transfer followed by share transfer

Regulation 4(1): share transfers

Sub-paragraph (a) covers the situation where company A. (the insolvent company) has transferred its property to its wholly-owned subsidiary, company (B.). Later the liquidator/receiver/administrator finds a purchaser (company C.) and company A. then effects a *share transfer* of its shares in company B. to company C. In such a case regulation 4 provides that the first transfer of property from A. to B. is not a relevant transfer for the purposes of the Regulations, but the position is held in suspense until A. sells its shares in company B. to C. At that moment, the employees left behind in company A. will automatically transfer into the employment of company B., and thus be part of company B. when its shares are acquired by C. However it should be noted that, the intermediate transfer between A. and B. is left in suspense only for as long as A. still owns *all* the shares in company B. The delayed transfer of the employees into company B. will take effect whether C. acquires all the shares in company B., or a controlling or minority shareholding.

Property transfer followed by business transfer

Regulation 4(b): business transfers

Sub-paragraph 4(b) covers the situation where company A. transfers its property to its wholly owned subsidiary company (B.). The liquidator/receiver/administrator then finds purchaser C., who wishes to take over the business of company B as a going concern, not its shares. A split second before the moment of the business transfer between company B. and C., regulation 4(1)(b) operates to transfer the employees left behind in company A. into the employment of company B., so that they will automatically transfer into the employment of company C. as part of the business transfer under the Regulations.

Effect of regulation 4

Thus regulation 4 introduces a state of suspension created by the hiving down operation. It seeks to make the Regulations work in such a context. There is, however, one major loophole in regulation 4. It appears that there is nothing stopping company C. requiring the liquidator/receiver/administrator for company A. to dismiss those employees it does not wish to inherit. If such dismissals are effected during the period of "suspension"—*i.e.* before anything is sold to company C.—regulation 5 will not operate on their contracts at the moment of transfer, because they would not have been in company A.'s employment at that key moment. This is because regulation 4 would not have transferred them into company B. at the crucial moment, since they would have ceased to have been employed by company A. at the time regulation 4 becomes operative—see *Harris* v. *Fiesana Ltd.* [1983] unreported (C.O.I.T. 1474/167).

This interpretation seems to defeat one of the objectives of the Regulations; and such dismissed employees will face the daunting prospect of trying to obtain their unfair dismissal compensatory award from the liquidator/receiver/administrator, in competition with other unsecured creditors. Their unfair dismissal basic award or redundancy pay and pay in lieu of statutory notice can be recovered from the Redundancy Fund, run by the Department of Employment. However this is subject to the rule in the *Litster* case (see p. 55 above) by which the employee is deemed to be still employed at the moment of transfer.

Insolvency and the Business Transfer Directive

It should be noted that, according to the E.C.J. in *Abels* v. *The Administrative Board of the Bedrijfsvereniging Voor De Metaal Industrie En De Electrotechnische Industrie* [1987] 2 C.M.L.R. 405, the Business Transfer Directive does not apply where insolvency proceedings have been commenced or a liquidator has been appointed by the court. However the Directive does apply disposals of insolvent companies which have not reached such a stage.

6 DISMISSALS ARISING FROM A BUSINESS TRANSFER

Background

It is fairly common that, on a business transfer, the purchaser is unwilling to take on all of the vendor's employees currently working in the business (or part) to be transferred. It has already been seen how regulation 5 apportions liability for those employees (*i.e.* including liabilities arising from dismissals) by making the purchaser responsible for any such employee whose employment contract is still alive on or after the moment of transfer, and leaving the vendor with liability in respect of the remainder of its employees (see p. 54 above). So the vendor is liable for any liability arising from any dismissal by it which has *taken effect* before the moment of transfer, and the purchaser is liable for its own and the vendor's dismissals which *take effect* from that moment onwards. From the purchaser's viewpoint, this is something of which it will be wary, since the way the vendor tries to put such dismissals into effect may either:

1. be such that the liability for the dismissals transfers over to the purchaser (contrary to the parties' intentions) or
2. such dismissals are unfair either on the basis of selection or procedurally (see Appendix A).

The vendor's position

From the vendor's viewpoint, it may find itself responsible for paying the liabilities arising from dismissals which the purchaser insisted (usually as a term of the acquisition agreement) the vendor put into effect prior to the moment of transfer. For example, the purchaser's basis of selection may be unfair, or the timescale in which redundancies take effect, could make such dismissals procedurally unfair because there has been no advance warning or consultation [see Appendix A]. Alternatively the purchaser's insistence on secrecy and a quick timescale may mean that the vendor has broken its obligations to inform and consult with recognised trade unions under E.P.A. s.99 [see Appendix A], or under regulation 10 (see p. 118 below).

Dismissals unconnected with the transfer

There is also the possibility that the vendor has given notice of dismissal to an employee for a reason wholly unconnected with the business transfer (*e.g.* for absenteeism or poor performance). If that notice does not expire until after the moment of transfer, the purchaser will inherit liability for any unfair dismissal compensation (*i.e.* if such dismissal was unfair, *e.g.* because the vendor had not given the employee concerned the requisite number of warnings). It will be recalled that regulation 5(2)(b) treats the purchaser as having perpetrated *all* the vendor's acts and omissions for those employees the purchaser inherits under regulation 5(1)—see p. 102 above.

Indemnities

For all these reasons, the vendor and purchaser will usually agree in the acquisition agreement who will pick up the liability in the final event *as between themselves*. The acquisition agreement cannot, of course, dictate the existence of the liability in the first place (see regulation 12—on page 46 above), nor can it dictate whom the dismissed employee must sue in order to claim the appropriate damages or compensation. Regulation 5 controls that issue (see p. 66). See also p. 162 and Appendix B p. 190 for more on indemnities.

Summary of liabilities arising on dismissal

This chapter is concerned with those liabilities which may arise from the dismissal of employees either before or after a business transfer takes place, and which occur in connection with the transfer. Such dismissals might be effected by the purchaser or vendor to reflect the purchaser's needs in respect of the vendor's workforce, or they might be initiated by an employee (*i.e.* a constructive dismissal) because the purchaser proposes to change the terms of employment contracts. There are five main areas where liability may arise. These are:

Areas where liability may arise

1. damages for wrongful dismissal (*i.e.* where a dismissal has been effected without full notice or before the expiry of a fixed term contract);
2. statutory redundancy pay (possibly together with damages in respect of any contractual enhanced redundancy pay provided for in an employer's redundancy policy);
3. a protective award for failure to inform and consult with recognised trade unions under E.P.A., s.99;
4. compensation for unlawful sex or race discrimination;
5. compensation for unfair dismissal.

The relevant employer's obligations and liabilities are summarised below.

Wrongful dismissal

What is "wrongful dismissal"?

An employee is wrongfully dismissed if his employment contract is terminated without due notice or (in the case of a fixed term contract) prior to the expiry of the fixed term. The claim is, in effect, for damages for breach of contract and it is therefore dealt with by the ordinary courts. The only defence available to an employer in respect of such a claim is to argue that it was entitled to dismiss the employee summarily on account of his repudiatory breach of contract—*i.e.* for gross misconduct or gross negligence. This is unlikely to be applicable for most dismissals occasioned by a business transfer, and therefore the relevant employer will be liable for damages for wrongful dismissal.

In many business transfers, the vendor will not be in a position to give full notice to those employees to be dismissed. This will especially be the case in respect of senior management and long-serving staff who will probably have notice periods of three months or longer. Thus the vendor will almost inevitably be in breach of contract if he is required to effect those dismissals before the moment of transfer—*i.e.* to stop regulation

Payment in lieu of notice

5 operating to transfer liability over to the purchaser. Therefore the vendor will probably give the dismissed employees pay in lieu of notice in respect of that part of their notice periods not worked. Where an employment contract gives the employer the right to give the employee pay in lieu of notice instead of full notice, a dismissal with pay in lieu will not be a breach of contract—*Parker & Ginsberg Ltd.* v. *Parker* [1988] I.R.L.R. 483 (see p. 130 for further implications on this). Where the dismissals are effected by the purchaser, timing is usually less important since regulation 5 has already operated to transfer the vendor's employees to him.

Calculation of payment in lieu of notice

Whether the employee is given pay in lieu of notice or he has to claim damages for wrongful dismissal, the moneys to which he is entitled are calculated on the same basis. In fact, pay in lieu of notice is, in effect, an out-of-court settlement by way of liquidated damages—*i.e.* the employer is paying to an employee a sum to cover his losses to save them both going to court. Therefore the pay-in-lieu of notice should cover the same items of net loss which the court would award if the wrongful dismissal claim was heard in court. These include:

1. net salary which the employee would have received, had he been given his full notice entitlement; and
2. the net value of any contractual benefits he would likewise have enjoyed during the remainder of his notice period (*e.g.* company car, private medical insurance, life assurance, pension contributions, etc.).

If the net value of these losses exceeds £30,000, then the excess above £30,000 must be grossed up at the employee's marginal rate of tax (see *Shove* v. *Downs Surgical* [1984] I.R.L.R. 17). This grossing up has to occur because the employee will be taxed on such excess.

Employee's duty to mitigate loss

However, as with all common law breach of contract claims, the innocent party to the breach of contract (*i.e.* the employee) has a duty to mitigate his loss. This means that he must:

1. take reasonable steps to look for other employment and
2. give his former employer credit for any sums he receives from new employment or self-employment in so far as these were earned in respect of the period which would have represented his notice period (had he been given it in full).

Injunctions restraining employer from breaching contract

It should be noted that employees dismissed with pay in lieu of notice may be able to apply to the courts for an injunction restraining that breach of contract (see p. 130); but they can only do so if they refuse to "accept" their employer's breach of contract. If they accept their pay in lieu of notice, the court is likely to regard them as having also accepted that their contract is at an end.

Redundancy pay

What is redundancy pay?

The relevant employer's obligation to make a statutory

redundancy payment is likely to occur where the purchaser tells the vendor that it does not need the services of all, or some, of the latter's employees. In such circumstances their dismissals will almost certainly fall within the statutory definition of redundancy—*i.e.* if their dismissals were wholly or mainly attributable to the fact that:

1. "the employer has ceased, or intends to cease, to carry on the business for the purpose of which the employee was employed . . . or . . . [to do so] at the place where the employee was employed; or
2. the requirements of that business for employees to carry out work of a particular kind . . . or . . . [to do so] . . . in the place where he was so employed have ceased or diminished or are expected to cease or diminish"—see E.P.C.A., s.81(2).

Conditions for statutory redundancy pay

Of course, an employee must have two years continuous service to be entitled to claim statutory redundancy pay. He must also have been dismissed. Thus, since regulation 5(1) prevents there being a dismissal by the mere fact of the business transfer, he will not be entitled to claim redundancy pay when he transfers into the purchaser's employment. This is so, even though the effect of the business transfer is that the reduction in the vendor's needs for employees falls within the statutory definition of redundancy.

So the right to redundancy pay will apply only to those employees actually dismissed (whether directly or constructively) by the vendor or the purchaser. There might be a dismissal by the vendor in response to the purchaser's requirement that certain of the vendor's employees are dismissed to avoid the transfer effect of regulation 5(1). There might also be a direct dismissal by the purchaser shortly after the business transfer has taken place and after the purchaser has had time to assess its staffing requirements. Alternatively, there might be a constructive dismissal by the purchaser where, on or after the transfer, it indicates to the employee an intention either not to honour his employment contract at all (see the *Premier Motors* case [1983] I.R.L.R. 471), or to change the employee's place of work in breach of contract.

Offers of alternative employment

E.P.C.A. 1978, ss. 82(3)–(7), and 84

Under normal redundancy law (*i.e.* E.P.C.A., s.82(3)–(7) and s.84), an employee will forfeit his statutory redundancy pay if he unreasonably refuses an offer of suitable alternative employment (see p. 167 for further details). So if the vendor makes an employee redundant from his existing job (*i.e.* because the purchaser does not want to take him on), but offers him suitable alternative employment elsewhere in the company, or in an associated company (*e.g.* company in the same group of companies), he will forfeit his statutory redundancy pay if he unreasonably refuses that offer (see E.P.C.A., s.82(7)). However that offer must have been made to the employee in question before the ending of his employment, and the new job must start no later than four weeks after his employment ended (see E.P.C.A., s.84)—see Appendix A p. 167 for further details.

Offers of alternative employment by the transferee E.P.C.A. 1978, s.94

Section 94 of the E.P.C.A. has the effect of applying this same rule where the transferee of a business (or part thereof) makes an offer of suitable alternative employment to an employee whom the transferor is to dismiss for redundancy (see p. 167 for a fuller explanation of this rule). This means that if the vendor of a business makes an employee redundant prior to a business transfer taking place but, before his dismissal takes effect, the purchaser makes him an offer of suitable alternative employment to start within four weeks of the end of his employment with the vendor, the employee will forfeit his redundancy pay if he unreasonably refuses that offer. If the vendor is to avoid a redundancy payment with the help of section 94, it must ensure that the purchaser makes the offer *before* the employee's contract ends and that the job is to begin within the four weeks of the employee's dismissal. In practice the vendor will usually require a stipulation to that effect in the acquisition agreement between the purchaser and itself. Where the offer of employment by the purchaser is made *after* the employee's contract with the vendor has ceased, he can have the best of both worlds—*i.e.* he will receive his redundancy payment from the vendor and a new job from the vendor, as happened in the *Spence* case [1986] I.R.L.R. 248.

Limiting the vendor's liability for damages

The vendor may limit its liability for damages for wrongful dismissal by this technique. If the offer from the purchaser is a suitable one, the employee will have failed in his common law duty to mitigate his loss if he refuses to accept it. Thus the vendor's liability for damages for wrongful dismissal may be reduced to the value of the employee's net salary and benefits in respect of gap in employment before the employee joins (or should have joined) the purchaser. If the terms offered by the purchaser are less favourable than those the employee enjoyed with the vendor, the wrongful dismissal damages will also extend to the difference between the two contracts for the relevant period which would have constituted his notice.

Effect on subsequent redundancy 1978, s.94

Where a vendor does make a redundancy payment to a dismissed employee who is subsequently engaged in accordance with s.94, the employee will have to requalify for entitlement to redundancy pay afresh with the purchaser, even though his employment is otherwise treated as continuous (E.P.C.A., para. 12, Sched. 13). In addition, his period of continuous service prior to the end of his employment with the vendor will be discounted for the purpose of calculating his redundancy pay due from the purchaser, in the event that the purchaser makes him redundant at some future date.

See Appendix A p. 165 for a fuller explanation of the law on redundancy.

Redundancy consultation with trade unions

Duty to consult trade unions: E.P.A. 1975, s.99

Under E.P.A. 1975, s.99 an employer is required to give certain information to, and to consult with, trade unions it recognises to any extent for collective bargaining in respect of any group of employees. However this obligation only arises once an employer has formulated a proposal to make some of those employees redundant.

Timing of consultations

Section 99 requires the consultation to commence at the "earliest opportunity" and in any event in time to allow for the statutory consultation periods to run their full length. These vary depending on the numbers of employees to be made redundant and the timescale in which the redundancies will be put into effect. The consultation periods are as follows:

1. 90 days—where 100 or more employees at one establishment are to be made redundant in 90 days or less;
2. 30 days—where 10 or more employees at one establishment are to be made redundant in 30 days or less;
3. an unspecified number days (but unlikely to be more than 30)—in any other case (*e.g.* where less than 10 employees are to be made redundant).

It is important to note that these consultation periods are calculated back from the date when the first employee is due to leave. The consultation process is usually started with the employer giving the union the information required by E.P.A., s.99(5)—*e.g.* reasons for redundancy, methods of selection and timing of redundancies, etc.

Calculating the protective award

What is a protective award and how is it calculated?

Where an employer fails to comply with section 99, the union can apply to an industrial tribunal for a "protective award." The maximum amount of the protective award varies depending on the relevant consultation period which should have been adhered to by the employer. These are as follows:

1. 90 day consultation period—90 days pay per employee
2. 30 day consultation period—30 days pay per employee
3. unspecified consultation period—28 days pay per employee.

Tribunals assess the size of protective awards on the basis of what they consider to be "just and equitable in all the circumstances, having regard to the seriousness of the employer's default." However employers may be able to avoid liability to pay a protective award, where they can convince a tribunal that there were "special circumstances which render it not reasonably practicable . . . to comply," and they have complied with section 99 as far as they reasonably could in the circumstances (E.P.A., s.99(8)). In practice, tribunals construe the scope of this defence very narrowly. As a general rule, the need to preserve the secrecy of a proposed business transfer will not constitute "special circumstances" for the purposes of the section 99(8) defence.

Offsetting the liability for a protective award

It should be noted, however, that an employer can offset its liability for a protective award by damages paid to an employee in respect (*e.g.* pay in lieu of notice) or any other payment made to the employee under his employment contract which relates to the period covered by the protective award. See Appendix A p. 177 for a fuller explanation of E.P.A., s.99.

Practical implications for vendors

Significance of E.P.A. 1975, s.99 for vendors

The importance of section 99 for the vendor is that, in most business transfers, the vendors is not going to be in a position to comply with section 99 in full (especially where the 90 day consultation period is applicable). This is probably because the purchaser will insist on complete secrecy until just before contracts are signed. Similarly the vendor will not want to start consulting with recognised unions over redundancies which may never occur, if the business transfer never takes place. Thus, unless there is sufficient time between exchange of contract and its completion in which to comply with section 99, the vendor probably will face liability for a protective award.

This has serious repercussions for the vendor because, according to the E.A.T. in *Angus Jowett & Co.* v. *N.U.T.G.W.* [1985] I.R.L.R. 326, regulation 5 does not transfer over liability for protective awards under section 99. In some cases, the vendor will manage to obtain an indemnity from the purchaser, especially where it is on the latter's insistence that the consultation process is delayed or not proceeded with at all.

Sex or race discrimination

In rare cases, dismissals arising out of a business transfer may result in claims for sex or race discrimination under the Sex Discrimination Act 1975 and Race Relations Act 1976 respectively. It is conceivable that a purchaser may insist on redundancy selections by the vendor which constitute unlawful sex or race discrimination. For example:

Race and sex discrimination in business transfers

1. It will be unlawful race discrimination where an employee is dismissed by the vendor because the purchaser will not, as a matter of policy, employ nationals of certain countries (*e.g.* some U.S. companies involved in high-tech defence equipment will not employ persons whose origins are from behind the Iron Curtain);
2. It will be indirect sex discrimination for an employer to select employees for redundancy on the basis that part-timers are selected ahead of full-time employees—see *Clarke & Powell* v. *IMI (Eley) Kinnock* [1983] I.C.R. 165.

Remedies for discrimination

Such claims are heard by industrial tribunals who have power to award compensation of up to £8,925. This compensation not only covers the employee's losses caused by the act of discrimination, but also damages for injury to feeling and (in serious cases of discrimination) aggravated damages. It is important to note that employees can bring a sex or race discrimination claim from their first day at work, and do not have to accrue a qualifying period of continuous employment.

Purchaser's liability for vendor's discrimination

If the vendor has committed an act of unlawful sex or race discrimination, liability for it will transfer automatically to the purchaser, if the employees concerned are still in the vendor's employment at the moment of transfer (see regulation 5(2) on p. 76 above).

Unfair dismissal

Right to claim unfair dismissal

Employees with over two years' continuous employment have

the right to bring an unfair dismissal claim in the industrial tribunal. Once it has been established that the employee has been dismissed, tribunals consider an unfair dismissal claim in two parts. First, the tribunal examines whether the employer has established that its reason for dismissal falls within the statutory list of reasons which are *capable* of being fair reasons for dismissal. The list of potentially fair reason for dismissal is: conduct, capability, redundancy, statutory ban and "some other substantial reason of a kind such as to justify the dismissal" (E.P.C.A., ss.57(1) & (2)). The last category is a "catch-all" in case the reason relied on by the employer does not fall within the first four reasons, but is nonetheless of a kind which could justify dismissal. In the past it has covered matters such as business reorganisations, dismissal of temporary replacements, off-duty conduct, etc.

Reason for dismissal E.P.C.A. 1978, s.57

Reasonableness of dismissal

Next the tribunal considers the reasonableness of the employer's decision to dismiss; and, in so doing, it must look at all the circumstances of the case, including the size and administrative resources of the employer in question—E.P.C.A., s.57(3). (See Appendix A p. 168 for a fuller explanation of basic unfair dismissal law).

Dismissals which are automatically unfair

In normal unfair dismissal cases there are only four circumstances where a tribunal must find a dismissal to be automatically unfair, regardless of how reasonable the employer has otherwise been:

1. redundancy selections in breach of an agreed procedure or customary arrangement (E.P.C.A., s.59(b)),
2. redundancy selections on grounds of an employee's union membership, union activities or non-membership of a union (E.P.C.A., s.59(a)),
3. dismissal on grounds of pregnancy in various circumstances (E.P.C.A., s.60),
4. refusing an employee to exercise her "job-back" rights on her return from maternity, in limited circumstances.

Regulation 8

Regulation 8 of the Transfer Regulations is the United Kingdom's implementation of article 4(1) of the Business Transfer Directive which states that:

> "the transfer of an undertaking, business or part of a business shall not in itself constitute grounds for dismissal by the transferor or transferee. This provision shall not stand in the way of dismissals that may take place for economic, technical or organisational reasons entailing changes in the workforce . . .".

Regulation 8 therefore represents an amendment to these normal unfair dismissal rules. It operates in two parts. First, it provides that any dismissal connected with a relevant transfer is automatically unfair (regulation 8(1)). If the law was left as that, it would clearly be unfair to employers who might want to make genuine redundancies in the context of a business transfer. Therefore regulation 8(2) provides an "escape route"—*i.e.* where the reason for dismissal is an "economic, technical or organisational reason entailing changes in the workforce." Secondly, if the employer can show its reason for dismissal falls within the scope of regulation 8(2), the dismissal will be treated as a "some other substantial reason of a kind justifying the dismissal." This means that the dismissal will have broken clear of the automatic unfairness rule in regulation 8(1), and the tribunal will then proceed to consider the reasonableness of the decision to dismiss in the circumstances. These two parts of regulation 8 need to be examined more closely to see how they work in practice. It should be remembered that regulation 8 applies to all types of dismissal under E.P.C.A., s.55(2)—*i.e.* direct employer dismissals, constructive dismissals and the non-renewal of fixed term contracts.

Automatic unfairness

The automatic unfairness rule is contained in regulation 8(1). It provides as follows:

> "Where either before or after a relevant transfer, any employee of the transferor or transferee is dismissed, that employee shall be treated . . . as unfairly dismissed if the transfer or a reason connected with it is the . . . principal reason for his dismissal."

When does regulation 8 apply?

First, it should be noted that regulation 8(1) only applies if there has been a relevant transfer—*i.e.* a business transfer to which the Transfer Regulations apply. It has no applicability where there is a business transfer of an undertaking not in the nature of a commercial venture (see p. 41) or to dismissals arising from share transfers.

Employees covered by regulation 8

Regulation 8(1) applies whether or not the dismissal is effected by the vendor or purchaser, and it is not dependent upon the employee having remained in the vendor's employment up to the moment of transfer. The words: "before or after a relevant transfer" have a wide meaning, and are not limited to any particular period of time each side of the business transfer in question—see regulation 8(3). Therefore regulation 8(1) will operate on the dismissals of the following groups of employees whose dismissals are *connected* with the business transfer:

1. employees engaged in the business (or part) to be transferred who are dismissed by the vendor prior to or with effect from the transfer (*e.g.* because the purchaser does not need their services);
2. employees who are transferred with the business to the purchaser and who are then subsequently dismissed by the purchaser after the transfer;
3. the vendor's employees who are not engaged in the business to be transferred, but who are dismissed by the vendor (*e.g.* to make room for another employee, who worked in the business to be transferred, but whom the vendor wishes to retain);
4. the purchaser's existing employees prior to the business transfer, who are dismissed before or following the transfer (*e.g.* as part of a reorganisation programme to merge the two operations into a single operating unit);
5. the vendor's employees retained after the business transfer has taken place, who are subsequently dismissed (*e.g.* because there is no work for them after all).

The wide scope of regulation 8(1) is reinforced by

regulation 8(3) which provides that regulation 8 applies to employees: "whether or not the employee in question is employed in the undertaking or part . . . transferred or to be transferred."

Dismissal "connected" with the transfer

The automatic unfairness rule in regulation 8(1) will only operate if the reason for the dismissal in question was either the transfer itself, or a reason *connected with it.* Therefore the fact that a dismissal takes place in close proximity to a business transfer does not necessarily activate regulation 8(1), since its timing may be merely coincidental. For example, if the vendor or purchaser dismissed an employee for misconduct or poor performance, regulation 8(1) will not apply to his case if that dismissal would have taken place regardless of the business transfer—see *Oliver* v. *Brian Reed Ltd.* [1983] unreported (C.O.I.T. 1353/101). The formal onus of proving that a dismissal is connected with a relevant transfer lies with the employee; however this may be a fairly easy burden to discharge (see the *Oliver* case [see above]). This issue is obviously a question of fact for the tribunal to decide; and although there is no legal presumption that a dismissal occurring about the time of the business transfer is linked with it, it is submitted that there is, in practice, an *evidential* burden on the employer to produce some evidence showing that the dismissal is not connected with the business transfer. In *P. Bork International AS* v. *Foreningen AF Arbejdsledere I Danmark* [1989] I.R.L.R. 41, the E.C.J. said:

> "in order to determine whether the only reason for dismissal was the transfer itself, account must be taken of the objective circumstances in which the dismissal occurred and, in particular, in a case like the present one, the fact that it took place on a date close to that of the transfer and that the workers concerned were re-engaged by the transferee."

There may be cases where a vendor proposes to dismiss an employee for misconduct or poor performance, but decides to bring forward the proposed date of dismissal (*e.g.* by giving pay in lieu of notice) in order to avoid regulation 5 operating to transfer that liability to the purchaser. Since the connection with the business transfer must be the *principal* reason for the dismissal, it is unlikely that such a case will fall within the ambit of regulation 8(1). This is because, the business transfer merely affected the timing of a dismissal that had already been decided upon. Of course, the vendor will have to produce evidence to a tribunal to show that the dismissal would have occurred in any event. The words "connected with" are clearly wide in their scope and would appear to cover both direct and indirect linkage with a dismissal.

Timing of operation of the automatic unfairness rule

Regulation 8(1) makes it clear that its automatic unfairness rule can apply to dismissals either before or after the date of the business transfer. However, there is no stipulated "cut-off" time either side of it, before or after which an employer can safely say that regulation 8 does not apply to a particular dismissal. But any dismissals by the vendor which occur prior to the start of negotiations over a proposed business transfer are unlikely to be regarded as "connected with" it, unless it can be said that the vendor effected such dismissals (for redundancy) in order to make its business appear a more attractive proposition for a prospective buyer. In practice, such a motive will be difficult for an employee to establish.

The reason for dismissal

The key to the linkage between a dismissal and a business transfer is to examine the underlying factor activating the decision to dismiss. For example in *Meikle* v. *McPhail (Charleston Arms)* [1983] I.R.L.R. 351, dismissals by the purchaser four days after the business transfer of a pub were held to be connected with that transfer, even though the purchaser had originally intended to retain those employees. In that case, the purchaser soon realised that he was, after all, overstaffed and could not run the business economically without a reduction in staff headcount. Similarly, if the purchaser makes some of its existing staff redundant some time after the business transfer has taken place, in order to accommodate the vendor's employees acquired as a result of the business transfer, there will be a similar connection. Alternatively, if the vendor makes redundancies (*e.g.* from among support staff) from its business consequent upon a transfer of part of it to the purchaser, this too will be a sufficient connection with the business transfer.

There is therefore no magical time after which the connection with the business transfer can safely be regarded as broken. It is necessary to examine whether the "chain of causation" between the business transfer and the dismissal has been broken. Employers will be able to do this by pointing to a particular event (*e.g.* loss of orders) or a decision of the Board which breaks that link (but which is not itself connected with the transfer). Obviously the longer the passage of time between the dismissal and the business transfer, the weaker that link.

It is also important to note that the automatic unfairness rule will not apply unless the business transfer is the *principal* reason for the dismissal. After a time, although a dismissal might still have some linkage with a business transfer, the *principal* reason for it will no longer be connected with the business transfer. For example in *Richmond Precision Engineering Ltd.* v. *Pearce* [1984] unreported (E.A.T. 148/84), the purchaser sought to change an employee's terms and conditions of employment in the February following a business transfer which had occurred in the previous November. In a strangely reasoned decision the E.A.T. upheld a tribunal decision that regulation 8 did not apply.

Significance of regulation 8(1) for purchasers

The importance of the apparently open-ended effect of regulation 8(1) has considerable repercussions for purchasers who attempt to harmonise terms and conditions of employment between their existing employees and those they have acquired in connection with a business transfer. Both groups of employees can rely on the protection of regulation 8(1). But, as explained below, the scope of the "escape route" under regulation 8(2) is narrow and does not cover the harmonisation of terms and conditions of employment pursuant to a business transfer—see *Delabole Slate Ltd.* v. *Berriman* [1985] I.R.L.R. 305; C.A. (see p. 101 below). As a result, if an employee resigns his employment because his employer is trying to harmonise his terms and conditions with those of other employees (in breach of contract), his constructive dismissal will be automatically unfair under regulation 8(1) and not saved by the regulation 8(2) escape route.

The regulation 8(2) "escape route": economic, technical or organisational reasons entailing changes in the workforce

Regulation 8(2)

Regulation 8(2) seeks to mitigate the effect of regulation 8(1), which would otherwise be unduly harsh and restrictive on employers. It provides that:

> "Where an economic, technical or organisational reason entailing changes in the workforce of either the transferor or transferee before or after a relevant transfer is the . . . principal reason for dismissing an employee—
> (a) para. (1) above shall not apply to his dismissal; but
> (b) without prejudice to the application of section 57(3) of the 1978 Act . . . (test of fair dismissal), the dismissal shall for the purposes of section 57(1)(b) of that Act . . . (substantial reason for dismissal) be regarded as having been for a substantial reason of a kind such as to justify the dismissal of an employee holding the position which that employee held."

The references to the 1978 Act relate to the E.P.C.A. 1978; and the same rules apply to the Northern Ireland equivalent of the unfair dismissal provisions contained in the Northern Ireland (Industrial Relations) Order 1976.

Effect of regulation 8(2)

Regulation 8(2) only comes into play where a dismissal runs the risk of being automatically unfair because it falls within the scope of regulation 8(1). It does two things. First, it cancels the operation of the regulation 8(1) automatic unfairness rule, and so brings the case back into the mainstream rules on unfair dismissal. Secondly, it provides that the reason for the dismissal is within the category of "some other substantial reason justifying dismissal"—*i.e.* it is a potentially fair reason for dismissal.

Reasonableness of dismissal

It is important to note that avoidance of automatic unfairness under regulation 8(1), does not mean the dismissal is automatically fair. It will only be fair if the tribunal is satisfied that the decision to dismiss was reasonable in all the circumstances under section 57(3)—see *McGrath* v. *Rank Leisure Ltd.* [1985] I.C.R. 527. This question of reasonableness is dealt with below. But first, the employer, having been caught by the automatic unfairness rule under regulation 8(1), must satisfy the tribunal that it can escape its effects by means of regulation 8(2).

The burden on the employer

The onus on showing that regulation 8(2) applies, lies with the employer—see *May & Hassell (West) Ltd.* v. *Jansen* [1983] (unreported E.A.T. 525/83), and *Forth Estuary Engineering Ltd.* v. *Litster* [1986] I.R.L.R. 59. An employer will only fall within the scope of regulation 8(2) if it can show that the principal reason for the dismissal in question satisfied two linked conditions:

1. the reason was an economic, technical or organisational one; *and*
2. that reason entailed changes in the workforce.

Interpretation of "economic, technical, or organisational reasons"

"Economic, technical or organisational reasons." Initially,

different divisions of the E.A.T. (notably in Scotland) took divergent views on the scope of these words. However, it is now generally acknowledged (on both sides of the border) that an "economic, technical or organisational" reason must be to do with the running of the business by either the vendor or the purchaser—see *Wheeler* v. *Patel & Another* [1987] I.R.L.R. 211.

"Economic reasons"

This category of reasons carries with it a connotation embodying a commercial objective—*e.g.* to save or make money. For example in *Meikle* v. *McPhail (Charleston Arms)* [see p. 94 above] the purchaser established an economic reason for dismissal when it made some employees redundant shortly after the business transfer, after it realised that the pub could not be run economically with such a high staff headcount. The same principle applies where the vendor is required by the purchaser to dismiss an employee ahead of the transfer because the purchaser considers that the business could not be run economically with that extra member of staff—see *Shipp* v. *D.J. Catering Ltd.* [1983] (unreported C.O.I.T. 1348/49). Thus most genuine redundancies will probably qualify as an economic reason.

Therefore where a purchaser requires the vendor to make genuine redundancies prior to the moment of transfer (often as a condition of the acquisition agreement), these will normally be regarded as resulting from an economic reason—*Secretary of State for Employment* v. *Spence* [1986] I.R.L.R. 248. In the *Litster* case (see above) Lord Oliver commented that the reason for the dismissals in the *Spence* case was an economic one since:

> "the sequence of events by the receivers (the transferor) and the transferees and there was no collusion between them and, secondly, the reason why the receivers decided to dismiss the workforce was that, until a contract could be re-negotiated with the company's principal customer, there was no prospect of any work for the business."

He distinguished the facts in the *Litster* case [see above] on the grounds that there was collusion between the transferor and transferee and the dismissals were clearly connected with the business transfer. Lord Oliver's dicta in this respect was *obiter* and should be treated with caution. It should be recalled that, in the *Litster* case, both the industrial tribunal and the E.A.T. proceeded on the basis the reason for dismissal was an economic one within the scope of regulation 8(2) and decided the case on reasonableness. In particular there is little, if any, analysis by the tribunal or the E.A.T. whether the reason did properly fall within the scope of regulation 8(2). For this reason, Lord Oliver's comments are a little confusing. Whilst it is clear that, if the vendor and purchaser collude, in the absence of genuine redundancies, so that employees are dismissed to prevent the Transfer Regulations applying to their employment contracts, then the reason for dismissal will not be an economic one within the scope of regulation 8(2). But, it seems, that where a purchaser genuinely does not require a specified number of the vendor's employees since it is already overstaffed in certain departments, then this would clearly seem to be either an economic or organisational reason within the scope of regulation 8(2).

But the vendor's and purchaser's motive is important. If the reason why the purchaser requires those dismissals to be effected by the vendor has nothing to do with the running of the business, it will not be regarded as an economic reason for the purposes of regulation 8(2)—see *Wheeler* v. *Patel & Another* [see above]. In that case the purchaser required the vendor to dismiss all its employees before the moment of transfer (so that regulation 5 would not operate to transfer them into the purchaser's employment with their existing employment terms intact). The vendor complied with this requirement. After the business transfer had taken place, the purchaser then offered employment to selected employees on different terms and conditions of employment. Mrs Wheeler was one of those who was not offered a job by the purchaser. The E.A.T. found that regulation 8(1) applied because her dismissal was clearly connected with the business transfer, but that the vendor could not rely on regulation 8(2) to avoid the operation of the automatic unfairness rule. The E.A.T. said that an "economic" reason within regulation 8(2) should be construed "*eiusdem generis*" with the words technical and operational; and as such an economic reason must be concerned with the conduct or running of the business. In the *Wheeler* case [see above], the vendor's reason for dismissing Mrs Wheeler was to secure a sale of the business, because the purchaser would not have bought the business if it was forced to engage all the vendor's staff on their existing conditions of employment. The E.A.T. said that the vendor's desire to achieve a better price for the business was not an "economic" reason within the eiusdem generis approach to regulation 8(2).

The *Wheeler* case [see above] seems to be in accord with the comments of Slynn A.G. in the *Wendelboe* case [1985] 1 C.M.L.R. 476, when he said "Where employees are dismissed, with a view to, and before, a transfer . . . and are re-engaged immediately by the transferee thereafter, their dismissal must be regarded as contrary to Article 4(1) . . . " (which only permits dismissals in the context of a business transfer for an economic, technical or organisational reason). However in two earlier cases [*Anderson & McAlonie* v. *Dalkeith Engineering* [1985] I.C.R. 66, and *Litster* v. *Forth Estuary Engineering Ltd.* [1986] I.R.L.R. 59], the E.A.T. seem to have assumed that the purchaser's insistance on dismissals prior to the business transfer was an economic reason within the scope of regulation 8(2). It is now generally accepted that the E.A.T.'s narrow interpretation of the word "economic" adopted in the *Wheeler* [1987] I.R.L.R. 211, and *Gateway* [1988] I.R.L.R. 287, cases is correct. However, obiter dicta by Lord Dunpark in the Court of Session hearing of the *Litster* case suggests support for a wider interpretation. The effect of the *Wheeler* case [see above] is to overrule an earlier decision by the E.A.T. in Scotland in *Anderson & McAlonie* v. *Dalkeith Engineering Ltd.* [see above] when the E.A.T. had suggested that the mere fact of the purchaser's demand for redundancies was sufficient for the vendor's reason for dismissals to fall within regulation 8(2). The E.A.T. in Scotland have now confirmed that the *Wheeler* approach to regulation 8(2) is correct—see *Gateway Hotels Ltd.* v. *Stewart & Others* [see above].

Significance of the Wheeler case for purchasers

The *Wheeler* case [see above] has important practical repercussions for purchasers where the vendor has made some or all of its employees redundant prior to the date of transfer. It seems the purchaser's liability for a finding of automatic unfairness under regulation 8(1) will turn on *why* the vendor made the dismissals before the business transfer. The purchaser's motive can also be relevant. If the purchaser requires the employees to be dismissed because it already has staff fulfilling those functions, such a reason appears to be concerned with the conduct of the business. However, if the purchaser's reasons are to avoid the automatic transfer effect of regulation 5 (thus enabling the purchaser to offer employment to selected employees and on different terms of employment), then this is not, according to the *Wheeler* case [see above], an economic reason within regulation 8(2). In the light of the House of Lords' decision in the *Litster* case [see above], it seems that the risk falls wholly on the purchaser. This is because, if the reason for any pre-transfer dismissals are found to be connected with a business transfer but *not* for "an economic, technical or organisational reason entailing changes in the workforce", then, under the *Litster* rule, those employees are deemed to be treated as still employed by the vendor with the consequence that the purchaser inherits all liability for them. This seems to apply regardless of whether the purchaser requested or even knew of such dismissals. Therefore to protect itself, the purchaser should:

1. ask the vendor to explain, in writing, its reasons for dismissing any of its employees over the previous months;
2. require the vendor to give a warranty in the acquisition agreement to the effect that no such employees were dismissed in connection with the business transfer other persons whom the purchaser expressed required to be dismissed;
3. insist on an indemnity from the venndor to cover the unfair dismissal compensation and legal costs incurred in the event a tribunal subsequently finds that the vendor's reason for dismissal does not fall within regulation 8(2).

Similarly, if the reason for the vendor acquiescing to the purchaser's demands is to achieve a sale of his business or to obtain a higher price, that too will not constitute an economic reason concerned with the running of the business.

"Technical reasons"

There have been no cases on the scope of this category of reason for dismissal. However it would appear to cover situations where an employee is dismissed because he does not have the necessary technical know-how or experience to do his job which has changed because of technological reasons, such as the use of new equipment. It may also apply to situations where the purchaser intends to introduce some technological innovation which will impact on the employee's job.

"Organisational reasons"

To some extent this may overlap with the economic reasons category of dismissals. For example redundancies are often the result of both economic and organisational decisions made by an employer—see the *Meikle* case [1983] I.R.L.R. 351. It seems that organisational reasons might also apply where, after the business transfer has taken place, the purchaser starts to merge its newly acquired staff into the same operational unit as its existing staff. This might involve changes to working practices, changes to hours of work or even relocation to different premises. If such changes are in breach of the employment contracts of the staff concerned, they can claim they have been constructively dismissed. But the purchaser will be able to argue about its fairness since such changes are operational ones. The same principle applies where a vendor has to reorganise its remaining workforce to consolidate its business operations, after the sale of a part of its business to the purchaser.

"Entailing changes in the workforce" condition

It is this part of the regulation 8(2) escape route which has the effect of narrowing its application. Not only must the reason for the employee's dismissal be an economic, technical or organisational one, but that *reason* must also entail changes in the relevant employer's workforce.

Meaning of "entail"

This question is important because, on it, hinges the scope of the regulation 8(2) escape route. There appear to be two alternative meanings, as follows:

1. that the changes in the workforce must be necessary; or
2. that the changes in the workforce are a necessary consequence of the economic, technical or organisational reason.

Case law on interpretation of "entail"

From what little judicial comment that there has been on this question, it appears that some form of "necessity" test is preferred. In *Delabole Slate Ltd* v. *Berriman* [1985] I.R.L.R. 305 the Court of Appeal said that the phrase meant that:

> "the change in the workforce is part of the economic, technical or organisational reason. The employer's plan must be to achieve changes in the workforce. It must be an objective of the plan, not just a possible consequence of it."

For example in *May & Hassell (West) Ltd.* v. *Jansen* [1983] unreported (E.A.T. 525/83), the employer sought to move Mr Jansen from his existing job to another very similar one but with 30 per cent. lower wages. The E.A.T. upheld his constructive unfair dismissal claim, and agreed with Mr Jansen's argument that his job, in reality, still remained to be done and therefore the proposed changes in his contract were not necessary in the context of the reorganisation programme. However the E.A.T.'s reasoning is rather sparse on this point and could be construed as meaning that the change in Mr Jansen's contract was not a *necessary consequence* of the business reorganisation. The wording of regulation 8(2) indicates that the word "entails" is being used in in the sense of changes to the workforce being the planned consequence of the economic, technical or organisational reason. This approach was taken by an industrial tribunal in *Batchelor* v. *Premier Motors* [1982] (unreported C.O.I.T. 1359/181) which commented that the word "entailing" meant "a necessary sequence of events." It seems likely that the tribunals will adopt a test similar to that used in ordinary business reorganisation cases—*i.e.* that the employer must demonstrate a sound commercial or business reason concerned with the running of its business and that the dismissal was a necessary consequence of that reason. In this respect there is a range of reasonable responses, and tribunals must not substitute their business judgement for that of the employer concerned. However, to fall within the ambit of regulation 8(2) employers will also have to demonstrate that the changes in its workforce were a reasonably necessary consequence of the relevant business decision.

What constitutes a change in the workforce?

In *Delabole Slate Ltd.* v. *Berriman* [1985] I.R.L.R. 305, the Court of Appeal held that "changes to the workforce" meant changes in the overall numbers or functions of the workforce. They said, "the word 'workforce' connotes the whole body of employees as an entity; it corresponds to the 'strength' or the 'establishment'." The case concerned an attempt by the purchaser of a business to impose changes in an employee's conditions of employment which were to his detriment. The employee refused those changes and claimed constructive (unfair) dismissal. The Court of Appeal held that regulation 8(2) did not apply since the change or harmonisation of terms and conditions did not "entail changes in the workforce." The purchaser's economic reasons for the variation in the employee's conditions of employment did not involve a reduction in the number or functions of employees, but rather it entailed changes in working conditions. The Court also firmly rejected the purchaser's ingenious argument that it had no place for anyone who would not work under its standard conditions of employment, and therefore when the employee left there would be a reduction in the workforce followed by a change of identity of the person undertaking the employee's job!

It is clear that changes in the workforce will cover redundancies, reorganisation of work and restructuring of business operations. However it will not include redundancies effected so that the purchaser can offer the employees re-employment on different terms and conditions—see *Bullard & Wilton* v. *Marchant & Patel* [1986] I.C.R. 389, E.A.T. To date the cases have not dealt with whether a change in shift times, or a relocation of workplace "entails changes in the workforce" for the purposes of regulation 8(2). It will be recalled that in the *Delabole Slate* case [see above], the Court of Appeal expressly referred to the changes to numbers and functions of employees. However, it is suggested that this was not intended to be an exhaustive list of circumstances which could be said to "entail changes in the workforce" and that changes to shift patterns or workplaces is as much a change to the body of employees or the establishment of employees, as is a redundancy. Both can affect either certain departments of the workforce or the whole of it. Neither regulation 8(2) nor the Court of Appeal's dicta in the *Delabole Slate* case [see above] require that the changes in question must affect all the workforce in question.

Harmonisation of conditions of employment

The effect of the *Delabole Slate* case [see above] is that it will be an automatically unfair dismissal for an employer to seek to harmonise terms and conditions of employees, for as long as such changes are connected with the business transfer. This illustrates the important impact of regulation 8, since such dismissals are normally fair if the employee is acting unreasonably in holding out against the harmonisation programe—see *Richmond Precision Engineering* v. *Pearce* [1984] unreported (E.A.T. 148/89).

Statutory redundancy pay and unfair dismissal

It will have become apparent from the above, that where an employee is, as a result of a relevant transfer, made redundant, regulation 8(2) treats the reason for his dismissal as an economic, technical, or organisational one entailing changes in the workforce. This does not, however, mean that the employee so dismissed cannot claim his statutory redundancy pay entitlement—see *Gorictree Ltd.* v. *Jenkinson* [1984] I.R.L.R. 391 (which is now regarded as overturning a contrary decision in *Canning* v. *Niaz* [1983] I.R.L.R. 431).

Reasonableness

Once an employer has shown that its dismissal is saved from automatic unfairness by regulation 8(2), the tribunal will nonetheless find the dismissal unfair unless it is satisfied that the employer's decision to dismiss was reasonable in all the circumstances—E.P.C.A., s.57(3). In this respect tribunals apply a "range of reasonable responses" test—see *British Leyland* v. *Swift* [1981] I.R.L.R. 91; C.A. This test involves an appreciation that there are often a range of things an employer can do when running its business. Some employers may dismiss the employee concerned, others might prefer an alternative course of action (*e.g.* job transfer or the selection of someone else for redundancy). Both courses of action might be reasonable. Consequently a dismissal will only be unfair if the decision to dismiss falls outside that range of options which a reasonable employer might take in the circumstances.

"Reasonableness" test

Procedural unfairness

It is important to note that redundancy or business reorganisation dismissals can be unfair both in substance and procedurally. In other words an otherwise fair decision to dismiss for redundancy or arising out of a business reorganisation can be rendered unfair because of the way it is handled—see *Polkey* v. *A.E. Dayton Services Ltd.* [1987] I.R.L.R. 503; H.L. A summary of unfair dismissal law in these respects is contained in Appendix A on page 171. These principles apply whether the redundancies are effected by the vendor or the purchaser.

Vendor's liability where purchaser stipulates redundancies

In many transactions the purchaser tells the vendor that it does not need all or some of the latter's employees and so the vendor is left with no choice but to make them redundant before the transfer is completed. In such cases it is often the purchaser who "calls the tune" in so far as the numbers of employees to be made redundant, their selection and the timing of such redundant (often with little advance warning or with insufficient time for consultations). The purchaser will not be liable to the employees if their redundancies are unfair (unless their dismissals took effect on or after the moment of transfer).

This puts the vendor in something of an invidious position, because the effect of the purchaser's demands in relation to the redundancies may be to make the dismissals effected by the vendor unfair—*e.g.* through unfair selection, lack of advance warning or consultation. For this reason the vendor might ask the purchaser for an indemnity to cover any unfair dismissal compensation, or an adjustment of the purchase price. An indemnity from the purchaser in relation to unfair dismissal compensation does not affect the vendor's liability to an employee claiming unfair dismissal—it simply allows the vendor to claim reimbursement from the purchaser in respect of any compensation it has to pay to that employee [see Appendix A p. 177].

Justifying dismissal by reference to purchaser's demands

Even if redundancies made by the vendor at the purchaser's request are genuine and therefore constitute an "economic, technical or organisational reason entailing changes in the workforce" under regulation 8(2) [see p. 95 above], tribunals appear undecided as to the extent to which a vendor can successfully argue that the purchaser's (unreasonable) demands justified the vendor acting as it did in relation to those dismissals complained of. In its most extreme form, the vendor's argument would be along the lines that if it did not comply with the purchaser's demands, the business transfer would not have taken place at all. This is sometimes known as the "purchaser's demand" defence. It is important to remember the distinction between the **reason** for dismissal (*e.g.* redundancy) and the reasonableness with which it is put into effect. It will be recalled that, in respect of the **reason** for dismissal, employers cannot argue that they had to comply or the sale would never have taken place [see the *Wheeler* v. *Patel* case [1987] I.R.L.R. 211; E.A.T.—p. 99]. However the "purchaser's demand" defence only comes into play once the tribunal comes to consider reasonableness—*i.e.* regulation 8(2) has been satisfied as to the reason for dismissal by the vendor establishing that the redundancies were genuine.

In *Anderson & McAlonie* v. *Dalkeith Engineering Ltd.* [1985] I.C.R. 66, the E.A.T. said that it was not easy to envisage circumstances where a demand for redundancies by a purchaser could make it unreasonable (within the scope of E.P.C.A., s.57(3)) for a liquidator of an otherwise insolvent company not to comply. In that case there was a clear requirement by the purchaser that the redundancies had to be effected or else the purchase would not be proceeded with. The case rested on two important facts.

First, the purchaser made it a condition of the purchase that the dismissals had to be effected before the transfer took place. It is unlikely that tribunals will be prepared even to consider a "purchaser's demand" defence unless there is clear evidence of:

1. what the purchaser has demanded,
2. the purchaser not being willing to proceed with the transaction unless its demands are met,
3. it was the vendor's compliance with the purchaser's demands which made the dismissals unfair, and
4. there was no other way by which the vendor could have met the purchaser's demands and still acted fairly.

The second key factor in the *Anderson* case [see above] was that the vendor was a liquidator—*i.e.* the employees would have been dismissed in any event if a purchaser could not be found. In addition, by complying with the purchaser's demands, the liquidator increased the assets of the business to be distributed among its creditors and enhanced the possibility that the purchaser might offer employment to at least some of the workforce. Indeed, the E.A.T. put some emphasis on the liquidator's duty to preserve and maximise the assets for the benefit of the creditors. It is a moot point whether a vendor can rely on the "purchaser's demand" defence where it has a real choice whether or not to sell the business or the relevant part. It is submitted that if the vendor does have a real choice, the "purchaser's demand" defence will not be available to it. Liability to pay unfair dismissal compensation is no doubt something which the vendor will take into account in deciding whether it has sold its business at a good price.

In contrast with the *Anderson* case [see above], the E.A.T. took a different view in *Forth Estuary Engineering Co. Ltd.* v. *Litster* [1986] I.R.L.R. 59, where the facts were very similar. In that case the E.A.T. held it was unfair for a vendor to have dismissed its entire workforce at the purchaser's insistence, because such dismissals had not been made a condition of the purchase. However, on appeal to the Court of Session, Lord Dunpark commented (*obiter*) that, although there was no express stipulation in the business transfer agreement requiring the dismissal of all the vendor's employees, there was nonetheless clear evidence that the purchaser would not have proceeded with the transaction unless this had been done. Lord Dunpark said it was not necessary that the purchaser's demands be included in the contract and he went on to conclude that the dismissals were fair. Since Lord Dunpark's comments were obiter, they do not override the E.A.T.'s ruling on that aspect of the case; however his remarks obviously carry some weight.

It is submitted that the E.A.T. in the *Litster* case [see above] went too far by insisting that the vendor can only rely on the "purchaser's demands" defence if there is an express requirement stipulated in the business transfer contract. It is a question of evidence, and an express stipulation in the contract is the best evidence on the point. But it should not exclude other evidence to the same effect, such as an oral or written request. The problem with not including such a stipulation in the business transfer contract is that the purchaser must make it clear that the transaction will not proceed unless its demands are met. Such an approach may have to be adopted in cases where contracts are exchanged and completion takes place on the same day (as is often the case in purchases from liquidators); and so it is a nonsense to make it a pre-condition on the contract that redundancies are effected in advance of the transfer.

Situations where purchaser's demands might justify dismissal

It should be noted, however, that neither the *Anderson* or *Litster* cases [see above] dealt with the question of procedural unfairness or redundancy selection. They both concerned the dismissal of the entire workforce of the vendor. It is suggested that a vendor will find it very difficult to rely on the "purchaser's demand" defence unless it can show that:

1. the selections for redundancy made by the purchaser were, in effect, conditions of the sale;
2. the vendor tried to persuade the purchaser to alter its redundancy selections which were unfair, but had been successful;
3. the vendor had exhausted all other reasonable alternatives to making those persons redundant;
4. any procedural failing (*e.g.* lack of advance warning or consultation) was an inevitable consequence of the secrecy which the purchaser had imposed as a condition of the

negotiations for the purchase continuing and the vendor has given as much advance warning and consultation as it reasonably could in the circumstances;

5. the vendor's need to sell the business (or part) outweighed its obligations to comply with the normal guidelines for fair redundancy dismissals [see Appendix A p. 171];
6. the vendor has offered any suitable vacancies elsewhere in its organisation, to those employees who would otherwise be redundant.

Both the *Anderson* and *Litster* cases [see above] proceeded on the basis that the pre-transfer dismissals had met the requirements of regulation 8(2); but the correctness of that assumption has been strongly doubted by the E.A.T. in the *Wheeler* case [1987] I.R.L.R. 211 [see p. 99]. However, there seems no reason why the purchaser's demands in respect of the redundancy selection should not be a relevant factor on the question of fairness. This assumes that the redundancies called for by the purchaser are genuine and meet the requirements of regulation 8(2) [see p. 96].

Redundancy selections by the purchaser

Where a purchaser is willing to take on only part of the vendor's employees, it is almost inevitable that it will be involved in the redundancy selections to be made by the vendor. It is possible that the purchaser's nomination of those employees it wishes to take on may result in unfair redundancy selection of some of the vendor's employees not chosen. This may arise from the vendor not complying with its agreed procedures or customary arrangements for redundancy selections and so such dismissals will be automatically unfair under E.P.C.A., s.59 [see Appendix A p. 171], or from the choice of arbitrary selection criteria by the purchaser. It seems likely that vendor may be able to rely on the purchaser's selections as a justification for contravening its own agreed or customary redundancy selection ·teria under E.P.C.A., s.59(b). For example, by way of analogy, in *GEC Energy Systems Ltd.* v. *Grufferty* [1988] unreported (E.A.T. 590/87) where the E.A.T. upheld a tribunal's decision that an employer could contravene his established redundancy selection criteria/agreement where this was demanded by a customer as part of a new contract between the two employers.

There has been very little tribunal caselaw on this point. However in *Bannister & Others* v. *Brasway plc* [1983] unreported (C.O.I.T. 1377/49), a tribunal indicated that there might be circumstances where the "purchaser's demands" defence might apply. However the tribunal indicated that, in such cases, the vendor must have played no part in the selections and the purchaser's selections must have been made a condition of the sale. The tribunal went on to comment that a vendor should nonetheless be prepared to be held responsible for its own dismissals and that it would be judged by the part in played in those dismissals. In one of the cases before that tribunal, the vendor in the *Bannister* case [see above] had provided inaccurate information to the purchaser in relation to some of the latter's choice of employees to be retained.

"Pool" of employees for redundancy selections

Caselaw has not yet decided whether redundancy dismissals by a vendor are unfair if the "pool" for selecting redundancies is limited to the vendor's employees. For example, a purchaser may already have its own printing department of 12 staff, but the business it is to acquire from the vendor also contains a large printing department of 30 printers. The purchaser therefore decides that its needs for printers after the acquisition is 20. It selects the 8 printers from the vendor's department of 30 and requires the vendor to make the remaining 22 printers redundant prior to the moment of transfer, so that they will not transfer over by virtue of regulation 5(1). The purchaser does not take into account any of its existing 12 printers in the "pool" from which the redundancies are to be made. Is it unfair for the redundancy selections to be restricted to the vendor's employees? There has been no reported case to date on this point; but it is submitted that, in such a situation, the choice of "pool" for redundancy selections is likely to be a matter which falls within the range of reasonable responses—*i.e.* the purchaser can reasonably exclude its existing employees from the "pool" for selection.

However where the purchaser puts the redundancies into effect after the transfer has taken place, it is unlikely that it will be regarded as acting reasonably if it limits the redundancies to its newly acquired employees (especially where the two departments have been merged).

Offers of alternative employment by purchaser

Vendors are also strongly advised to request a purchaser to offer any suitable available vacancies elsewhere in the purchaser's organisation, to those of the vendor's employees to be made redundant as a result of the business transfer. If the vendor makes reasonable attempts to persuade the purchaser to offer such vacancies to its otherwise redundant employees, but the purchaser refuses to do so, it is unlikely that the vendor will be criticised by an industrial tribunal for failing to make reasonable efforts to re-deploy staff.

The effect on a dismissal if it is automatically unfair under regulation 8(1)

There has been some confusion over the status of a dismissal which is connected with a business transfer, but is automatically unfair under regulation 8(1), because the employer has not satisfied a tribunal that it was for "an economic, technical or organisational reason entailing changes in the workforce." The confusion has arisen over certain dicta contained in the E.C.J.'s judgment in *P. Bork International AS* v. *Foreningen AF Arbejdsledere I Danmark* [1989] I.R.L.R. 41:

> "It follows that workers employed by the undertaking whose contract of employment or employment relationship has been terminated with effect on a date before that of the transfer, in breach of Article 4(1) of the Directive, must be considered *as still employed* (author's emphasis) by the undertaking on the date of the transfer with the consequence, in particular, that the obligations of an employer towards them are fully transferred from the transferor to the transferee, in accordance with Article 3(1) of the Directive."

Similar comments were also made by the House of Lords in

Litster v. *Forth Estuary Engineering Ltd.* [1989] (H.L. 16.3.89). Lord Keith said:

> "So there must be implied in regulation 5(3) words indicating that where a person has been unfairly dismissed in the circumstances described in regulation 8(1), *he is deemed to have been employed in the undertaking immediately before the transfer* . . ." (author's emphasis).

Lord Oliver (who gave the main speech in the Lords, which was endorsed by the other four Law Lords) said:

> ". . . a dismissal effected before the transfer and solely because of the transfer of the business is, in effect, prohibited and is *for the purpose of considering the application of article 3(1), required to be treated as ineffective* . . ." (author's emphasis).

> "It follows from the construction that I attach to regulation 5(3) that where an employee is dismissed before and by reason of the transfer, *the employment is statutorily continued with the transferee* . . ." (author's emphasis).

At first sight it might be thought that these cases suggest that such a pre-transfer dismissal is nullified—*i.e.* treated as never having occurred. However it is submitted that this is not a correct interpretation of the above dicta. All that they are saying (especially the House of Lords in the *Litster* case) is that any dismissal which breaches article 4(1) of the Directive (*i.e.* one which is automatically unfair under regulation 8(1) of the Transfer Regulations), is *deemed* to be statutorily continued for the purpose of ascertaining who is responsible for the vendor's liabilities to the employee so dismissed. Whilst both interpretations are respectable, it is submitted that the latter one is correct for the following reasons.

1. The dicta by the E.C.J. in the *P. Bork International* case should be understood in the context of the European composition of the E.C.J. In some EEC countries, labour law contains the concept of a "nullified dismissal" for either all unlawful dismissal or certain classes of dismissal—*e.g.* Netherlands, W. Germany, Italy etc. There is no such concept of a nullified dismissal known to English law. The difference in remedies under the labour laws of Member States was recognised by Sir Gordon Slynn A-G in the *Wendelboe* case [1985] E.C.R. 457 when he said:

> "where employees are dismissed, with a view to and before, a transfer falling within the Directive and are re-engaged immediately by the transferee thereafter, their dismissal must be regarded as contrary to article 4(1), subject to the exceptions specified in that paragraph. Whether the remedy for such an unlawful dismissal consists in a court order declaring that dismissal to be a nullity or the award of damages or some other effective remedy, is for the Member States to determine."

2. In *Von Colson & Kamann* v. *Land Norhrhein-Westfalen* [1984] E.C.R. 1891, the E.C.J. made it clear that it was up

to Member States to adopt whatever remedy considered appropriate to infringements of their national laws, which implement EEC Directives. The only proviso was that these remedies must be effective. Whilst some other EEC countries have adopted the concept of a nullified dismissal, the United Kingdom has adopted compensation as the remedy for dismissals in breach of regulation 8(1). It is another question whether the United Kingdom's remedy is effective [see below], but in none of the dicta was that even referred to. So, neither case is authority for the proposition that compensation for an automatically unfair dismissal is an inadequate remedy.

3. Article 4(1) does not state that employees cannot be dismissed for a reason connected with a business transfer. It merely states that such a dismissal will not constitute lawful grounds, unless it is "for an economic, technical or organisational reason entailing changes in the workforce."
4. In the *Litster* case, the Lords were considering the narrow point of whether the employees were, or should be treated, as still employed by the vendor up to the moment of transfer—with the consequence that the purchaser would take over the vendor's liabilities in respect of them. If the Lords had intended to overturn the common law, one would have expected them to have said so more explicitly—especially as the ramifications of the introduction of the concept of a nullified dismissal are so wide-ranging for English employment law. Instead Lord Keith referred to the employee being *"deemed" to have been employed* up to the moment of transfer and Lord Oliver talks of *the employment being "statutorily continued"*. When looked at in the context of the issue in the case and the words which the House of Lords implied into regulation 5(3) (see p. 107), it is clear that they were referring to the employment being artificially extended so that the employee is treated as falling within the scope of regulation 5(3)—*i.e.* he is treated as being employed in the business up to immediately before the transfer.
5. The words which the Lords implied into regulation 5(3) also indicate a statutory deeming of employment for limited purposes. Indeed both Lords Keith and Oliver refer to the employee as having been unfairly dismissed. Lord Oliver's implied additional wording makes regulation 5(3) read as follows: ". . . employed immediately before the transfer or *would have been so employed if he had not been unfairly dismissed in the circumstances described by regulation 8(1).*" If Lord Oliver had intended there to have been a nullified dismissal, why would he refer to the employee as having been unfairly dismissed?
6. Both the E.C.J. and the House of Lords referred to the deemed continuation of employment, *for the purposes of article 3(1) or regulation 5*. Both of these provisions contain the automatic transfer principle. In particular article 3(1) states that "the transferor's rights and obligations arising from a contract of employment or from an employment relationship existing on the date of a transfer . . . shall . . . be transferred to the transferee." It is concerned with

rights and liabilities of the vendor as at the date of transfer. It does not require the transfer of employees to the purchaser if they are no longer in the vendor's employ on the transfer date—protection against dismissal is provided by article 4(1) and is governed by effective remedies in Member States. In the *P. Bork case* [see above], the E.C.J. said the employment was continued "with the consequence . . . that the obligations of an employer towards them are fully transferred from the transferor to the transferee *in accordance with Article 3(1) of the Directive.*" In the *Litster* case, Lord Oliver said such an unlawful dismissal ". . . is in effect prohibited and is, *for the purpose of considering the application of article 3(1),* required to be treated as ineffective." In other words, in both cases the deemed continuation of the employment is preserved only for the purpose of transferring liability to the transferee.

7. At the end of the *Litster* case, an application was made for the case to be remitted back to the tribunal to consider the reason and reasonableness of the dismissal. This was refused on the grounds that those issues had already been addressed and decisions made on them. If Lord Oliver had intended to mean that the dismissal was nullified for all purposes, surely he would have given, as his reason for refusing that application, that the issue was irrelevant since their dismissal is treated as never having occurred.
8. In both cases, the dicta refers to the deemed employment applying in respect of pre-transfer dismissals which contravene article 4(1) or regulation 8(1). Yet those provisions also apply to dismissals connected with the business transfer which occur after it has taken place (unless for an economic, technical or organisational reason etc.). This is more consistent with the dicta relating to the transfer of liabilities to the transferee—which was the issue with which both cases were concerned—and not a nullification of the dismissal for all purposes.

Are the two interpretations any different? In short, the answer is "yes." The differences include the following:

1. In the case of a nullified dismissal, the employee is treated as never having been dismissed by the vendor for *all* purposes. As a consequence, the purchaser is responsible for all back-pay and value of benefits due from the date of the purported dismissal to the present date, and the employee would not be entitled to redundancy pay, damages for wrongful dismissal or compensation for unfair dismissal. This state of affairs would continue until the employee was dismissed for a reason which took the case outside regulation 8(1). In contrast, in the case of a transfer of liability, the employee is treated as having been dismissed by the purchaser who is responsible for all liabilities (except for pensions) due to the dismissed employee. These liabilities might include back-pay or accrued holiday pay up to the actual termination date, redundancy pay, damages for wrongful dismissal (or pay in lieu of notice) and compensation for unfair dismissal. In practice, where a dismissed employee asks for re-

instatement as his primary remedy, industrial tribunals are more likely than not to grant it. This is because, to give effect to Directive, tribunals should, wherever possible, be prepared to grant the primary remedy for unfair dismissal. In practice, this means that the re-instatement order will require the purchaser to re-instate the dismissed employee on his existing terms and conditions of employment (as if he had not been dismissed), *and* to pay the employee a sum representing his losses (*e.g.* for salary and employment benefits) from the date of dismissal to the date when the re-instatement order must be complied with. Thus, so far, the purchaser's liability is the same under, both interpretations. The important difference comes where the purchaser declines to comply with that order and is willing to pay the additional award (which has a current maximum in these circumstances of £4,472). Due to the current maxima on the unfair dismissal basic award of £172 for a week's pay and £8,925 for the compensatory award, it may be that the purchaser considers it cheaper to pay unfair dismissal compensation of up to an absolute maximum of £18,557, rather than comply with the re-instatement order (which will inevitably include an award of compensation).

2. If a dismissal in breach of regulation 8(1) is nullified, whether it occurs before or after the business transfer, then the purchaser can never effect a dismissal of the employee whilst the causal connection with the business transfer is in existence, unless the purchaser has found an "economic, technical or organisational reason entailing changes in the workforce" enabling him to do so. This means that whenever the purchaser attempted a dismissal in breach of article 4(1) or regulation 8(1), the employee could go to the High Court for a declaration that the dismissal was continuing after the business transfer. Such an option would not be available to employees where only liability is transferred to the purchaser.
3. The precise "effective date of termination" would be different in both cases. This might have an impact on whether the employee in question has sufficient service to claim unfair dismissal or whether the three month time limit for presenting unfair dismissal applications has expired.

Does United Kingdom law provide an adequate remedy? As stated above, the absolute maximum unfair dismissal compensation is £18,557. Even so, this assumes that the employee in question is aged 60 or more, has 20 years' continuous employment, and his losses match or exceed the £8,925 maximum compensatory award. In most cases, the maximum compensation is much less and more likely to be in the region of about £14,000 to £15,000. In addition, the employee may have a claim for damages for wrongful dismissal if due notice of termination (or pay in lieu of notice) was not given to him. However, it should be noted that an employee who has been both wrongfully and unfairly dismissed cannot claim twice over damages or compensation in respect of the same loss (*e.g.* lost wages for the same period of time).

In the case of highly paid executives (who are often the casualties in business transfers), it may be arguable that the limits placed by the E.P.C.A. 1978 do not provide an adquate or effective remedy since the compensatory award will act as a low ceiling limiting the recovery of their actual losses. This may be especially the case where the executive is aged 50 or more and will face difficulties in finding comparable employment. However, it must be doubted whether the E.C.J. would consider the current limits placed on recoverable damages by English law could properly be regarded as so ineffective (as in the *Von Colson* case [see above] that the industrial tribunals would not regard themselves as bound by them. The only case which has begun to approach this issue is *Marshall* v. *S.W. Hants Health Authority (No. 2)* [1988] I.R.L.R. 325 where the industrial tribunal considered themselves not bound by the, then, maximum of £6,250 for sex discrimination claims and awarded Mrs Marshall just over £19,000. However the *Marshall* case should be distinguished by one important consideration—the tribunals was considering the *direct application* of the Equal Pay Directive, not the application of domestic legislation which sought to implement it. The tribunal were able to do so because Mrs Marshall's employer, the Health Authority, was an organ of the State and was therefore capable of being sued directly under the Directive. In such circumstances, the tribunal were entitled to say that, since the claim was brought directly under the Directive, not the Sex Discrimination Act 1975, they were not bound by the latter Act's limitations. In contrast, it is very unlikely that claims will be able to be brought in the United Kingdom directly under the Business Transfer Directive, since in the vast majority of cases the purchaser will be in the private sector and therefore cannot be sued directly under that Directive.

7 EFFECT OF TRANSFER REGULATIONS ON COLLECTIVE AGREEMENTS AND COLLECTIVE BARGAINING ARRANGEMENTS

Background: the position under the Business Transfer Directive

Article 5 of the Business Transfer Directive requires EEC Member states to preserve the status of "employee representation" (*e.g.* union representation) in a business transferred. Regulations 6 and 9 of the Transfer Regulations seek to give effect to article 5 by providing, in effect, for the continuation by the purchaser of collective agreements and collective bargaining arrangements which trade unions enjoyed with the vendor in respect of the business (or part) transferred.

Collective agreements

Regulation 6

Regulation 6 deals with the preservation of collective agreements. It provides as follows:

> "Where at the time of a relevant transfer there exists a collective agreement made by or on behalf of the transferor with a trade union recognised by the transferor in respect of any employee whose employment is preserved by reg. 5(1), . . . then,
>
> (a) without prejudice to s.18 of the 1974 Act [*i.e.* T.U.L.R.A. 1974] or Art. 63 of the 1976 Order [*i.e.* the Industrial Relations (N. Ireland) Order 1976] (collective agreements presumed to be unenforceable in specified circumstances) that agreement, in its application in relation to the employee, shall after the transfer, have effect as if made by or on behalf of the transferee, and accordingly anything done under or in connection with, in its application as aforesaid, by or in relation to the transferor before the transfer, shall, after the transfer, be deemed to have been done by or in relation to the transferee; and
>
> (b) any order made in respect of that agreement, in its application in relation to the employee, shall, after the transfer, have effect as if the transferee were a party to the agreement."

Interpretation of regulation 6

The above text is really a long-winded way of saying that the purchaser steps into the shoes of the vendor in so far as collective agreements relating to the transferring employees are concerned. Section 18 of the T.U.L.R.A. (and its Northern Ireland equivalent in the 1976 Order) provides that collective agreements between employers and trade unions are unenforceable as between those two parties, unless there is a statement in writing in the body of the collective agreement stating that the parties wish it to be legally binding between them. In practice, very few collective agreements in the United Kingdom are legally binding as between employer and union. However, much of the contents of collective agreements also form part of employees' contracts of employment by way of incorporation. For example the employees' written statement of terms and conditions of employment may expressly cross-refer to, and incorporate, the terms of a collective agreement between either their employer and a trade union, or an employer's association and trade unions (*e.g.* the EEF/CSEU National Agreement). Rates of pay, overtime and shift premia, working hours, flexible working practices and other employment benefits are usually covered by a collective agreement.

Incorporation of collective agreements into employee's contracts of employment

In so far as parts of a collective agreement are incorporated into employees' contracts of employment, regulation 6 is superfluous because those terms are transferred with the employees to the purchaser under regulation 5. However not all parts of collective agreements are so incorporated, but only those which relate to individual's pay, benefits and conditions and how he performs his duties. The courts are reluctant to incorporate those parts of collective agreements which are concerned with the trade union's organisation and activities. For example, in *British Leyland U.K. Ltd* v. *McQuilken* [1978] I.R.L.R. 245, the E.A.T. held that a reorganisation policy contained in a collective agreement was not incorporated into individual employment contracts; and in *NCB* v. *NUM and Others* [1986] I.R.L.R. 439 the court held that a disputes conciliation procedure was not so incorporated. In practice the following parts of collective agreements will not normally be regarded as capable of being incorporated into individual employment contracts: disputes procedures, recognition/bargaining rights, facilities for shop stewards, provision of information, certain aspects of flexible working agreements, redundancy selection procedures, "understandings" with trade unions regarding business reorganisation. It is these at which regulation 6 is directed, with the effect that they are transferred to the purchaser at the moment of transfer, along with the rest of the business.

What is a collective agreement?: T.U.L.R.A. 1974, s.30

A collective agreement is defined by T.U.L.R.A. 1974, s.30 as follows:

> "any agreement or arrangement made by or on behalf of one or more trade unions and one or more employers or employers associations, and relating to one or more of the matters mentioned in section 29(1). . . . "

Section 29 lists a wide range of matters including terms and conditions of employment, engagement/non-engagement of workers, suspension of workers, allocation of work between workers, disciplinary matters, union membership/non-membership, trade union facilities, negotiating/consultative procedures, etc. It should be noted that the definition in section 30 includes "arrangements," which appears wide enough to embrace unwritten "understandings" between the employer and trade unions.

Significance of regulation 6

At first sight regulation 6 seems a bit irrelevant since those parts of collective agreements, which are not incorporated into individual employment contracts, are not legally enforceable in any event. However, regulation 6 does have a material impact in respect of those aspects of statutory employment protection legislation which expressly or impliedly take account of the contents of collective agreements. This can arise in the following areas.

Transfer of redundancy selection criteria

Under section 59(b) of the E.P.C.A. a redundancy dismissal is automatically unfair if the complainant has been selected in contravention of an agreed procedure or customary arrangement. An employer can only succeed in defending such a selection if it can show "special reasons justifying a departure from" the agreement or procedure. In many highly-unionised workplaces, employers have negotiated redundancy selection criteria with trade unions, and these will transfer across to the purchaser under regulation 6.

Where such a redundancy selection procedure does transfer across under regulation 6, the purchaser can sometimes face a problem if these criteria are different to those it has agreed with trade unions recognised for its existing employees. This is exacerbated where the two workforces are merged, since the purchaser cannot but be in breach of one of the collective agreements (thus rendering some dismissals automatically unfair). In such circumstances, the purchaser should try to negotiate a new redundancy selection procedure covering both groups. If agreement cannot be reached, the purchaser may terminate both collective agreements and start afresh. However this action should be taken before the process of making the redundancy selections starts.

Time off for union duties, training and activities

Under section 27 E.P.C.A., officials of recognised unions are entitled to paid time off to carry out their industrial relations duties or to undergo training in respect of them. Under section 28 E.P.C.A. ordinary members of recognised unions are entitled to take unpaid time off during working hours to participate in union activities (*e.g.* a mass meeting to discuss the employer's offer to increase wages). However both rights are subject to the test of reasonableness. The ACAS Code of Practice on Time Off puts particular emphasis on agreed procedures for time off; and thus compliance with those procedures by employers and unions is a major factor tribunals take into account when deciding whether an employer has unreasonably refused time off in the circumstances. Therefore a purchaser needs to be aware of what the vendor's agreed procedures were for time-off for union officials and union members.

Dismissals or victimisation of union members

Under section 58(1)(b) and section 23(1)(b) E.P.C.A. union members are only protected from dismissal or action short of dismissal on account of their participation in union activities, if those activities took place "at an appropriate time." Sections 58(2) and 23(2) E.P.C.A. define "an appropriate time" as either outside working hours, or during working hours but at times in accordance with agreed procedures or with the employer's consent. Thus, again, collective agreements are important in defining the protection given to union members participating in their union's activities. Since the definition of "collective agreement" includes arrangements between the employer and a union, it appears to embrace unwritten "understandings" relating to the times when union members can carry out their union activities during working hours. These understandings can be implied through a course of conduct, or custom and practice, over the years. Again, the purchaser needs to know details about these.

Enhanced redundancy pay agreements

Some trade unions, whilst steadfastly refusing (for "policy" reasons) to sign any agreement with an employer regarding redundancy, nonetheless have understandings with employers that, in the event of redundancies, the employer will make enhanced redundancy payments in excess of its statutory obligations. These understandings will also transfer across under regulation 6 but will not have appeared in employees' written employment contracts.

Regulation 6(a) also says that anything done by the vendor in respect of a collective agreement is treated as having been done by the purchaser. This would seem to include commitments made by the vendor during wages negotiations (*e.g.* that a certain issue would be addressed at the following year's negotiations) or offers made to trade unions during negotiations. In the latter case, if business transfer takes place midway through the annual wage negotiations, the purchaser will be regarded as having made the same offer as last made by the vendor.

Regulation 6(b) is likely to be of minimal importance, and it deals with the application of an "order," made in respect of collective agreements, to the purchaser in the same way as it applied to the vendor. Unfortunately, the Regulations do not explain to what sort of orders regulation 6(b) applies. It is thought these include orders of the C.A.C. after a collective agreement has been referred to it, by agreement, for the arbitration of a dispute.

Pensions

In so far as any collective agreement relates to pensions (*e.g.* where union representatives have negotiated improvements in pension benefits), these will not transfer over under regulation 6. This is because regulation 7 excludes occupational pension schemes from the ambit of both regulations 5 and 6 [see p. 71].

Recognition and collective bargaining

Transfer of union recognition to purchaser: regulation 9

In the United Kingdom, union recognition is conducted on a voluntary basis. There is therefore no legal recourse against a purchaser who decides that it does not wish to recognise a trade union previously recognised by the vendor in respect of those employees transferring across with the business. However regulation 9 nonetheless requires the purchaser to continue to recognise such unions on the same basis as the vendor had recognised them for the transferring employees prior to the transfer. But this obligation on the purchaser only arises:

> "where, after the relevant transfer, the undertaking or part of the undertaking transferred maintains an identity distinct from the remainder of the transferee's undertaking."

This means that, if the purchaser merges the newly acquired business with its own existing business to the extent that the acquired business loses its identity, then regulation 9 ceases to apply [see regulation 9(1)].

The effect of regulation 9 is to put the onus of cancelling any inherited union recognition on to the purchaser. Although there are no direct *legal* repercussions for the purchaser on withdrawing recognition, there are very likely to be material industrial relations consequences, especially where the union retains a significant presence amongst the workforce. Courts are very reluctant to imply the recognition of a union as a term of individual employment contracts.

Regulation 9 applies to transfer recognition to the purchaser, only if, and to the extent that, a trade union is recognised by the vendor prior to the business transfer *in respect of those employees transferring across* to the purchaser under the Regulations. So, if the vendor had only recognised a union for representation rights in respect of the transferring employees, the purchaser will inherit that same basis of recognition.

In practice, the question of recognition is not a legal issue, but an industrial relations one. A purchaser will have to consider how the transferred recognised unions will fit into its existing collective bargaining structures—particularly where there are joint shop steward committees or national bargaining. In practice the purchaser will try to negotiate a revised bargaining structure with all the unions involved. If agreement cannot be reached, then the purchaser can decide which union it wishes to recognise for the relevant employees. A rather surprising result of regulation 9 is that it could create an inter-union dispute over who has the right to negotiate for the relevant employees.

Consequences of recognition

Although recognition, in itself, is voluntary, its consequences are legal. For example certain rights are only afforded to recognised trade unions and their members. These include the following:

1. the right for the union to be consulted and given specified information prior to redundancies (E.P.A., s.99)—see p. 89 below;
2. the right for the union to be consulted and given specified information prior to a business transfer under the Transfer Regulations (regulation 10—see chapter 8 below);
3. the right of trade union officials to paid time off to carry out their union duties and to undergo training in respect of them (E.P.C.A., s.27);
4. the right of ordinary union members to unpaid time off to participate in their union's activities (E.P.C.A., s.28);
5. the right of unions to appoint safety representatives and safety committees (with the applicable paid time off for those representatives to perform such duties and undergo training in respect of them) [Safety Representatives & Safety Committees Regulations 1977];
6. the union's right to the disclosure of information to enable it to negotiate with the employer (E.P.A., s.17).

Implied recognition of a trade union

Therefore where a purchaser inherits a recognised union from the vendor under regulation 9, it is legally obliged to observe those employment protection rights unless and until recognition is withdrawn. Where, on initial enquiries, a vendor indicates that it does not recognise any union, the purchaser should double-check to ensure that there is no recognition implied through a course of dealings between the vendor and any trade union. In *NUGSAT* v. *Albury Bros. Ltd.* [1979] I.C.R. 84, the Court of Appeal held that recognition need not be expressly granted by an employer, but could be implied through a course of dealings with a union. However in the latter case, the burden on the union in showing that it is recognised by implication is a high one—*i.e.* mere casual contact between an employer and a union will not normally be sufficient. See *NUTGW* v. *Charles Ingram & Co. Ltd.* [1977] I.C.R. 530; E.A.T. and *Joshua Wilson & Bros. Ltd.* v. *USDAW* for two examples where union recognition was implied from such a course of conduct.

The issue of implied recognition is important for the purchaser for industrial relations reasons, since the last thing the purchaser will want on acquiring a business is a dispute with a union over recognition.

Regulation 9(2)(b) does envisage the possibility of the purchaser varying or withdrawing recognition when it says: "any agreement for recognition may be varied or rescinded accordingly."

8 INFORMING AND CONSULTING TRADE UNIONS

Introduction

Background: the requirements of the Business Transfer Directive article 6

Article 6 of the EEC Business Transfer Directive requires Member States to make provision in their domestic legislation for trade unions to be informed about various aspects of a business transfer and to be consulted about it. Accordingly regulation 10 purports to comply with this requirement by imposing on employers an obligation to inform and consult with recognised trade unions about a proposed business transfer. It does *not* apply to proposed pure assets transfers or to share transfers. It also exists independently of any obligation to inform and consult recognised trade unions about proposed collective redundancies—see Appendix A p. 177 below. However, as will be shown later in this chapter, these two obligations are interrelated.

The obligations in regulation 10

Regulation 10, in fact, contains two separate obligations:

1. to give trade unions certain specified information, and
2. to consult with them about it.

It should be noted that whilst the former will always be applicable, the latter may not. This is because the obligation on the employer to consult with a trade union only arises if the employer in question proposes "to take measures" in respect of "affected employees" for whom that union is recognised by the employer [regulation 10(5)].

What is a "relevant transfer"?

It is important to note that the duty to inform and consult under regulation 10 only applies if the business transfer is a "relevant transfer"—*i.e.* one to which the Transfer Regulations apply [see p. 40]. For example in *TGWU* v. *BICC Capacitors Ltd.* it was held that regulation 10 did not apply to share transfers (even one which involved a sale of a majority shareholding). Similarly in *BIFU* v. *Barclays Bank plc* [1987] I.C.R. 495, the E.A.T. held that regulation 10 did not apply where the employer concerned seconded its employees to *another* employer who then acquired the business from another company within the same group of companies. In that case the employees' own employer was neither the transferor or transferee of the business transferred, and the supply of labour was not a business in its own right in the circumstances of the case.

Duty to inform trade unions

Regulation 10(2)

Regulation 10(2) provides that:

"Long enough before a relevant transfer to enable

> consultations to take place between the employer of any affected employees of a description in respect of which an independent trade union is recognised by him and that union's representatives, the employer shall inform those representatives of . . . "

certain specified information [see below]. This obligation is drafted in such a way that it anticipates that, in practice, a period of consultation will probably take place between the employer and the relevant recognised union, even if there may be no legal obligation on the employer to consult. In practice, once an employer tells its recognised trade unions about a proposed business transfer, the unions are sure to want to discuss it; and, in an industrial relations context, such a request for meetings will be difficult for employers to refuse.

What is an "affected employee?"

The duty to inform trade unions only applies where the employer in question recognises that trade union in respect of any "affected employees." Regulation 10(1) defines these in wide terms as follows:

> " . . . in relation to a relevant transfer, any employee of the transferor or the transferee (whether or not employed in the undertaking or part . . . to be transferred) who may be affected by the transfer or may be affected by measures taken in connection with it. . . . "

This means that the purchaser or vendor must supply the specified information to any trade union which it recognises for any class of employee who *may* be affected by the business transfer in question. The use of the word "may" indicates that the duty to inform will be activated even if there is a *possibility* that certain employees may be affected in some way by the business transfer.

The extent of the duty

It is no defence for the employer to argue that it had no proposal to take any action in respect of those employees. Thus the duty to inform may (and probably will) arise, not only in respect of those employees transferring to the purchaser along with the business, but also those remaining with the vendor and the purchaser's existing employees. The effect of a group of employees moving from one employer to another may affect other groups of employees in respect of matters such as allocation of work, revisions to collective bargaining arrangements, transfer payments out of pension funds, etc.

Timing of information

Regulation 10(2) says "long enough before a . . . transfer to enable consultations to take place. . . . " This is not particularly helpful since it suggests that the timescale will vary depending on the extent of the consultations which may or may not take place. However it seems that the greater the ramifications of the business transfer upon the relevant group of affected employees, the longer the timescale which should be allowed between the date when the specified information is supplied to the trade union and the date of the relevant transfer. At a very minimum, the timescale should allow for the trade union to make representations to the employer and for the employer to respond to those representations.

The process of consultation

The linking the date when the specified information must be given to the process of consultation is rather confusing, especially in those cases where there is no legal duty to consult the union. This will occur where neither the purchaser nor the vendor is planning to take any measures in respect of the affected employees. It is submitted that the reason why regulation 10(2) has been drafted in such terms, is to recognise the industrial relations reality that once the information about the business transfer has been given to the trade union, it is bound to want to start discussions with the employer about the effects of the business transfer on the position of its members and itself—even if it is asking for reassurance. The best advice that can be given to employers is that they should endeavour to provide the specified information to the trade unions as soon as is reasonably practicable. The negotiations and confidentiality surrounding a proposed business transfer is likely to dictate when this will be.

"Long enough before the relevant transfer"

It is a moot point whether the words "long enough before a relevant transfer" relate to the moment of exchange of contracts or completion. It is submitted that they relate to the date of completion. Although there is no E.A.T. case on point, this view was taken by an industrial tribunal in *N.A.T.T.K.E.* v. *Rank Leisure Ltd.* [1983] unreported (C.O.I.T. 1388/134). This interpretation is also supported by the following:

1. where a particular provision of the Transfer Regulations operates from a precise moment in time (*e.g.* regulation 5) the courts have held it to be from the moment of completion—see the *Spence* case [1986] I.R.L.R. 248;
2. there is (*obiter*) *dicta* in *B.I.F.U.* v. *Barclays Bank plc* [1987] I.C.R. 495, which indicates that a union can bring a complaint for breach of regulation 10 without waiting for the transaction to be completed;
3. unlike E.P.A., s.99 [see Appendix A p. 177], regulation 10 does not use the word "proposed" to describe a relevant transfer, but treats the transfer as a fact which is to take place;
4. regulation 10(2)(a) specifies in the list of information to be supplied to the trade union "the fact that the relevant transfer is to take place and when approximately . . ."—this suggests that contracts have been exchanged;
5. in practice very few employers indeed are going to be in a position to tell third parties (including recognised trade unions) in advance of an exchange of contracts that a business transfer is to take place, without severely prejudicing their negotiating position or running the risk of the other party claiming that such a communication constitutes an unconditional acceptance of its offer;
6. the business transfer may be conditional upon the vendor or purchaser undertaking certain acts prior to completion, and therefore these conditions may never be satisfied;
7. in the *Wheeler* case [1987] I.R.L.R. 211, the E.A.T. said that a "relevant transfer" took place on completion, not on exchange of contracts [see p. 57 above].

Contract exchange and completion on the same day

A problem arises in those business transfers where exchange of contracts and completion take place on the same day. In such circumstances, the employer will be in breach of regulation 10(2) if it fails to give the union the specified information ahead of that date. In practice, the vendor and purchaser will recognise there is a potential liability under regulation 10 and provide accordingly by either adjusting the purchase price or by way of indemnity. In any event the information must be provided sufficiently before the business transfer to allow for consultations to take place. In *B.I.F.U.* v. *Barclays Bank plc* [see above] the E.A.T. commented that:

> "it would be quite contrary to the whole spirit of the legislation and to the Directive if there were to be no sanction for a failure to consult in relation to a proposed transfer which happened not to take place."

Information to be given

Regulation 10(2) specifies the following information must be given to the relevant recognised trade union(s):

1. the fact of the business transfer and when, approximately, it will take place;
2. the reasons for the business transfer;
3. the legal, economic and social implications of the transfer for the affected employees;
4. the measures with the employer envisages it will be taking in connection with those affected employees (and, if no measures are to be taken, then that fact);
5. the measures which the purchaser envisages it will be taking in connection with those affected employees transferred to it under regulation 5(1) [see p. 52] (and, if no measures are to be taken, then that fact).

"Legal, economic and social implications"

The first two categories of information are quite straightforward. The "legal, economic and social implications" category seems wide-ranging and most certainly include matters such as the effect on employees' duties, terms and conditions of employment, continuity of employment, the fact they will automatically transfer into the purchaser's employment, effect on collective agreements and collective bargaining arrangements, the identity of the purchaser etc. It would also include what is going to happen to the employees' pension rights—although these are excluded from the automatic transfer principle in regulation 5, they are not excluded from the ambit of regulation 10. In practice the transfer of funds from a pension scheme or the purchase of annuities, or the distribution of any excess surplus in the pension fund are highly relevant matters which fall within this category of information. In some cases, it will often be difficult too for employers to give much information by way of the social implications of the business transfer. Employers are best advised not to guess or speculate on such matters or state anything in such a letter which they are not prepared to honour. This is because the communication to the union might be regarded as a contractual representation to employees about what will happen to their conditions of employment or job security, etc.

"Measures envisaged"

The penultimate category relates to measures which the vendor and purchaser "envisage" they will take in respect of their *own* employees. The final category only applies to the vendor, and relates to any measures which the purchaser intends to take in respect of the employees transferring to its employment under regulation 5(1). It should be noted that regulation 10(3) expressly requires the purchaser to furnish the vendor with this information "at such time as will enable the transferor to perform the duty imposed on him. . . . " Since all the information must be supplied to the union by the vendor "long enough before the . . . transfer to enable consultations to take place," this suggests the the purchaser must have given the relevant information to the vendor by that time. However in *I.P.C.S.* v. *Secretary of State for Defence* [1987] I.R.L.R. 373, the High Court interpreted this as meaning "as soon as measures are envisaged and, if possible, long enough before the transfer. . . . " It will be recalled that where either the vendor or the purchaser intend to take no measures in respect of the relevant affected employees, then the information provided must state that fact. The *I.P.C.S.* case [see above] indicates that there will often be cases where the employer will at one point in time have envisaged taking no measures, but later (on examining the effects of the proposed business transfer more closely) changes its mind. The High Court suggested that where there is a change of mind, this should be communicated to the relevant trade union as soon as possible.

The key to the last two categories of information (and the obligation to consult) lies in the meaning of the words "envisage" and "measures."

The meaning of the word "envisage"

In the *I.P.C.S.* case, the High Court said that the word "envisage" connotes the formulation of some definite plan or proposal which the employer intends to implement if necessary as a result of, or on or after, the business transfer. This means that there is no duty to inform trade unions of measures which:

1. the employer had contemplated as mere possibilities and without any actual or contingent decision of putting them into effect;
2. have no causal or time connection with the business transfer (*i.e.* those measures which would have occurred in any event whether or not the business transfer was to take place).

The meaning of the word "measures"

As a general rule the word "measures" is wide in scope and includes any positive act or omission by the employer taken in respect of the affected employees in question—*e.g.* redundancies, changes in terms and conditions of employment or collective bargaining arrangements etc. It would also seem to cover the situation where the vendor intends to make a transfer payment out of the pension fund, or where the purchaser intends to offer the transferring employees lesser or no pension benefits. However matters such as manpower predictions are not regarded as measures, since they do not involve a positive act or omission—see the *I.P.C.S.* case [see above].

The *I.P.C.S.* case [see above] also makes it clear that where the information supplied by the employer is not of a factual nature, but based on the employer's appraisal or judgment, the employer is not obliged to supply to the trade union the calculations or assumptions upon which such appraisal or judgment is based.

The format of the information

The right to be supplied information under regulation 10 does not extend to union being entitled to see the original source documents containing that information. It is open to the employer to extract the information from one or more sources and give the union a summary of the details required. Thus the union cannot insist on the format in which the information is given—see the *I.P.C.S.* case [see above].

The information must be supplied in writing to the union representative or the union's head office [regulation 10(4)]. It is no defence for an employer to argue that the union representative knew what was going on and therefore did not need to be given the relevant information in writing—see *N.A.T.T.K.E.* v. *Rank Leisure Ltd.* [1983] unreported (C.O.I.T. 1603/80); I.T.

A recognised trade union's rights to information under regulation 10 do not diminish its rights to information to be disclosed for collective bargaining purposes under E.P.A. 1975, s.17.

Duty to consult

Regulation 10(5)

By virtue of regulation 10(5) this is only activated if the employer in question envisages that it will be taking any measures in respect of its *own* "affected employees" in connection with the business transfer. This means that the vendor is not required to consult with his trade unions recognised by him, if measures are envisaged by the purchaser but not himself. The interpretation of the word "envisages in connection with the relevant transfer taking measures" is the same as described by the relevant employer there is no duty to consult—see *N.A.T.T.K.E.* v. *Rank Leisure Ltd.* [see above]. It is also important to note that the purchaser has no obligation to consult with the trade unions recognised by the vendor in respect of the transferring employees. This is, perhaps, surprising, since the one person to whom those unions will want to have discussions is the purchaser—who will soon be the employer of their members.

What is consultation?

It is clear from regulation 10 that the consultation process is commenced by the delivery to the trade union of the specified information. Regulation 10(6) specifies that, as a minimum, the consultation process must comprise of at least:

1. the consideration by the employer of any representations which the union may wish to make, and
2. a response by the employer to those representations together with reasons for rejecting them (if applicable).

If the employer puts the measures into effect at the same time (or shortly after) giving the information to the union, there, is a risk that a tribunal may conclude that no meaningful consultations have taken place—see *Green & Sons (Castings) Ltd.* v. *A.S.T.M.S. & A.U.E.W.* [1984] I.R.L.R. 135; E.A.T. This produces something of a problem for employers, especially if a tribunal was to consider that there had been no meaningful consultation with the trade union simply on the grounds that the consultation process started after contracts for the sale of the business had been exchanged. It is submitted that the *N.A.T.T.K.E.* case [see above] is correct in its interpretation that the obligations to inform and consult arise on the moment of exchange of contracts, and therefore regulation 10 consultations are not concerned with the *fact* of the business transfer, but only with *measures* taken by the employer in connection with it.

Employer's defence

What are special circumstances?

An employer is only excused its obligations under regulation 10 if it can demonstrate that there were "... special circumstances which render it not reasonably practicable for an employer to ..." do so. However, in such cases, the employer must be able to demonstrate that it took all reasonably practical steps to comply in the circumstances. The wording of this defence is almost identical to that applicable to the obligation to inform and consult unions prior to redundancies under E.P.A. 1975, s.99 [see Appendix A p. 177]; and it is likely that will be construed along similarly narrow lines. In section 99 cases, an employer can only rely on this defence if it can show that the redundancy was genuinely forced upon the employer with no advance notice and "there was no writing on the wall." In the only case to date where this issue has been considered, the tribunal held that the urgency with which the business transfer had to be completed was a "special circumstance" (see the *N.A.T.T.K.E.* case [see above]); however the employers could not rely on the defence because they had not taken all reasonable means to deliver the information to the union. The tribunal said the employers should have arranged for it to be delivered by hand within one day of exchange of contracts.

Secrecy as a defence

Although there is no case on the point, it seems likely that tribunals will be reluctant to allow employers to rely on the "secrecy" of a proposed business transfer except in rare circumstances. This might include the situation where there is clear evidence that the transfer would not have taken place unless the complete secrecy had been maintained and there was a real and genuine need to preserve such secrecy. Where there is a gap between the dates of exchange of contract and completion, tribunals are likely to be highly sceptical about the need to preserve such secrecy once contracts have been exchanged.

The problem is more acute where exchange of contracts and completion take place on the same day. A tribunal may be prepared to accept the need for secrecy where the purchaser is negotiating to buy an insolvent company in competition with others, and the liquidator can only obtain the best price for creditors and save some jobs, if the purchaser's demands for secrecy are complied with. Even in these situations, the employer must till try to comply with regulation 10 as best it can in the circumstances.

The burden of proof in the "special circumstances" defence

It should be noted that the onus of proving there were "special circumstances" justifying the employer's failure to comply with regulation 10 *and* that the employer had complied with its obligations under regulation 10 as was reasonably practicable in those circumstances, lies with the employer in question [see regulation 11(2)]. Where a vendor seeks to argue that he was prevented from giving the relevant information to the trade union because of the purchaser's failure to supply to him with details of measures it envisaged taking in respect of the transferring employees, he must give the purchaser notice of that fact. As a consequence the purchaser will be joined as a party to the proceedings [regulation 11(3)].

Remedies for breach of regulation 10?

Where a trade union considers that an employer has not complied with its obligations under regulation 10, it may present a claim to a tribunal (regulation 11(1)). However it must do so within three months of the date on which the relevant transfer was completed [regulation 11(8)(a)]. However there is nothing stopping a union from lodging its application before the transfer has been completed—see *B.I.F.U.* v. *Barclays Bank plc* [1987] I.C.R. 495; E.A.T. An employee cannot bring a claim to a tribunal on grounds that the employer has failed to comply with regulation 10.

Tribunal's powers

If the tribunal finds that the employer has contravened regulation 10, it must make a declaration to that effect. It has a discretion to order the payment of such award as it considers: "just and equitable having regard to the seriousness of the failure of the employer to comply with his duty" (regulation 11(4) & (11)). However there is a maximum of two weeks pay in respect of each affected employee in respect of which the tribunal found the employer had failed to comply with regulation 10 (regulation 11(4) & (11)).

Where the vendor's failure to comply with regulation 10 arises out of the purchaser's failure to give him the requisite information, the tribunal may order the purchaser to pay the award instead of the vendor. However, the vendor must have served notice on the purchaser of its intention to show that fact (regulation 11(3) & (4)(b)). In all other cases, the vendor and purchaser are responsible for paying the awards to their own affected employees arising out of their own breaches of regulation 10. It should be noted that in calculating the award, there is no maximum on the amount of a week's pay and the award is paid gross (*i.e.* without deduction for tax or national insurance). The normal rules for calculating a week's pay in E.P.C.A., Sched. 14 are applicable [regulation 11(12)].

It is open to tribunals to award nil compensation; but it is likely that they will only do so where the breach of regulation 10 is only technical and the affected employees have not sufferred any loss as a result—see *N.A.T.T.K.E.* v. *Rank Leisure* [1983] unreported (C.O.I.T. 1388/134), where the vendor had tried to comply with its obligations under regulation 10 but was merely a little too slow in doing so and there was no obligation to consult with the union. However where the employer's breach is blatant and deprives the union of its right to be consulted over the proposed measures, the tribunal will probably make an award near the top of the scale—see *N.A.T.T.K.E.* v. *Andego Enterprises Ltd.* [1984] unreported (C.O.I.T. 1603/80).

In making the award, the tribunal will normally specify the date when the employer must pay the awards to the affected employees. If the employer fails to pay the awards, the employee can return to the tribunal for an order requiring the employer to pay it to him (regulation 11(5) & (6)), but he must do so within three months of the date of the tribunal's award or order (regulation 11(8)(b)).

Offsetting remedy against other claims

Where an employer has breached its obligations under

section 99 to inform and consult recognised trade unions in respect of proposed redundancies as well as having contravened regulation 10, it may nonetheless offset this against its liability for a protective award under section 99 [see Appendix A p. 180], or any liability for breach of contract in respect of the period covered by the protective award (regulation 11(7)(a)). Similarly any remuneration payable or paid to the employee under his employment contract, or as damages for breach of contract, in respect of the period covered by the protective award, can be offset against the employer's liability to pay an award for breach of regulation 10 (regulation 11(7)(b)).

Appeals

Appeals against a tribunal's decisions can be made to the E.A.T. on points of law only—regulation 11(10).

Liability to pay the award after the transfer

In the light of the E.A.T.'s decision in *Angus Jowett & Co* v. *N.U.T.G.W.* [1985] I.R.L.R. 326, the vendor's liability to pay the tribunal's award under regulation 11 apparently does not transfer to the purchaser under regulation 5, but remains with the vendor (see p. 75 above). However, it seems at least arguable that if, by the time of the transfer, the tribunal had already made that award, then liability would be inherited by the purchaser. This is because, whilst a contravention of regulation 10 is something for which an individual employee cannot bring a claim, the non-payment of the award (once made) to him certainly is (see regulation 11(5)). It therefore becomes a liability "in connection" with his employment contract and is capable of transfer to the purchaser along with other liabilities uinder regulation 5. This, of course, assumes that the employee's contract is transferred to the purchaser under regulation 5. If it is not, then liability to pay the award will stay with the vendor.

9 PRACTICAL ISSUES ARISING OUT OF THE TRANSFER REGULATIONS

It has been seen from Chapters 4 to 8 above how dramatic an impact the Transfer Regulations have had on the respective liabilities of the vendor and purchaser on the transfer of a business. In practice, there will be occasions where the purchaser does not want to inherit those liabilities; or the vendor does not want to lose certain employees to the purchaser, but wishes to retain them in that part of its business it is retaining. This chapter is concerned with various ways in which steps can be taken by the vendor and purchaser to minimise the effects of the Transfer Regulations. However it must always be borne in mind that regulation 12 renders void any provision in any contract (whether a contract of employment or otherwise) which purports to exclude or limit the operation of the Transfer Regulations. However, this does not stop the vendor and purchaser arranging matters so that desired results are produced when the Transfer Regulations do operate.

Regulating which employees transfer to the purchaser

Ways of avoiding the effects of regulation 5

Both the vendor and purchaser may have reasons for wanting to determine which of the vendor's employees are automatically transferred to the purchaser under regulation 5(1). The basic rule is that all those employees of the vendor employed (or deemed employed) in the business (or part) transferred at the moment of transfer will be automatically transferred to the purchaser. Accordingly if attempts are to be made to influence which employees are so transferred, they must be effected before the moment of transfer by removing the employees concerned from the business or part to be transferred. It is too late to avoid the effects of regulation 5 if these changes take place at the moment of transfer, as in the *Premier Motors* case [1983] I.R.L.R. 471 (see p. 37 above), or if a dismissal is regarded as in contravention of regulation 8(1).

This can be achieved in two ways. First, the vendor can dismiss the relevant employees (for an "economic, technical or organisational reason" entailing changes in the workforce) so that their employment contracts have ceased to exist as at the moment of the business transfer. Secondly, the vendor may transfer them to a part of its business that it is not selling or to an associated company within the same group. However, the act of dismissing employees brings with it the liability to pay damages for wrongful dismissal (or pay in lieu of notice), redundancy pay or compensation for unfair dismissal. These are cost liabilities in respect of which the vendor and purchaser can agree to apportion between themselves in the commercial contract the eventual costs.

Redeployment of staff within vendor's business

If the vendor has the contractual right to redeploy staff elsewhere within its organisation, then it should be straightforward for it to redeploy to jobs in other parts of its business those of its staff it wishes to retain. Where there is no such contractual right either to assign his contract to another company within the vendor's group of companies or to redeploy him in another job within the vendor's retained business and the employee refuses his consent to such a change, the vendor may face the same three claims (through a constructive dismissal).

It should also be realised that there will often be cases where a particular employee does not wish to join the purchaser (*e.g.* because his pension rights will be adversely affected and he is in his last years before retirement). Accordingly he may well be quite happy to accept such a redeployment.

Separating employees who will transfer from those who will not

In some cases employees provide services for various identifiable parts of their employer's business, and it is necessary to separate those who are to go to the purchaser with the part sold from those who are to stay with the vendor's remaining part. This can be done either by creating a division which is wholly comprised of the part of the business to be transferred and allocating the transferring staff to work in that division. The commercial contract will then describe the business transfer of that distinct division. It can also be achieved by persuading such employees to transfer to an "off-the-shelf" company, which is then sold on to the purchaser together with its employees—see the *B.I.F.U.* v. *Barclays Bank* case [1987] I.C.R. 495.

Co-operation between vendor and purchaser

In most cases the purchaser will liaise closely with the vendor over exactly which employees it wants to be transferred to it under the Transfer Regulations. In effect, the purchaser hopes to get the vendor to arrange his workforce so that only those agreed employees transfer across automatically under the Transfer Regulations. This obviously assumes a willingness on the part of the vendor to co-operate in this respect. However there may be cases where the vendor is simply not prepared to co-operate without the benefit of appropriate indemnities in the business transfer contract, or the purchaser refuses to continue with the negotiations unless the vendor complies with its requirements to divest the business of certain employees by the time of the transfer.

Transfer of licences and concessions

There are also circumstances where a business is treated as being transferred even though the transferee is not willing to take over its operations. This may occur, for example, on the surrender of licences or tenancies which often do constitute businesses (see p. 21). For example, company A may run various concessions under licence at different premises. Such licences are either for a fixed term or terminable on specified notice, and will therefore terminate on the expiry of that term or the notice. The termination will constitute the business transfer back to the licensor. In such a case the licensor will, by virtue of the Transfer Regulations, acquire all the licensee's employees working in the particular concession in respect of which the licence has been surrendered. The licensor has no bargaining power to force the licensee to dismiss those employees ahead of the surrender of the licence. The licensor will either have to offer the licensee a cash sum or an indemnity to induce him to effect such dismissals.

There is also a further complicating factor—*i.e.* the licensee may decline to effect such dismissals and may also choose to deploy in its other concessions those of its good employees it wishes to retain, and replace them in the concession it is surrendering with all its "troublemakers." Thus the licensor will be left with a surrendered concession it does not want and employees it would rather not have. This scenario would seem to apply to tenancies, licences, contracting out services (*e.g.* contract catering) all of which are terminable on notice or expiry of a fixed term. To avoid such an horrendous liability, licensors should include an express clause in their licences/tenancies, etc., to the effect that prior to the surrender of the licence/tenancy, the licensee must dismiss all its employees before the date the surrender takes effect [see Appendix B p. 202]. Further, compliance with such an obligation should be made a precondition of the surrender being effective; and there should be an indemnity in favour of the licensor in the event that they are deemed to be employed in the undertaking at the moment of transfer.

Where there is a contract manufacturing agreement entered into as part of a series of transactions, the purchaser will want to ensure that those of the vendor's employees engaged in manufacture do not transfer across to his employment either on the initial sale or on the expiry of the contract manufacturing agreement. This is normally protected by means of warranties and indemnities—see Appendix B pp. 182 and 190.

Effecting dismissals to avoid regulation 5 operating

Dismissal of employees prior to transfer

It is clear that regulation 5 will operate to make the purchaser inherit the employment contracts and liabilities of the vendor's employees, if their contracts of employment with the vendor are still in force at the moment of transfer—see the *Spence* case. Case law has established that a gap of just one or two hours between dismissals taking effect and the moment of transfer is sufficient. Where there is to be a gap of less than 24 clear hours between the time the dismissals take effect and the moment of transfer, care should be taken to ensure that these two moments in time can be pin-pointed with precision. For example, if a vendor dismisses employees on a Thursday and the business transfer is completed on the Friday, there is a risk that a tribunal may conclude that the dismissals took effect at midnight on the Thursday and the business transfer occurred at one minute past midnight on the Friday. In such a case, the effect of regulation 5 would not have been avoided.

When and how the dismissals should be effected

For a dismissal to be effective, it must be communicated to the employee concerned by the employer. Where dismissals are communicated to employees by post, care should be taken to ensure that the letters are received before the critical time. Where employees are on holiday, such dismissals may not have effect before the moment of transfer, but only when they return home and open their letters. But, by then, the purchaser would have inherited liability for such dismissals initiated by the vendor.

It is best if such dismissal letters are given out by hand and in the presence of a witness. The letter should also clearly state the date and, where appropriate, the time when the dismissal takes effect. Failure to do so carries with it the risk that a tribunal may consider that the moment of dismissal was midnight on that day. It should also be remembered that any ambiguity in the dismissal letter will be construed against the writer of the letter (*e.g.* the vendor)—see for example *Adams* v. *G.K.N. Sankey Ltd.* [1980] I.R.L.R. 416; E.A.T.

Evidence of when the transfer takes place

Where a business transfer is to take effect in close proximity to the dismissals, it is advisable that some evidence is kept of the time when the business transfer takes place. Although there have been no cases where the gap between the dismissals and the business transfer has been less than one hour, it is quite probable that some tribunals may adopt the "*de minimis*" rule where the gap is only a matter of minutes. Indeed, in the *Litster* case, Lord Oliver confirmed such an approach [see p. 57 above]. The documentation should therefore take that matter into account. See Appendix B p. 192 for examples of letters.

The granting of injunctions

In many cases the dismissal will be without full contractual notice but with pay in lieu of notice; and in such circumstances the employer will be in repudiatory breach of contract. The employee therefore has a right to elect not to accept the breach and seek an injunction to restrain the dismissal from taking effect until due notice has expired. It seems likely that the courts may be willing to grant such a remedy since trust and confidence between the vendor and its employees will still be intact and damages will be an ineffective remedy (*e.g.* where the vendor is insolvent)—see *Hill* v. *Parsons* [1972] 1 Ch.D. 305; C.A. However, where a vendor has the contractual right to give employees pay in lieu of notice, there will be no breach of contract where he does so—see *Stewart Rex Jefferies, Parker Ginsberg Ltd.* v. *Parker* [1988] I.R.L.R. 483. Further, where the vendor has no such contractual right to give pay in lieu of notice, but the employees accept the money, they will be be regarded as having accepted that repudiatory breach and will not be entitled to seek an injunction.

Inducing breach of contract

Where a purchaser requires the vendor to act in such a way that the latter is *bound* to act in breach of contract (*e.g.* by dismissing certain employees without due notice), the purchaser will be at risk for damages for the tort of inducing a breach of contract. However, liability under such a tort will be much more difficult for the employee to prove where, although his dismissal was at the behest of the purchaser, it was not inevitable that it would have been effected in breach of contract.

Indemnities

Purchasers should be aware of such a possibility and ensure that they have an indemnity from the vendor to cover such a contingency. Where the vendor is insolvent, the purchaser would be well-advised to require that a sum of money is held in escrow to finance a claim under such an indemnity.

Negotiations prior to transfer over redundancies

Redundancies prior to the business transfer

In many business transfers, the purchaser requires the vendor to dismiss all or certain of the vendor's employees before the moment of transfer, so that the purchaser will only inherit those employees he actually wants. In such cases, the purchaser will usually choose those employees whom he wants to be retained in the business unit and leave it to the vendor to ensure that the remainder are no longer employed in it. Thus, the purchaser indirectly makes the vendor's redundancy selections for him; but will not be liable for any of the unfair dismissal compensation, wrongful dismissal damages and redundancy pay arising from these redundancy selections unless the dismissals are unfair under regulation 8(1).

In these circumstances, the vendor is taking on the liability for notice pay and redundancy pay, and the risk that any redundancy selections forced upon him by the purchaser may be unfair (see p. 102). In practice the vendor and purchaser will negotiate over who is to pick up the cost of these liabilities, and the purchaser may be willing either to give the vendor an indemnity or to increase the purchase price. Whether or not such an indemnity is given by the purchaser, it is in the interests of both the vendor and purchaser that they liaise closely over redundancy selections. This involves the vendor in supplying the purchaser with the relevant and accurate information about those employees concerned and of the existence of any agreed procedure or customary arrangements for redundancy selection.

Procedure of pre-transfer redundancies

The procedural side of pre-transfer redundancies also has to be dealt with by the vendor (see p. 103). It may be that the timing of redundancies puts the vendor in breach of E.P.A., s.99 by failing to commence union consultations until too late (see p. 177), or renders the dismissals unfair due to insufficient advance warning. Alternatively, there may be insufficient time for consultation with those employees to be made redundant or for offers of alternative employment to be made by the vendor or considered by the employees concerned. Although the purchaser might be prepared to give the vendor an indemnity in respect of those redundancy selections he has forced the purchaser to make, care should be taken to ensure that the indemnity does not cover compensation for those dismissals which are unfair on account of the vendor's unfair manner of putting those redundancies into effect except to the extent that such unfairness was caused by the purchaser's timetable imposed on the vendor (see p. 162 for more on indemnities and Appendix B p. 190 for sample wording).

Harmonising terms and conditions

In many business transfers, the purchaser wants those employees he has acquired from the vendor to work under his standard terms and conditions already applied to his existing employees, or to accept less favourable terms and conditions. It will be recalled that a transferring employee carries with him into the employment of the purchaser his existing terms and conditions of employment in all respects except pensions (see p. 67); and that if these are changed without his consent any resulting (constructive) dismissal will be automatically unfair under regulation 8 (see p. 93). It will also be remembered that, under the Transfer Regulations, a transferring employee can refuse to accept a bundle of revised terms and conditions of employment which are no less favourable than those he enjoyed with the vendor. Although, at first sight, the law may appear to put the purchaser in something of a cleft stick, there are various ways the purchaser can achieve its objective. These are discussed below.

Obtaining the employees' consent

Needless to say, where the transferring employee consents to the proposed changes in terms and conditions of employment, no constructive dismissal claim will arise. On some occasions such consent will be forthcoming because the package of terms and conditions offered by the purchaser will be more favourable. On others, the purchaser may have to induce the employees' consent by offering a one-off bonus to "buy out" their rights or by increasing pay.

In some cases, the purchaser may want these changes to be arranged prior to the business transfer taking place. This may be linked to the purchaser's refusal to proceed with the transaction unless a minimum number of employees agree to the new package of terms and conditions (see the sample warranty set out in Appendix B p. 182). Obviously the vendor will be unwilling to effect such changes prior to at least exchange of contracts or without an indemnity from the purchaser. The purchaser may therefore offer the transferring employees revised terms and conditions ahead of the business transfer taking place. This offer by the purchaser will be made strictly conditional on the proposed business transfer taking place and will be subject to the employees' acceptance by a specified date before the date of the business transfer. The transferring employees will be required to indicate in writing to the purchaser their acceptances of the conditional offer by that deadline. In addition, there may be a condition precedent in the commercial agreement between the vendor and purchaser to the effect that the transaction will be cancelled unless a minimum number of acceptances have been received by the purchaser by the specified deadline. That agreement may also require the vendor to ensure that any non-accepting employees have ceased to be employed in the business (or part) to be transferred at the moment of transfer. However, it should be recognised that liability in respect of such employees will nevertheless transfer to the purchaser under regulation 5, since their dismissals will be automatically unfair under regulation 8(1)—see the *Litster* case (p. 54) and the *Delabole Slate* case.

Regulation 12

One *possible* risk in this method lies in regulation 12—*i.e.* a tribunal might conclude that the purpose of such an agreement between the purchaser and his prospective new employee is to preclude the operation of the Transfer Regulations and is therefore void. There has been no case on this point, although some reliance could be placed on *Tocher* v. *General Motors* [1981] I.R.L.R. 55; E.A.T., where an agreement by a union on behalf of an employee (which had the effect of stopping him claiming redundancy pay) was held by the E.A.T. to contravene E.P.C.A., s.140 which is worded similarly to regulation 12. However it should be noted that, in practice, tribunals may be reluctant to find that a freely-agreed variation in contract will be rendered void, especially where the employee receives some benefit as a result of the variation of employment terms and conditions. Indeed, there are dicta in the E.C.J.'s judgment in the *Daddy's Dance Hall* case [1988] I.R.L.R. 315, which makes it clear that, where existing law allows the parties to agree or enforce variations in terms and conditions of employment, there is nothing in the Acquired Rights Directive which takes that away.

"Red-circling"

The purchaser may be prepared to allow those transferring employees who are not prepared to agree to the revised terms and conditions offered by the purchaser, to remain as anomalies in his workforce. This is sometimes known as "red-circling." They might be told that they will not be given pay increases or offered participation in any new benefits schemes until they are prepared to agree to the purchaser's standard terms and conditions of employment. In other words, the relevant employees are given a choice: either to remain on their existing terms and conditions (except for pensions) or to accept the purchaser's standard terms and conditions package (in which event they will be entitled to any improvements in employee benefits, etc.).

In practice many of those employees who are not sufficiently motivated to agree to work under the purchaser's standard terms and conditions will only be anomalies for a limited period. They will either leave the purchaser's employment in due course (with their replacements engaged on the standard terms and conditions) or they will realise that their career and financial prospects with the purchaser will be better served by agreeing to the standard terms and conditions or leaving.

A variant on this approach is to offer pay increases on the condition that employees accept a package of revisions in terms and conditions of employment. If an employee is not prepared to accept the burdens of the package, he will not be given the benefits.

Obviously, in some circumstances, it may not be practical for the purchaser to administer two sets of employees engaged on very different terms and conditions of employment. In practice the "red-circling" technique is used where the number of employees concerned is relatively small. It may also be appropriate for "red-circling" to be applied only to certain terms and conditions which a particular employee is not prepared to forgo.

Postponing harmonisation

It will be recalled that the automatic unfairness rule under regulation 8(1) only applies where any dismissal (constructive or otherwise) is connected with a business transfer (see p. 93). It may be possible for the purchaser to implement the harmonisation programme as part of a later reorganisation exercise (see p. 174). In some cases, the reorganisation programme may mean that certain jobs disappear and certain redefined jobs are created. The latter jobs may be offered to the relevant employees as an alternative to redundancy, but on the purchaser's standard terms and conditions of employment. However, in such cases, the differences between the old and redefined jobs must be of substance.

Terminating old contract and offering a new one

Where an employer wishes to force through new terms and conditions of employment which are unpopular with some of his employees, it is sometimes achieved by serving due notice of terminating the employees' old contracts and offering new contracts to start with effect from the expiry of the notice. This technique certainly avoids breach of contract claims; but, as it necessarily involves a dismissal, it will not avoid the automatic unfairness rule under regulation 8 of the Transfer Regulations—unless there has been a considerable delay since the date of the business transfer so that the connection with the business transfer has been broken.

Terms and conditions which cannot be transferred

In some cases, the nature of certain terms and conditions of employment with the vendor are such that they cannot be transferred to the purchaser. Alternatively, the effect of the business transfer may be to activate participation or entitlement in these schemes (*e.g.* stock options).

Non-transferable terms

It will be recalled that, under the Transfer Regulations, the purchaser will automatically inherit all the transferring employees' terms and conditions of employment except for pensions. But an employee may enjoy entitlement to stock options with the vendor which cannot be transferred to the purchaser (even if it can properly be said to be part of his contract of employment).

Alternatively he may be entitled to a bonus or profit-share which is based on the performance of either or both of the business (or part) transferred and/or the wider group of which that business forms a part. The purchaser may decide to merge his newly-acquired business (or part) with his existing business in circumstances where separate accounts are not kept for the acquired business (or part). It will therefore be impossible to assess bonus entitlement against the performance of the business in which the transferring employee previously worked. Similarly it will be wholly inappropriate for the purchaser to assess his own employees' bonus or profit-share based on the performance of the group of companies to which the vendor belonged.

It is clear that the purchaser must maintain a bonus or profit-share scheme which will bring to the employee broadly equivalent rewards if 100 per cent. performance has been achieved. It seems likely that, in circumstances such as these, it will be sufficient if the purchaser devises a different scheme for his employees provided it is a of a similar type and it provides corresponding levels of bonus or profit-share.

In some cases, the purchaser may be unable or unwilling to introduce such a substitute scheme. He will therefore either have to "buy out" the employee's entitlement to bonus/profit-share, or persuade him to waive his right to it. Alternatively the vendor can minimise this contingent liability for a potential purchaser by including a suitable clause in the scheme (see Appendix B p. 201).

Benefits which do not transfer to the purchaser

Some employers grant stock options to their employees and, depending on the circumstances, these may not form part of their conditions of employment but represent separate "collateral" contracts. It is normal for such schemes to provide for early exercise of stock options in certain specified circumstances, including redundancy. The *Chapman* v. *C.P.S. Computers* case [1987] I.R.L.R. 462; C.A. (see p. 68), illustrates that a business transfer may be regarded as constituting a redundancy for stock option purposes, thus giving rise to an early exercise of stock option rights. Similarly, it will be recalled that rights or benefits under occupational pensions schemes do not transfer to the purchaser (regulation 7—see p. 71). Accordingly a business transfer may give rise to a cause of action against the vendor in this respect (see p. 74).

It is submitted that a vendor can prevent these liabilities from arising on a business transfer by inserting a clause in the relevant stock option and pension scheme expressly excluding such claims in the event of a business transfer—see Appendix B p. 202.

Confidentiality agreements and restraints

Some employees have post-termination restraints contained in employment contracts with the vendor. Others sign separate "Confidentiality Agreements" or deeds (under seal) containing such restraints. These will usually prohibit the employee from working for a competitor, or soliciting the vendor's customers or employees, or divulging/using the vendor's trade secrets and confidential information.

It will be recalled that, as a general rule, these post-termination restraints are only enforceable if they are necessary and reasonable for the protection of the employer's legitimate business interests. The wording of these restraints usually refers to "the Company" (*i.e.* the vendor) and relate to the "Company's customers" or the "Company's products." Where, on a business transfer, an employee of the vendor is transferred to the purchaser, this may have the effect of rendering a post-termination restraint (which was previously reasonable in respect of the vendor) unreasonable in respect of the purchaser. This may be because the purchaser's range of products and activities is much wider than the vendor's and includes those with which the relevant employee was not at all concerned. It is therefore necessary that these post-termination restraints are reviewed and amended (if appropriate). In any event the restraint clauses should contain a clause making it clear that the word "Company" relates also to the vendor's successors in title and assigns; and the commercial agreement between the vendor and purchaser should (if necessary) assign the benefit of those covenants.

Amending the restraints on a transfer

Position where restraints does not form part of the contract of employment

In some cases, the agreement containing the post-termination restraint does not form part of the employment contract (*e.g.* where the post-termination restraints were entered into as part of an earlier share sale agreement by an employee shareholder). If so, the Transfer Regulations will not transfer their benefit to the purchaser under the Transfer Regulations. The purchaser should therefore review these and, if appropriate, require the assignment of these agreements to it. Notice of assignment should also be served on the relevant employees. However, it may be preferable if new agreements are entered into with the employees.

10 LIABILITY OF VENDOR AND PURCHASER ON BUSINESS TRANSFERS ARISING APART FROM THE TRANSFER REGULATIONS

Background: common law protection for employees

As already indicated at the start of this book, the common law and statutory employment protection legislation provide some minimum ground rules dealing with employment rights in the context of a business transfer. Some of these apply to all business transfers (regardless whether the Transfer Regulations apply). Others have been either overridden or rendered obsolete by the Transfer Regulations, but nonetheless continue to apply in the relatively small class of cases where the Regulations do not apply (*e.g.* the transfer of an undertaking not in the nature of a commercial venture). This chapter seeks to collate these together in one place.

Notice of termination

Employers duty to give notice

Since the effect of regulation 5(1) is a statutory novation of an employee's contract of employment, he will not be able to claim he has been dismissed by his employer (the vendor) when the latter transfers its business to the purchaser. Therefore where an employee's contract is automatically transferred to the purchaser under regulation 5(1) there is no dismissal, and so the vendor will be under no obligation to give its employees due notice of termination of employment, or pay in lieu of notice.

However, where the Transfer Regulations do not apply to a business transfer, the common law rules will operate. For reasons already explained earlier in some detail (see p. 48), it is submitted that the effect, at common law, of a business transfer on the employment contract may be a repudiatory breach of it.

Employee's remedy for a repudiatory breach of contract

If it is a repudiatory breach of contract (as will normally be the case where the whole of the vendor's business is transferred to the purchaser), then the employee will have a claim for damages for wrongful dismissal at common law. These damages will include the employee's net lost salary and other benfits of employment (*e.g.* pension contributions, company car, private medical insurance, etc.) which he would have enjoyed had he received his full notice of termination. Needless to say, if the vendor gives him his full notice, then there is no claim for wrongful dismissal. If the employee is given short notice, then his claim for damages will be limited to his lost pay and benefits for the period by which the actual notice given falls short of his notice entitlement.

Offers of alternative employment

The vendor's liability to pay damages for wrongful dismissal or to give pay in lieu of notice may be reduced where the purchaser offers the vendor's dismissed employees suitable alternative employment. If the employees accept such offers, then the earnings and benefits enjoyed by them in their new employment with the purchaser will be offset against any wrongful dismissal damages—but only in so far as these were earned during any period which would have been their notice period with the vendor, had it been given in full. If the employees unreasonably refuse to accept such offers from the purchaser, the vendor will be able to argue that they have not taken reasonable steps to mitigate their loss. To maximise this way of reducing liability, the vendor might insert a clause in the sale agreement requiring the purchaser to offer the employees jobs on terms and conditions not less favourable than they enjoy with the vendor.

Continuity of employment

The application of E.P.C.A. 1978, Sched.13

Whether or not the Transfer Regulations apply, E.P.C.A., para. 17(2), Sched. 13 operates to preserve employees' accrued period of continuous employment where they are taken into the employment of the purchaser. If such protection was not there, employees would have to re-qualify for their various statutory employment rights—*e.g.* two years for unfair dismissal, redundancy pay and maternity rights. Paragraph 17(2) provides as follows:

> "If a trade or business or an undertaking . . . is transferred from one person to another, the period of employment of an employee in the trade or business or undertaking at the time of the transfer shall count as a period of employment with the transferee, and the transfer shall not break the continuity of the period of employment."

What is a "trade, business or undertaking"?

The meaning of a "trade, business or undertaking" under paragraph 17(2) is the same as that applicable to the Transfer Regulations, with the one exception that it also covers undertakings not in the nature of a commercial venture (see p. 12 for meaning of a trade, business or undertaking). The E.A.T. has said that, this exception apart, the meaning of trade, business and undertaking in paragraph 17(2) and the Transfer Regulations should be construed in the same way. It is therefore clear that paragraph 17(2) does cover non-commercial venture—see *Robinson* v. *The Council of the County Borough of Bournemouth* [1970] 5 I.T.R. 100; I.T., where a transfer of a surveying department from one technical college in Bournemouth to a polytechnic in Portsmouth was held to be a transfer of a business within the scope of paragraph 17(2). It would clearly not have been covered by the Transfer Regulations.

The extent of paragraph 17(2)

Paragraph 17(2) is relevant only where the purchaser either offers employment to the vendor's employee or his employment is transferred over under the Transfer Regulations. However, paragraph 17(2) only operates where the relevant employee is still employed in the vendor's business (or part) to be transferred at the time of the transfer. *In Brook Lane Finance Co. Ltd.* v. *Bradley* [1988] I.R.L.R. 283, the E.A.T. held that this meant the moment of transfer (*i.e.* the completion of the business transfer). In that case the applicant transferred to the employment of the purchaser about two weeks prior to the time of completion in order to prepare the way for the business transfer to take place. With some reluctance, the E.A.T. held that, as the strict wording of regulation 5 and paragraph 17(2) required him to have been in the vendor's employ at the moment of transfer, he lost his period of continuous employment with the vendor.

Vendors dismissed employee offered employment by purchaser

Thus, it seems, if the vendor's employee is no longer in the vendor's employment before the moment of transfer, but is subsequently offered employment by the purchaser after the date of the business transfer, he will not be able to rely on paragraph 17(2) to carry forward any accrued continuous employment into his employment with the purchaser. This is because he was not in the vendor's employment at the time of the transfer. The onus of proving that paragraph 17(2) operates to preserve continuity of employment lies with the employee—see *Secretary of State for Employment* v. *Cohen* [1987] I.R.L.R. 169; E.A.T.

Vendors employee does not transfer to purchaser immediately

It appears that paragraph 17(2) may operate to preserve an employee's period of continuous employment, where he remains with the vendor up to the moment of transfer, but does not commence employment with the purchaser until shortly afterwards. For example, an employee might remain employed by the vendor until the moment of transfer on the Monday of week 1, and not start his employment with the purchaser until the Friday of week 2. Under E.P.C.A., para. 4, Sched. 13 a whole week counts for continuity purposes, if during part of it the employee's relations are governed by a contract of employment normally involving 16+ hours per week. In the above example, week 1 was a week during which the employee worked under such a contract, and so was week 2. It does not matter that he did not actually work 16+ hours in either week—the key point is that in each week he worked under an employment contract which normally provided for those hours. Therefore both weeks count for continuity purposes and the ostensible "break" in continuity caused by the business transfer is cured by paragraph 17(2) because the employee had remained with the vendor until the time of the transfer—see *Edgar* v. *Robert Elliott Ltd.* [1986] (unreported E.A.T. 581/85).

Temporary cessation of work

The above application of paragraph 4 of the continuity rules only operates to preserve employees' accrued periods of continuous employment if the gap between leaving the vendor and joining the purchaser is under two weeks (a week runs from Sunday to Saturday—see E.P.C.A., para. 24(1), Sched. 13). It may also be possible to argue that continuity might be preserved through a longer gap by E.P.C.A., para. 9, Sched. 13 which treats as a period of continuous employment any week during the whole or part of which the employee is "absent from work on account of a temporary cessation of work." Paragraph 9 of the continuity rules applies whether or not there is a contract of employment in force during the period of the absence from work. It is intended to cover absences such as temporary lay-offs. However it does seem at least arguable that it might operate to preserve continuous service of a vendor's employee who is offered his former job by the purchaser to begin several weeks after the business transfer has taken place. It is submitted that for continuity to be preserved in such a case the following conditions must be satisfied:

1. the employee must have remained with the vendor until the time of the transfer, and
2. the purchaser's offer must have been made before his employment with the vendor had ended, and
3. the job offer by the purchaser must relate to the employee's former job with the vendor.

E.P.C.A. 1978, Sched. 13, para. 17(1)

However, some doubt must be cast on this method of preserving continuous employment since E.P.C.A., para. 17(1), Sched. 13 says that, apart from the provisions of paragraphs 17 and 18, the continuity rules of Schedule 13 ". . . relate only to employment by one employer. . . ." It is unclear whether this would prevent an employee relying on a temporary cessation of work with a new employer which occurs at the start of his employment.

Change of partners: E.P.C.A. 1978, Sched. 13, para. 17(5)

Continuity of employment may also be preserved on a change of partners in a business. Paragraph 17(5) provides that:

> "If there is a change in the partners . . . who employ any person, the employee's period of employment at the time of the change shall count as a period of employment with the partners . . . after the change, and the change shall not break the continuity of the period of employment."

This is couched in very similar terms to paragraph 17(2) [see above] and should be construed accordingly.

It should be noted that where the change in partners results in only one partner remaining, paragraph 17(5) will not apply—see *Harold Fielding Ltd.* v. *Mansi* [1974] I.R.L.R. 79. This is because paragraph 17(5) apparently envisages there being more than one partner after the relevant change. This interpretation also applies where there is a change from a sole partner to two or more partners—see *Wynne* v. *Hair Control* [1978] I.C.R. 870; E.A.T. However in that case, the E.A.T. suggested that the employee could have relied on the protection given by paragraph 17(2)—see also *Allen & Son* v. *Coventry* [1979] I.R.L.R. 399; E.A.T. Similarly in *Jeetle* v. *Elster* [1985] I.R.L.R. 227, the E.A.T. held that the dissolution of a four partner practice followed by a single partner practice did constitute a business transfer under paragraph 17(2).

Associated employers E.P.C.A. 1978, Sched. 13, para. 18

Groups of companies may decide to restructure their group-wide businesses for a variety of reasons. Where this involves the transfer of assets in the nature of a going concern, the Transfer Regulations will apply to preserve continuity. In any event paragraph 18 operates to preserve continuity of employment between associated employers. Paragraph 18 provides that:

> "If an employee of an employer is taken into the employment of another employer who, at the time when the employee enters his employment is an associated employer

of the first-mentioned employer, the employee's period of employment at that time shall count as a period of employment with the second-mentioned employer and the change of employer shall not break continuity of employment."

Scope and significance of para. 18

This means that where an employee transfers between associated employers, he carries with him his accrued period of continuous employment. However for paragraph 18 to operate, the employer whom he is leaving and that whom he is joining must be associated. It does not matter that they subsequently cease to be associated at a later date.

An "associated employer" is defined in E.P.C.A., s.153(4) and is limited to companies. Two companies are associated: "if one is a company of which the other directly or indirectly has control, or if both are companies of which a third person directly or indirectly has control. . . . " The concept of "control" means control of the voting shares of the company—see *Secretary of State for Employment* v. *Newbold & Another* [1981] I.R.L.R. 305; E.A.T. This means the holding or control of more than 50 per cent. of the shares in the company—see *Hair Colour Consultants Ltd.* v. *Mena* [1984] I.C.R. 671; E.A.T. In this respect, the control of a company can reside in more than one person, provided that those persons holding the controlling shares vote together in practice—see *Zarb & Samuels* v. *British & Brazilian Produce Co.* [1978] I.R.L.R. 78; E.A.T. In such a case, there is no presumption that various shareholders always vote together (*e.g.* where a husband and wife hold the controlling shares between them), but evidence of joint voting must be produced—see *South-West Launderettes Ltd.* v. *Laidler* [1986] I.C.R. 455 C.A.

Redundancy pay

Eligibility for redundancy pay

Where the Transfer Regulations apply, employees who are automatically transferred into the employment of the purchaser will not have been dismissed, and therefore cannot claim statutory redundancy pay. Where the vendor makes an employee redundant and his dismissal takes effect on or after the business transfer has taken place, then the purchaser will inherit liability for redundancy pay if the Transfer Regulations apply to the business transfer—see the *Premier Motors* case [1983] I.R.L.R. 471; E.A.T. In all other respects any liability for redundancy pay remains with the vendor, provided the redundancy is genuine.

There may be a few business transfers where the Transfer Regulations do not apply—*e.g.* where the business transferred is not in the nature of a commercial venture. In such a case, the occurrence of a business transfer will usually result in the dismissal of the employee thereby giving him the chance to claim statutory redundancy pay. This might result in a measure of unfairness for the vendor, especially where the purchaser offers employment to some or all of the vendor's former employees. The employee would receive a windfall of the redundancy pay, and still have a job.

To prevent this unfair result, E.P.C.A., s.94 operates to provide a defence to paying statutory redundancy pay to employees who are offered jobs by the purchaser. Section 94 applies where two conditions have been satisfied:

1. there has been a change in the ownership of a business or part of one, and
2. the employer terminates an employee's employment (with or without notice), in connection with that change.

If these two conditions are satisfied then the employee will forfeit his right to statutory redundancy pay from the vendor in either of the following two situations:

Employees right to statutory redundancy pay is forfeited

1. The employee agrees with the new owner of the business to his contract being renewed or to being re-engaged by the owner on new terms and conditions (E.P.C.A., s.94(2)). In such a case E.P.C.A., s.84 and s.90 apply—*i.e.* the employee is treated as never having been dismissed by the vendor for the purposes of redundancy (see Appendix A p. 168).
2. The employee unreasonably refuses an offer of suitable alternative employment made by the new owner, or unreasonably terminates such new employment during the four week statutory trial period (E.P.C.A., s.94(3)). See also Appendix A p. 168).

In respect of both of these rules on forfeiture of statutory redundancy pay, no account is taken of the change of identity of the new owner of the business (E.P.C.A., s.94(4)). It should also be noted that the meaning of a "business" under section 94 is construed consistently with paragraph 17(2) and the Transfer Regulations (see p. 12 above).

It is unclear whether the second of the above forfeiture rules only applies where the new owner of the business has made an offer to the vendor's employees before their contracts had been terminated—see *White & Hunnisett* v. *Liquidator of Warmwell Bakeries Ltd. & Another* [1979] (unreported E.A.T. 172/79). However it is generally thought that the offer must have been made before the termination of employment with the vendor has taken effect. If the offer is made after the employees' contracts with the vendor have been terminated, it seems that they will not forfeit their redundancy pay entitlement even though they have accepted new jobs with the purchaser—see *Secretary of State for Employment* v. *Spence* [1986] I.R.L.R. 248; C.A. Accordingly if employers wish to be able to rely on E.P.C.A., s.94 they should ensure that:

Conditions for the application of E.P.C.A. 1978, s.94

1. the offer is made to the employees in question before their employment contracts with the vendor terminate, and
2. the offer is in writing (although this is not, strictly speaking, required by law); and
3. the job offered must start within four weeks of the date his employment ended.

Employee receipt of redundancy pay and entry into purchaser's employment

Receipt of redundancy pay. It can be seen from the above rules that there can be cases where the vendor's employees receive statutory redundancy pay, but still enter the employment of the purchaser. This might occur either where the vendor mistakenly gives redundancy pay, because he does not realise that the Transfer Regulations absolves him from that duty in respect of the transferring employees, or because the purchaser made an offer of employment too late for section 94 to operate. Where employees do receive redundancy pay in such cases, E.P.C.A., para. 12 Sched. 13 applies to stop the employee receiving it twice if he is subsequently made redundant from the employment of the purchaser. In fact, paragraph 12 not only says that the period of employment before the dismissal is disregarded for the purposes of calculating the amount of a future redundancy payment, it also provides that the employee must re-serve the requisite two years continuous employment. From the wording of paragraph 12, it also seems that its provisions apply even if a redundancy payment was wrongly paid to an employee. But they do not apply unless the employer has paid the employee's full redundancy pay entitlement.

Maternity "job-back" rights

E.P.C.A. 1978, ss.33, 45–48

Under E.P.C.A., s.33 and ss.45–48 a woman has the right to return to work after maternity leave provided she has satisfied certain conditions (*e.g.* she has two years continuous service as at the 11th week before the expected week of confinement, and she exercises her right to leave and return to work in accordance with the prescribed procedures). Section 45(1) provides that the right to return to work after maternity leave includes the right to return to the employment of any successor of her employer. This "job-back" right relates to:

> "... the job in which she was employed under the original contract of employment and on terms not less favourable than those which would have been applicable to her if she had not been so absent" (E.P.C.A., s.45(1)).

Meaning of a "successor" T.U.L.R.A. 1974, s.30(3) and E.P.C.A. 1978, s.153(1)

It therefore seems that an employee on maternity leave can enforce her statutory right to return to work against a purchaser of her former employer's business. However, this will only apply if the purchaser falls within the definition of a "successor." For this purpose the definition in T.U.L.R.A., s.30(3) is applicable (see E.P.C.A., s.153(1)). A "successor" is defined as:

> "... a person who, in consequence of a change occurring ... in the ownership of the undertaking or part ... for the purposes of which the employee was employed, has become the owner of the undertaking or of that part of it ... " (T.U.L.R.A., s.30(3)).

It is clear that the change in the ownership of the business (or part in which the woman was employed) can be effected by any method whatsoever.

Therefore a woman's statutory "job-back" rights can be enforced against a new owner of a business which has been transferred during her maternity leave—even though she had ceased to be employed by her former employer during her maternity leave. This applies regardless of the applicability of the Transfer Regulations (which only operate on the employment contracts of those persons still employed by the vendor at the moment of the business transfer). Where a woman has been refused her statutory "job-back" rights, she can claim she has been unfairly dismissed under E.P.C.A., s.56.

Industrial action

E.P.C.A. 1978, s.62

Where employees have been dismissed whilst taking part in industrial action or have been locked out as part of an industrial dispute, special unfair dismissal rules apply—see E.P.C.A., s.62. In effect section 62 provides that a tribunal has no jurisdiction to hear the merits of such a dismissal unless the employer has discriminated between "relevant employees." Section 62(2) specifies the two types of discrimination which can lose an employer this immunity from unfair dismissal claims: *i.e.*—where:

What constitutes "discrimination" for purposes of s.62

1. not all relevant employees have been dismissed; and
2. a relevant employee has been offered re-engagement within three months of his date of dismissal, but no such offer has been made to the complainant of unfair dismissal.

The relevance of this rule to business transfers lies in the rather wide definition of an offer of re-engagement. Section 62(4)(c) defines this as: " . . . an offer (made either by the original employer or by a successor of that employer . . .) to re-engage an employee. . . . " The definition of a successor is the wide one contained in T.U.L.R.A., s.30(3) (see p. 142 above in relation to maternity "job-back" rights).

The problem here is one for the vendor, since the purchaser will have no liability for such dismissals effected by the vendor before the moment of transfer. It may be that the vendor dismissed some of its employees whilst taking industrial action in the three months prior to a business transfer. If the purchaser then offers a job to one or more of the within three months of their dismissal, the vendor will suddenly lose its immunity under section 62 from unfair dismissal claims. This loss of immunity would apply even though the vendor was unaware of the purchaser's offer, or the purchaser was unaware that the former employee had been dismissed for taking industrial action. In such circumstances, a vendor may request an indemnity from the purchaser if the latter offers re-employment to any such employees within a period of three months.

Other common law actions

Representations made to employees

In most business transfers both the vendor and purchaser are keen to give the transferring employees as much re-assurance as possible, so that the transaction will be smoothly completed. This is particularly the case where the purchaser wants to ensure that certain key employees transfer across with the business. In some transactions the transfer of certain employees is the most important asset being sold. Either the purchaser or the vendor may say things to those employees with the intent of providing that re-assurance, without first considering the full implications of the such statements. In other words, those statements may create further legal obligations upon the purchaser or the vendor.

For example, the purchaser may say to some of the vendor's employees that he will honour their existing terms and conditions of employment or their period of continuous service.

Whilst the Transfer Regulations may transfer across to the purchaser the vast majority of an employee's remuneration package, they do not transfer occupational pension benefits, etc., (see p. 71). So such a wide comment may bind the purchaser to maintain a similar pension scheme or other benefits of employment which were peculiar to the vendor (*e.g.* stock option scheme).

Vendor as purchasers agent

Purchasers should be particularly wary of vendors who make such comments—*i.e.* that the purchaser will honour existing contracts of employments. Vendors might feel constrained to make such reassuring "noises" where it is a pre-condition of a business transfer that certain named employees agree to transfer with the business into the employment of the purchaser. In the normal course of events, the purchaser will not be liable for the rash comments of the vendor made to those employees who do not transfer to him under regulation 5. But the purchaser will be liable if he has held out the vendor as his agent in discussions with the transferring employees. Such an inference might be easily drawn where the purchaser and vendor make joint announcements to and have joint meetings with the vendor's staff.

Application of regulation 5(2)

Even if the purchaser is not liable for the vendor's statements under the normal principles of agency, it will be liable under regulation 5(2) Transfer Regulations which provide that:

> "anything done before the transfer is completed by or in relation to the transferor in respect of that contract or a person employed in that undertaking or part shall be deemed to have been done by or in relation to the transferee."

So if the vendor has done or said anything that can be legally enforceable against the vendor in respect of a transferring employee, the purchaser will be treated as having done or said that thing. Purchasers are therefore strongly advised that they approve every communication to transferring employees in relation to what will happen after the business transfer has been completed. This can either be done at meetings at which the purchaser is present, or in letters which the purchaser has approved in advance. In addition, purchasers might ask the vendor to give a warranty in the business transfer contract to the effect that the vendor has made no promises or representations in respect of the transferring employees except those approved (in writing) by the purchaser or dealt with in the disclosure letter (see Appendix B p. 183).

In the context of this background, it is now appropriate to examine how such additional common law liabilities might arise.

Breach of contract

Breach of contract will probably be the most common basis upon which a claim might be brought. However, it is a basic tenet of common law that a contract, or variation of contract, will only be binding if there is "consideration" moving from both sides. "Consideration" is a legal concept to the effect that, for a contract to "stick," both parties must give something either to the other or to a third party. However, "consideration" cannot be provided in retrospect—*i.e.* it cannot be provided by something done or not done in the past.

In fact it will probably be the employer's consideration which is the matter which has given rise to the breach of contract claim in the first place. There may be difficulty in finding such consideration moving from an employee, since he will be giving nothing positive in return. However it may be argued that, since consideration does not have to be "for value," the employee's willingness to remain employed so that his contract will be transferred to the purchaser is sufficient consideration. This will especially be the case where the purchaser has made certain representations to persuade the employee not to resign his employment with the vendor on the business transfer.

It must also be remembered that, for a contract term to be legally enforceable, it must be expressed with reasonable certainty and precision. For example, a statement that "we hope to start up a bonus scheme" is unlikely to be regarded by the courts as having sufficient certainty and precision to enable the court to ascertain exactly what the speaker promised to do. However, employers should beware of making such statements because a court may try hard to reduce sufficient certainty from other surrounding facts to render it enforceable.

Where there has been a breach of contract, the employee can sue for damages in the ordinary courts. These damages are limited to all losses he has suffered as a result of the breach of contract and which were reasonably foreseeable. However, the employee nonetheless has to take reasonable steps to mitigate his loss.

Estoppel

Estoppel is an equitable concept in law which stops a person from denying the truth of something he has said or written to another person. There are two areas where it might be used:

1. promissory estoppel and
2. estoppel of fact.

Promissary estoppel. This arises where Mr. X. makes a representation or promise to Mr. Y. (*e.g.* that he will or will not do something), and Mr. Y. acts on that promises to his detriment. The important thing about promissory estoppel is that Mr. X. will be bound by his promise even though Mr. Y. has given no consideration. In effect, equity steps in to stop Mr. X. taking advantage of his unfulfilled promises upon which Mr. Y. had acted to his detriment. However, the courts have decided that Mr. Y. cannot rely that promise as founding a cause of legal action in its own right, but he can only use it as a defence to a claim against him by Mr. X. In the context of a business transfer, there seems limited scope for this doctrine to apply in respect of contractual rights. In the light of the House of Lords decision in *Secretary of State for Employment* v. *Globe Elastic Thread Co. Ltd. & Another* [1979] I.C.R. 706, it appears that the concept of promissory estoppel cannot be used to hold employers to promises given in respect of the statutory rights such as honouring past periods of employment with former employers.

Estoppel of fact. This is not really a cause of action or a defence, but more akin to a rule of evidence. For example, if an employer says to an employee that a certain fact exists (*e.g.* that he has or has not done something), the employer will not be allowed to deny that fact, even though it is untrue. For example in *Smith* v. *Blandford Gee Cementation Co. Ltd.* [1970] 3 All E.R. 154; C.A., the employee had understood he had been employed by the N.C.B., although he subsequently received from B.G.C. Ltd. a document containing his terms and conditions of employment which stated that B.G.C. Ltd. was his employer. When he subsequently sued B.G.C. Ltd. for his redundancy pay, B.G.C. Ltd. were stopped from denying the contents of that document in which they had admitted that he was their employee.

Representations of fact and opinion

It is theoretically possible for an employee to claim that he was induced to enter into a contract with the purchaser, or to vary a term of a contract, by a misrepresentation by the purchaser. However a claim will only arise where the employee alleges that there was a misrepresentation of fact. It seems likely that, in the context of a business transfer, most representations will be expressions of opinion rather than of fact. Further, these representations may not be such that they can appropriately be regarded as a term of an employment contract (*e.g.* future plans or the profitability of the purchaser). A cause of action may arise under the Misrepresentation Act 1967 where the purchaser induces a person to leave his employment upon a representation that he is qualified to perform a specific job for the purchaser and then subsequently dismisses him for not having the relevant qualifications—see *McNally* v. *Welltrade International Ltd. & Others* [1978] I.R.L.R. 497; H.C. However it is unlikely that misrepresentation will be a fruitful legal action for transferring employees who find themselves disillusioned with the purchaser after the "honeymoon" of new employment is over.

Inducement to break a contract

It seems that where the purchaser requires the vendor to dismiss certain employees prior to the business transfer in circumstances where it is inevitable that the vendor will break their employment contracts (*e.g.* by not giving due notice), the purchaser will be at risk for a claim for damages for the tort of inducement to break a contract. The damages will be limited to the employees' losses caused by the relevant breach of contract—usually in respect of their notice period which has not already been paid by the vendor.

However, where the vendor can dismiss those employees lawfully with pay in lieu of notice (see *Rex Stewart Jefferies, Parker Ginsberg Ltd.* v. *Parker* [1988] I.R.L.R. 483 or it is at least possible for those dismissals to be effected with due notice, no such claim will lie.

Anticipatory breach of contract

Where one party to a contract tells another that it does not intend to honour its terms at some future date, the "innocent" party can elect to treat that statement as an "anticipatory breach of contract." He can thus elect to accept the repudiation of contract or to sue for damages without waiting for the breach to occur. In the context of a business transfer, such an anticipatory breach might arise where the purchaser tells a transferring employee that he will be employed on lesser terms and conditions once the transfer has taken place—see *Batchelor* v. *Premier Motors* [1982] (unreported C.O.I.T. 1359/181).

For such a claim to succeed, the employee must show both that:

1. he has a contract with the purchaser, and
2. the purchaser has evinced a firm intention to break the contract at some time in the future.

In some cases, the employee may face a problem demonstrating that he has a contract with the purchaser—since no contract will exist until regulation 5(1) operates to transfer his contract of employment from the vendor to the purchaser. However it may be possible for him to argue that an anticipatory breach arises if he has been told by the purchaser that his contract will definitely be transferred over with the business. The employee may also find an obstacle in persuading a court or tribunal that the purchaser had evinced a firm intention to break his contract—the purchaser may argue that his statement to vary the employee's terms and conditions was only a proposal to which, it was hoped, the vendor would agree.

11 THE PRACTICAL APPROACH

Introduction

So far, this book has dealt with the employment law implications and liabilities arising out of business and sale transfers. The Transfer Regulations have had the effect of creating additional employment law problems which the parties to a business transfer have dealt with by negotiation. If a purchaser of a business does not want to take on the vendor's employees, he has either to persuade the vendor to dismiss them ahead of the moment of transfer or decide that the additional liabilities he will inherit by virtue of the Transfer Regulations make the transaction no longer an attractive one to pursue. The issue whether or not to dismiss the vendor's employees is not such a difficult one as who is to pick up the legal and compensation liabilities arising from those dismissals (*e.g.* the redundancy pay, unfair dismissal compensation and damages for wrongful dismissal). In other words, having established that there is an imminent or contingent liability, the vendor and purchaser must decide who will bear it. This is often done either by an adjustment in the purchase price or by way of indemnities [see pp. 162 and 190 below].

Potential sources of problems

Practical experience suggests that parties to a business transfer are likely to find that most of the problems in respect of the employment aspects of the transaction have their roots in one or more of the following five sources

Lack of knowledge

The purchaser needs to know exactly what employment law liabilities he is taking on—*i.e.* the nature of the vendor's workforce, the numbers employed and their jobs, the employment cost, details of those unions recognised in respect of them, etc. The vendor also needs to know about the purchaser's intentions regarding those employees to be transferred—*e.g.* whether he intends to make redundancies or change their terms and conditions of employment.

Changes

Since the prime purpose of the Transfer Regulations is to transfer to the purchaser those employees working in the business together with their existing terms and conditions (except for pensions), the more changes the purchaser wants to make in connection with the business transfer, the greater the employment law liability. This will especially be the case where the purchaser requires the vendor to effect those changes ahead of the date of the business transfer.

Lack of time

In most business and share transfers, there is insufficient time for the vendor to meet its employment law obligations to its employees and trade unions—*e.g.* redundancy consultations and looking for alternative employment, or to give due notice of termination of employment.

The "purity" of employment law

Seeing the transfer in its commercial context

It is important to remember that the employment law liabilities (especially those created by the Transfer Regulations) are merely part of the commercial equation which makes up the costs incurred in a business transfer. It may be that the purchaser requires the vendor to dismiss certain employees in circumstances such that the dismissals are sure to be unfair and wrongful. But the vendor may consider that the compensation and damages liability flowing from such dismissals still make the purchase price very attractive. Similarly, the vendor may only be prepared to effect such dismissals required by the purchaser on the basis of a full indemnity. Yet the purchaser (having calculated his total contingent exposure to pay compensation or damages), may consider that the price he has to pay for the vendor's business is still good value in wider commercial terms.

This approach may seem a little callous. It is not suggested that employers should ride rough-shod over their employment law obligations. However these should be regarded in their proper commercial context. If employers treat their employment law obligations as inviolate principles, then they are likely to find either that the proposed business transfer collapses or their operational employment costs become unsustainable. In practice, employers should try to achieve change by agreement and within a reasonable timescale. However, if the circumstances do not permit this, the parties should then weigh up the cost of infringing employees' rights.

Negotiating weakness

Negotiating the terms of the transfer

In practice, the parties negotiate over who is to bear the cost of any employment law obligations. If the purchaser's negotiating position is strong (as is often the case where the vendor's business is trading unprofitably), the vendor may find himself in a weak position to resist the purchaser's demands that he make changes prior to the transfer date.

Steps in a share or business transfer

This chapter is concerned with the practical approach to dealing with the employment law aspects of a share or business transfer. It involves the following steps:

1. obtaining information from the other party;
2. making decisions;
3. warranties;
4. preconditions to completion of the transaction;
5. indemnities

6. anticipatory/preparatory steps.

Obtaining information—the purchaser

The importance of obtaining information

The common law maxim "*caveat emptor*" (buyer beware) applies to business and share transfers, just as much as in other transactions. It is therefore crucial that, as far as employment matters are concerned, the purchaser ascertains exactly what he is acquiring. If the weekly employment costs are higher than the purchaser had anticipated or, after the business transfer has been completed, he finds he has inherited a strike-prone workforce or a host of industrial tribunal cases or a series of potential equal pay claims, he cannot later complain or seek redress from the vendor unless he has protected himself by a warranty or indemnity. Therefore, as far as the purchaser is concerned, the information-seeking process prior to signing any contract is absolutely crucial. The results of that exercise will probably result in the purchaser asking for an adjustment in the purchase price, warranties or indemnities. Just as in the case of a house-purchase survey, its results may cause the purchaser to even reconsider whether it wishes to proceed with its proposed purchase or to require the vendor to rectify certain matters as a precondition of completion of the purchase.

The information-gathering exercise will also tell the purchaser to what extent, if any, he will have to make changes or take measures in respect of the transferring employees or his own employees. These changes may include redundancies, reorganisation of work or harmonisation of terms and conditions of employment. Where the purchaser recognises a trade union for either his own or the transferring employees, the decision to "take measures" in respect of them will operate the obligation to consult with that trade union under regulation 10 (and, possibly, under E.P.A., s.99)—see p. 177. In any event the purchaser will have to tell the vendor what, if any, measures it envisages taking in respect of the transferring employees and, if no measures are envisaged, then that fact (see regulation 10—p. 121). The purchaser will have to do the same in respect of those trade unions he recognises for his existing employees "affected" by the business transfer.

Methods of disclosure

There is no prescribed way this disclosure process has to be performed. However since liability under warranties and indemnities is usually linked to such disclosure the vendor will almost always provide it in written form in a disclosure letter. That way, there can be no dispute over whether or what the purchaser has been told by the vendor by way of disclosure. In practice, the purchaser's solicitors will serve a detailed list of questions on the vendor's solicitors. Many of these can be answered by the vendor simply sending copies of documents (*e.g.* a schedule containing employees' names, addresses, ages, start dates, salaries and notice periods; or copies of standard employment contracts and collective agreements, etc.). Other questions will need a specific written answer. Below is a list of topics/questions on employment issues about which the purchaser may request information, depending on the circumstances of the transaction. It must be stressed that in some cases, the purchaser will only want, or the vendor only has time to give, the bare minimum amount of information. In others, some of the topics listed below are not matters about which the purchaser is concerned. The list is therefore a collection of items, some of which will be relevant and others not.

Details of employees

1. Names and addresses
2. Birth dates
3. Date of start of continuous service
4. Salaries
5. Other earnings (*e.g.* commissions, bonuses, etc.)
6. Normal working hours per week
7. Participation in other employment benefit schemes (*e.g.* BUPA, P.H.I., life assurance, pension, company cars or car allowance, etc.)
8. Whether director status
9. Notice entitlement
10. Job titles and grade.

Commentary. From these details the purchaser will be able to work out, amongst other things:

1. the financial entitlements of each employee;
2. who has unfair dismissal and redundancy pay rights;
3. the cost of making redundancies;
4. who may have to be removed as directors;
5. whether, and to what extent, harmonisation of terms and conditions will be necessary.

Breakdown of employee types

1. Numbers of hourly, weekly and monthly paid employees
2. The grading structure
3. Total employment costs
4. Numbers of temporary and part-time staff
5. Numbers and identity of "consultants," casual workers, "self-employed" workers, and trainees on Government training schemes
6. Salary structure for relevant grades.

Commentary. Details received on question 4 may reveal potential sex discrimination claims (*e.g.* if part-timers are treated less favourably than full-time employees). The answers to question 5 may reveal the existence of persons who, although categorised by the vendor as "self-employed" are nonetheless employees for the wide definition of the Transfer Regulations. In any event, the purchaser in a share sale will want to know of their existence.

Where the purchaser intends to merge the business he hopes to buy, with his existing operations, the grading and salary structure will identify potential problem areas in this respect.

Workforce profile

1. Ages of workforce

2. Ethnic breakdown of workforce (across jobs and grades)
3. Sex breakdown of workforce (across jobs and grades)

Commentary. The responses to these questions may highlight a potential race or sex discrimination problem. In addition a "top-heavy" workforce nearing retirement ages will forewarn the purchaser of a future loss of experienced staff.

Copies of employment contracts

What to look for in employees' contracts

The purchaser will want to have sight of these in respect of all levels of staff (including directors). These may come in several formats: formal contracts, letters, or a written statement of main terms and conditions of employment with cross-reference to works rules or an employee handbook or benefits manual. The purchaser may look out for the following:

1. Flexibility clauses in respect of hours of work, job functions, place of work, etc.;
2. Inventions and confidential information clauses;
3. Restrictive covenants;
4. Start and finish times of the working days;
5. Defects in the existing documentation (*e.g.* the absence of a clause giving the employer the right to make deductions from wages).

Commentary. The details of questions 1 and 4 are going to be very important where the purchaser plans job changes or a change of workplace or working hours to take effect after the business transfer has occurred. The answers to questions 2, 3 and 5 may reveal to the purchaser that it will have to offer revised contracts to the transferring employees. For example the effect of the business transfer may make the vendor's restrictive covenants too wide to be enforced by the purchaser.

Benefits schemes/policies

Assessing how conditions of employment may need to be changed

1. Holiday
2. Sick pay
3. Pensions
4. Company car policies or car/petrol allowances
5. Relocation
6. Maternity
7. Mortgage subsidy
8. Life assurance
9. Permanent health or disability or accident insurance
10. Redundancy (selection criteria and severance benefits).

Commentary. These details will indicate the extent to which the transferring employees' conditions of employment may need to be changed. Question 10 will be particularly important where there are to be redundancies before or after the transaction has taken place (especially where the purchaser has agreed to bear the cost of those redundancies by way of indemnity or operates different redundancy election criteria).

Senior executives

1. Copies of service contracts

2. Copies of confidentiality agreements
3. Details of special benefits (*e.g.* company flats and special bonus/share option schemes, etc).

Bonus or profit share schemes/commissions

1. Copies of prevailing and proposed bonus/profit share and commission schemes
2. Details of individual employees' earnings under these schemes in last three years and projected earnings for current year
3. Details of any discretionary bonuses paid in last three years.

Stock option schemes

1. Details and copies of all stock option schemes
2. Details and copies of all grants of options made

Pensions

1. Copies of all pension schemes (including employee booklets, trust deed and rules)
2. Names of all members of (each) scheme
3. Whether a contracting-out certificate is in force
4. Details of employee representation on pensions committee and identity of trustees.

Trade union presence

1. Identities of all recognised unions
2. Extent of recognition afforded (*e.g.* any excluded matters?)
3. Copies of all collective agreements
4. Details of any "*de facto*" closed shops or sole bargaining arrangements
5. Full details of all agreements, arrangements and "understandings" between the vendor and trade unions (*e.g.* working practices, redundancy terms, flexible manning, etc.)
6. Trade union facilities afforded
7. Presence of staff associations
8. Approximate strength of union membership.

Industrial disputes

Summary of all official and unofficial disputes in the last five years including the following details:

1. Cause of dispute
2. Settlement reached
3. Categories of employee and the union(s) involved
4. Number of man-days lost in each dispute
5. Type of industrial action taken in each dispute (*e.g.* strike, go-slow, work-to-rule, etc.).

Arbitration/mediation awards

1. Details of all arbitration or mediation awards affecting transferring employees

2. Whether such awards have been implemented or are still in effect.

Areas of dispute

1. Details of each current or anticipated dispute with trade unions
2. Which unions are involved
3. Nature of dispute
4. Current state of negotiations
5. Concessions made to date to the union during negotiations
6. Proposed settlement plans
7. Proposals for pay increases or improvements in benefits for next annual pay negotiations (including details of any formal and informal commitments or "understandings" already given to trade unions
8. Details of any current disputes or of any matters which could give rise to a dispute by any trade union.

Wages councils

1. Whether any of the transferring employees are covered by a Wages Council;
2. If so, which Wages Council?
3. Which employees are so covered?

Redundancy arrangements

1. Copies of any redundancy agreements, and details of redundancy arrangements or "understandings" with trade unions
2. Redundancy selection criteria agreed or operated by custom and practice
3. Details of all redundancy programmes over the last five years (*e.g.* types of employee involved, timescale, numbers involved, basis of selection, redundancy payments made)
4. Redundancy pay terms (in excess of statutory redundancy pay)
5. Details of any proposed redundancies.

Personal commitments given to individual employees

1. Details of any particular commitments given to individual employees which are personal variations to the vendor's standard conditions of employment (*e.g.* a promise that a workplace mobility clause will not be implemented in their case or special start and finish times)
2. Identities of those employees concerned.

Directors

1. Names of all executive and non-executive directors
2. Details of all director's fees paid in last five years and due to be paid in current year
3. Details of all directors' other interests (*e.g.* other directorships, interests in other companies).

Sex and race discrimination

1. Details of any non-discrimination notices issued or formal investigations existing or threatened by the C.R.E. or E.O.C.
2. Details of any equal opportunities policies
3. Copies of any Industrial Tribunal Awards or Recommendations relating to sex or race discrimination in the last five years
4. Details of any job evaluation exercise carried out affecting the transferring employees.

Health and safety

1. Details of the health and safety policy
2. Details of any health and safety committees or safety representatives
3. Details of any health and safety matters brought to the vendor's attention by safety representatives, safety committees, factory inspectors and individual employees in the last five years and the steps taken thereon
4. Details of any health and safety or personal injury claims in the last five years
5. Details of any adverse reports from factory inspectors (including the issue of prohibition or improvement notices).

Salary reviews

1. Frequency of salary reviews (when and how often)
2. Previous undertakings or understandings about future salary reviews
3. Current state of any negotiations on salary reviews
4. Basis upon which salaries are reviewed (*e.g.* cost of living, merit, changed responsibilities, incremental?)

Lay-off and guarantee pay

1. Details of current contractual rights and collective agreements on lay-offs and short-time working
2. Details of previous periods of lay-off and short-time working over the last five years
3. Pay obligations for employees laid off or on short-time working.

Outstanding employment litigation

Full details of all existing, pending, threatened litigation, and of all matters which could give rise to such litigation, on the following types of claim:

1. Industrial Tribunal (*e.g.* unfair dismissal, redundancy pay, sex or race discrimination, equal pay, or any other claims under employment protection legislation
2. County court or High Court litigation (*e.g.* for wrongful dismissal, breach of contract enforcing or resisting breach of restrictive covenant, inducement to breach a contract)

3. Claims against trade unions (*e.g.* under E.P.A., s.99 or seeking an injunction to restrain unlawful industrial action)
4. Claims made by a trade union to the C.A.C. (*e.g.* for disclosure of information
5. Litigation with existing and former employees over intellectual property rights (*e.g.* patents, copyright, designs, etc.) including applications to the Comptroller of Patents.
6. All claims and applications relating to health and safety and personal injury (and details of all incidents which could give rise to such a claim)
7. Details of all judgments against the vendor and in favour of an employee by any court or tribunal or arbitrator in the last five years
8. Details of all dismissals made by the vendor in the 12 months preceding the transfer date.

Commentary. The details in 8 above are necessary to enable the purchaser to assess whether there have been any dismissals connected with the business transfer for which he may inherit liability, notwithstanding that those persons have ceased to be employees—see the *Litster* case (p. 55).

Disciplinary and grievance policies/procedures

1. Full details of each of these (including whether they form part of employment contracts)
2. Names of persons who have currently implemented the grievance or disciplinary appeals procedures and the nature of each grievance or appeal.

Dual employment

1. Details of those employees who work under two or more employment contracts
2. Copies of those other employment contracts
3. Details of time spent on each such contract.

Maternity and other leave

1. The names and addresses of those persons (existing and former employees) who are on maternity leave and have reserved their right to return to work
2. The names and addresses of those employees on unpaid or other leave of absence.

Obtaining information—vendor

Importance of obtaining information for the vendor

Although the "*caveat emptor*" rule does not, of course, apply to a vendor, he does nonetheless have two reasons for wanting to obtain information. First, he will normally be giving warranties to the purchaser that certain facts are true (*e.g.* in the disclosure letter), and will want to ensure that these warranties are correct and can be supported. In this respect the vendor will be making internal inquiries within its own business.

Secondly the vendor will want to ask the purchaser for information for two reasons:

1. to comply with his obligation to inform recognised trade unions of any measures which the purchaser envisages taking in respect of the transferring employees, and
2. to protect himself in the event that the purchaser asks him to take any measures prior to the transfer (*e.g.* to dismiss staff).

In addition, the vendor will no doubt want to be in a position to answer the many inquiries from those employees to be transferred about the purchaser. Below is a list of matters upon which the vendor may ask the purchaser for information.

Measures to be taken by purchaser

1. Proposed post-transfer redundancies?
2. Changes in terms and conditions of employment (*e.g.* what is to happen regarding pensions?)
3. Changes in workplace, working hours or job duties?

Pre-transfer redundancies

In some transactions, the purchaser may require the vendor to make all or some of its employees redundant prior to the moment of transfer. In respect of such redundancies the vendor will want to know of the purchaser:

1. Who is to be made redundant
2. The basis of redundancy selection
3. The timescale for the redundancies to take effect
4. Any suitable vacancies in the purchaser's existing business for otherwise redundant employees.

Collective bargaining arrangements

The vendor's trade unions may be concerned about the purchaser's attitude towards trade unions and whether it recognises other trade unions in respect of the same class of workers.

Directors

In many cases of business transfers and in some share transfers, the purchaser may wish to replace certain directors.

Stock options/profit share/pensions

Transferring employees may be concerned about the effect of the business transfer on their stock options, profit-share and pension schemes.

Decisions—for the purchaser

Once the purchaser has obtained a picture of what he is acquiring (in an employment context), certain decisions have to be made. These include the following:

Redundancies

1. Are all the vendor's employees to be transferred over?

2. If not, who is not to be transferred?
3. How are the non-transferring employees to be selected and by whom?
4. Are there to be redundancies after the transaction has been completed?
5. If so, how are the redundancy selections to be made (*i.e.* using the vendor's or the purchaser's selection criteria)?
6. What is the timing for the redundancies either *post* or *ante* the business transfer?
7. Who is to bear the cost of those redundancies?

Union organisation

1. Is the union still to be recognised?
2. Are collective agreements still to be honoured?
3. How do the vendor's trade unions fit into the purchaser's existing collective bargaining structure and do changes have to be made?

Work organisation

1. Are the transferring employees to continue to do their existing jobs?
2. If not, what changes are there to be?
3. Are there to be changes in working hours?
4. Are there to be changes in workplace (*e.g.* the merger of two factories)?
5. What is to happen with regard to any restrictive practices or lack of job flexibility?
6. Is the vendor's business transferred to be operated as a separate and identifiable unit, or to be assimilated into the purchaser's existing organisation?

Terms and conditions of employment

1. Are the transferring employees to continue on their existing terms and conditions of employment?
2. If not, what changes are to be made?
3. What is to happen to pensions?
4. How is the purchaser to achieve variations to employment contracts (*e.g.* by "buy-out," offer of alternative package—see p. 131)?
5. When are these changes to be effected (*e.g.* prior to or after the transaction)?
6. Who is to effect these changes?
7. Is the transaction conditional upon either a fixed percentage of acceptances of conditional offers or upon certain key employees agreeing to transfer on revised terms and conditions?
8. Are any employees required to resign as a director?
9. Do any restrictive covenants need to be revised and, if so, whose and to what extent?
10. Do stock options have to be cancelled or bought out?
11. What is to happen to those employment schemes which, by their very nature, cannot be transferred?
12. Does the basis of calculating bonus or profit-share need to be changed, and if so, how?

13. Is the overall employment cost satisfactory?

Other measures

1. What are the social, economic, technical, organisational or legal implications for the purchaser's existing workforce and trade unions?
2. Do any changes have to be made for the purchaser's existing employees?
3. If so, what are they (*e.g.* redundancies, harmonisation of terms and conditions, reorganisation of work, etc.)?
4. When can the relevant trade unions be told of the proposed transfer?

Inherited liabilities

Whether the proposed transaction is a share or business transfer, are there any liabilities which the purchaser will inherit from the vendor which he is not prepared to bear—*e.g.*

1. existing, threatened or pending litigation?
2. commitment made to trade unions?
3. the cost of redundancy dismissals?

Decisions—for the vendor

There are, in effect, many fewer decisions which the vendor has to take; and, in any event, those decisions which may arise will often be a reaction to the purchaser's proposed course of action. The vendor's decisions on employment matters may include the following:

The vendor's remaining business needs

1. Does it wish to retain certain employees?
2. If so, which ones?
3. How are these to be retained (*e.g.* in which jobs)?
4. Are redundancies needed from the vendor's remaining workforce, as a result of the business transfer? If so, what is the timing of these?
5. Does the vendor's remaining business need reorganisation (*e.g.* hours of work, job content, or place of work) arising from the sale of part of its business, and if so, what changes are required?

The vendor's response to the purchaser's proposals

1. Is the vendor prepared to make redundancies required by the purchaser ahead of the business transfer?
2. If so, is the vendor prepared to pick up all or some of the costs of those redundancies?
3. Is the vendor prepared to select employees for redundancy on the basis chosen by the purchaser?
4. Is the vendor prepared to bear the cost of any unfair

dismissal compensation awarded to dismissed employees where the unfairness arose out of the purchaser's selection or timing requirements?
5. Is the vendor prepared to co-operate in any pre-transfer changes in terms and conditions of employment for the transferring employees, and if so, to what extent?
6. Is there to be a transfer payment out of the vendor's pension scheme, and if so, how much and how does it affect the funding for the vendor's remaining employees?

Warranties

Importance of warranties

As a general rule, most of the warranties are given by the vendor to the purchaser. There are, in effect, representations that certain statements or information given by the vendor to the purchaser are true and accurate at the time given. These are contained in the share or business transfer agreement, often in a detailed schedule. Much of the detail is contained in a disclosure letter which is incorporated into the transfer agreement by cross-reference.

Since the warranties form part of the share or business transfer agreement, if they turn out to be inaccurate, the recipient of the defective warranty (usually the purchaser) will have a claim for damages against its giver (*e.g.* usually the vendor). It is therefore absolutely crucial that the party giving the warranty is quite certain that the statements warranted are true and accurate at the relevant time. Where there is some doubt, the party giving the warranty might give it on a qualified basis.

Warranties of fact

What are warranties of fact?

These warranties are that certain facts exist at the relevant date. There will be cross-reference to a disclosure letter or a schedule of details. These documents will bring to the purchaser's attention various facts and omissions often by incorporating copies of other documents (*e.g.* service or employment contracts, or pension schemes, a schedule of details about individual employees, copies of collective agreements). For example, a warranty of fact may state that there are no employees with service contracts and no collective agreements other than those indicated in, and attached to, the disclosure letter. Therefore if the vendor has overlooked something which should have been disclosed in the disclosure letter, he will be in breach of warranty. It is for this reason that the information-gathering exercise described above is so important. Examples of typical warranties given by the vendor are included in Appendix B on p. 182. They may often cover the following areas (depending on the circumstances):

Areas commonly covered by warranties

1. union recognition and collective bargaining arrangements
2. employees' details
3. terms and conditions of employment
4. industrial action
5. existing, threatened or pending litigation and matters which could give rise to litigation

6. identification of employees
7. consultancy and other "personal services" contracts
8. offers of employment made
9. persons on maternity leave
10. payment of all taxes and N.I. contributions and obligations to employees
11. E.O.C./C.R.E. formal investigations or non-discrimination notices, or industrial tribunal recommendations
12. issue of all notices under the Social Security Pensions Act 1975.

It will be noticed that the giving of some warranties necessitates the vendor taking certain action to ensure that they are true and accurate as at the relevant date. For example, a warranty may state that only those employees listed in Schedule X are employees of the vendor's business as at the relevant date. This may necessitate the vendor taking steps to ensure that its employees not named in Schedule X are removed from the business to be transferred (*e.g.* either by dismissal or redeployment to another part of the vendor's remaining business operations).

In some circumstances, the purchaser might require the vendor to warrant that its reasons for the dismissal of its employees connected with the business transfer is an "economic, technical or organisational one entailing changes in the workforce".

See Appendix B p. 182 for areas where the vendor might consider asking for a warranty.

Warranties of action/inaction

As well as requiring warranties as to facts, the purchaser may also want the vendor to warrant in addition that he will not do certain things, or to undertake to do certain things, by the contract completion date. This will arise where contracts are exchanged on one day and completed several weeks later. The purchaser will want to make sure that the vendor does not do anything which will incur the purchaser with unforeseen liabilities prior to completion. These warranties include that the vendor will:

1. not offer employment to or dismiss anyone or treat anyone unfavourably without the purchaser's consent
2. not vary terms or conditions of employment without the purchaser's consent
3. make representations about the proposed share or business transfer except in terms agreed with the purchaser (*e.g.* draft letters are often attached to the agreement)
4. comply with its obligations to consult and inform trade unions under E.P.A., s.99 or regulation 10 Transfer Regulations
5. effect certain named redundancies, or changes in terms and conditions of employment of the transferring employees
6. deliver prescribed letters to the transferring employees
7. do anything likely to represent a material change in the matters set out in the disclosure letter.

See Appendix B p. 182 for sample wording of these and other warranty clauses.

The vendor may also require such pro-active or restrictive warranties from the purchaser (usually the latter)—*e.g.* that the purchaser will not offer employment to certain employees for a specified period (normally at least three months). See Appendix B p. 182 for examples of these.

Preconditions to completion

Conditions attached to completion

In some share or business transfers, the purchaser will make it a condition precedent to the completion of the transaction that certain matters are rectified or objectives are met. These may cover some of the same ground as warranties of a pro-active nature (see above). However the difference is that in the case of a breach of warranty, the purchaser will normally be looking to damages as his prime remedy—*i.e.* he still wants the business but requires compensation for the unforeseen liability. In comparison, where a condition precedent has not been met, then the whole transaction falls through and the purchaser may sue for damages (unless the parties agree otherwise). Condition precedents might include the following issues:

1. the vendor effecting specified dismissals prior to the moment of completion of the transaction
2. the vendor obtaining employees' consents to specified revisions in their employment contracts (*e.g.* restrictive covenants or certain bonus schemes)
3. a specified number of the vendor's employees (or key persons) agreeing to the purchaser's conditional offers of employment (see p. 186)
4. the vendor agreeing with the union the removal of certain restrictive practices or revised working arrangements.

It is unusual for employment matters to form part of the conditions precedent, since they are unlikely to be such that the purchaser will want to change his mind about buying the business. He will normally prefer to protect himself from liabilities by way of warranty and indemnity.

Indemnities

Significance of indemnities

In some cases, the parties cannot precisely cost a liability, or a particular liability may be contingent (*e.g.* upon a dismissed employee winning an unfair dismissal claim. Where the parties to a share or business transfer identify an actual or contingent liability (or a risk of one), they will decide between themselves who is to bear the cost. For example, the purchaser may insist that the vendor makes certain employees redundant ahead of the transfer date. This may produce an immediate liability for the vendor of:

1. damages for wrongful dismissal or pay in lieu of notice

2. statutory redundancy pay and, in some cases, contractual redundancy pay.

It will also produce a contingent liability for compensation for unfair dismissal—*e.g.* if an industrial tribunal finds the dismissal was unfair because of the basis of selection or the manner of dismissal (*e.g.* lack of advance warning or consultation). It may also produce a contingent liability for a protective award under E.P.A., s.99 (see p. 177) where there has been insufficient union consultation.

During negotiations the purchaser and vendor will agree which of them picks up the costs of these liabilities and make provision for it either by adjusting the purchase price accordingly or by way of an indemnity. Commonly the contingent liabilities are covered in the indemnity.

Samples of standard indemnity clauses are set out in Appendix B p. 191. However it must be noted that these have to be drafted to reflect accurately what the parties have agreed. It has been seen earlier in this book how the Transfer Regulations have created new liabilities (especially for the purchaser of a business). Indemnities are simply the commercial solution to the relevant employment law problems. The issues which may come to bear on the scope of an indemnity include the following:

Negotiating indemnities

1. Who bears the cost of contractual and statutory redundancy pay?
2. Who bears the cost of damages for wrongful dismissal or pay in lieu of notice and how is mitigation of loss to be catered for?
3. Who bears the cost of any unfair dismissal claims—and does the indemnity cover the whole compensation awarded or just the basic or compensatory (or additional or special) awards?
4. Who bears the cost of other claims (*e.g.* sex or race discrimination or under E.P.A., s.99 or regulation 10 Transfer Regulations)?
5. Will the vendor indemnify the purchaser for redundancy pay and notice pay in respect of dismissals effected up to (for example) three months after the transfer date?
6. Will the purchaser indemnify the vendor for dismissals insisted upon by the purchaser and which are unfair because of the reason or selection imposed by the purchaser (in such cases the indemnity might be limited to the compensatory award only)?
7. Are the parties to share the liability and, if so, in what proportions?
8. Who picks up the liability for litigation, the material facts of which occurred prior to the transfer date?
9. In cases of share transfers, who bears the costs of unsuccessful litigation by former employees?
10. Who will receive the benefit of any redundancy rebate (if payable?)
11. Is the purchaser to be indemnified by the vendor from claims by the vendor's existing or former employees who do not transfer to his employment?

What should the indemnities cover?

It should also be remembered that the indemnities should cover all costs, expenses and financial consequences arising out of the contingent liability concerned. There may be cases where the purchaser or vendor is quite confident that if such a claim is brought, he will be successful in defending it. However he may incur considerable legal costs and management time in doing so. The indemnities should therefore cover these financial consequences.

Sums held in escrow

Where the purchaser is concerned over the vendor's future ability to pay out under an indemnity, he might require that a specified sum is held in escrow in the joint names of their respective solicitors for a fixed period of time to fund such claims. However where the vendor is a receiver or liquidator, he might be unwilling to give any indemnity or warranties at all. Thus the purchaser will have to rely of the extent of information he has gleaned from the information-gathering exercise. The purchaser may therefore decide to require the liquidator/receiver to hive down the business from the employees and then require their dismissals ahead of the business or share transfer taking place.

APPENDIX A

This Appendix contains a summary of the basic law on redundancy pay, redundancy consultations with recognised trade unions and unfair dismissal. Space does not permit a more exhaustive explanation. It should therefore be remembered that there are various exceptions and qualifications to the law summarised below.

Redundancy pay

Entitlement to statutory redundancy pay is governed by sections 81 to 120 of the E.P.C.A. 1978.

Entitlement to claim

A person can only claim statutory redundancy pay if he is an employee—*i.e.* he must work under a contract of employment (E.P.C.A., s.153(1)). It should be noted that this definition of an "employee" is narrower than the definition under the Transfer Regulations (see p. 53). An employee must also satisfy all the following criteria—*i.e.* he:

1. has two or more years of continuous employment (E.P.C.A., s.81(4));
2. ordinarily works inside Great Britain (E.P.C.A., s.141(3)), unless on the relevant date he is inside Great Britain in accordance with instructions given to him by his employer (E.P.C.A., s.141(4));
3. is not aged 65 or over (or 60 years, in the case of a woman, although this distinction is to be removed by the Employment Bill 1989 and put on a similar basis for unfair dismissal (see p. 170, para. 7) (E.P.C.A., s.82(1));
4. is not engaged in one of the occupations excluded by the E.P.C.A.—*e.g.* certain seafarers, dockers, etc. (E.P.C.A., ss.144/145);
5. has not waived his right to claim on the expiry of a fixed-term contract of at least two years' duration (E.P.C.A., s.142(4)), or under a severance agreement conciliated by ACAS (E.P.C.A., s.140(2));
6. has been dismissed within the statutory definition of dismissal—*i.e.* direct termination by the employer (either with or without notice), or the expiry of a fixed-term contract without being renewed, or constructive dismissal (*i.e.* where the employee resigns because of his employer's repudiatory breach of contract) (E.P.C.A., s.83);
7. has lodged his claim with the industrial tribunal within six months of his effective date of termination.

Meaning of redundancy

An employee is only entitled to statutory redundancy pay if his dismissal is "wholly or mainly attributable" to a redundancy situation. Section 81(2) of the E.P.C.A. defines in very precise terms what circumstances can constitute a redundancy. It should be noted that if the circumstances of an employee's dismissal do not fall within the statutory definition, he is not entitled to redundancy pay. Section 81(2) provides that a redundancy occurs where:

> "(a) . . . his employer has ceased, or intends to cease, to carry on the business for the purposes of which the employee was employed by him, or has ceased or intends to cease, to carry on that business in the place where the employee was so employed, or
> (b) the requirements of that business for employees to carry out work of a particular kind, or for employees to carry out work of a particular kind in the place where he was so employed, have ceased or diminished, or are expected to cease or diminish."

It is clear that, for the purposes of ascertaining whether there has been a cessation or diminution, regard may be had to "the business of the employer together with the businesses of associated employers" (E.P.C.A., s.81(2)). A redundancy situation may also occur whether the cessation or diminution referred to in the statutory definition occurs on a temporary or permanent basis.

When applying this statutory test of redundancy, industrial tribunals are required to examine whether there has been a reduction in the *number of employees* needed to undertake particular work, and not simply whether the actual workload has diminished. In addition, when identifying "work of a particular kind," regard is had not only to the work which the employee is actually doing, but also to work which he can be required to do under his employment contract—see *Nelson* v. *BBC* [1977] I.C.R. 649; C.A. and *Cowen* v. *Haden* [1983] I.C.R. 1; E.A.T. Therefore, if under the terms of an employee's contract of employment, he can be required to do a wide range of duties, there will be no redundancy if his employer wishes to run down a product line on which the employee works and transfer him to another product line (within the scope of his contract). Case law has established the following guidelines in ascertaining whether circumstances constitute a redundancy within the scope of E.P.C.A., s.81(2):

1. Employers do not normally have to justify their announcement of a redundancy nor prove that it is an economically correct decision—see *Moon & Others* v. *Homeworthy Furniture (Northern) Ltd.* [1976] I.R.L.R. 298; E.A.T. The numbers of employees needed to run a business efficiently is a matter for the employer to decide; however in some cases tribunals may expect employers to show that they came to their business decision based on reasonable information—see *Orr* v. *Vaughan* [1981] I.R.L.R. 63; E.A.T.
2. A business requirement that the same volume of work is done by fewer employees does constitute a redundancy

situation—see *Sutton* v. *Revlon Overseas Corporation Ltd.* [1973] I.R.L.R. 72; C.A. and *Carry All Motors Ltd.* v. *Pennington* [1980] I.C.R. 806; E.A.T.

3. The sub-contracting of work to a third party will normally be a redundancy situation (as will be the surrender of a licence or franchise, etc.)—see *Bromby & Hoare Ltd.* v. *Evans & Another* [1972] I.T.R. 76; N.I.R.C.
4. The word "requirements" should be construed in an operational context, rather than the ideal needs of the business (if money was no object)—see *A.U.T.* v. *University of Newcastle* [1987] I.C.R. 317.
5. Reorganisations of working hours will not normally fit into the statutory definition of redundancy, if the same number of employees are required to do the work. This is because the employer's needs for employees remains the same, but all that changes is the time of day when such work is performed—see *Johnson* v. *Notts Combined Police Authority* [1974] 1 W.L.R. 358; C.A.
6. A reorganisation involving a substantial change in the particular kind of work to be done, can result in a redundancy situation even though the employer continues to need the same number of employees. This might arise where an employer changes its equipment and needs employees with different skills to operate the new equipment—see *Murphy* v. *Epsom College* [1984] I.R.L.R. 271; C.A.
7. A sale of a business or part of a business can constitute a redundancy (see *Chapman & Another* v. *CPS Computer Group* [1987] I.R.L.R. 462; C.A.)—although the Transfer Regulations may operate to prevent there from being a dismissal (see p. 48).
8. A relocation of workplace will constitute a redundancy situation where the employer has no contractual right to relocate that employee—see *Air Canada* v. *Lee* [1978] I.C.R. 1202; E.A.T.

Suitable alternative employment

An employee will forfeit his redundancy pay if he unreasonably refuses an offer of suitable alternative employment made by his employer, an associated employer, or a successor to his employer (see E.P.C.A., ss.82(3) & 94). However such an offer must be made before the employee's contract terminates and the new job must start within four weeks of that date. Sections 82(4) & 84 of the E.P.C.A. provide for a four-week statutory trial period during which the employee maintains his right to statutory redundancy pay provided he reasonably resigns from the new job before the trial period has expired. If he either resigns unreasonably during the trial period, or he resigns (whether reasonably or not) after the trial period has expired, he will forfeit his right to redundancy pay. Similarly he will lose his redundancy pay if he unreasonably refuses to take up the job on a trial basis.

When assessing whether an employee has unreasonably refused an offer of suitable alternative employment, tribunals look at both the suitability of the job offered and the individual employee's reasons for rejecting it. The suitability of a job will usually be reflected in the wages, terms and conditions, working environment, job duties and responsibilities, etc. The suitability of the job has to be assessed in relation to the employee as an individual.

Where a tribunal is satisfied that a job offer is suitable, the employee will be at risk of forfeiting his redundancy pay unless he can satisfy the tribunal that his reasons for refusing it are reasonable. The reasonableness of a refusal may vary depending on individual circumstances. For example, a redundancy situation may arise from an office relocation. The address of the new office might involve roughly the same mileage for employee A to travel to work, but represent a substantial increase for employee B. In such a case, employee A's refusal will be regarded as unreasonable (and so he will forfeit his redundancy pay), but employee B's refusal will be regarded as reasonable. Different employees will have varying domestic situations which may impact differently on the reasonableness of their refusals.

Calculation of redundancy pay

Entitlement to redundancy pay is based on a sliding scale which takes into account age, length of continuous service and gross salary. The calculation formula is contained in E.P.C.A., Sched. 4 and it allocates a specified multiplier of a "week's pay" in respect of each complete year of continuous employment:

1. Each complete year in which the employee was not below age 41—one-and-a-half weeks' pay
2. Each complete year the employee was not below age 22—one week's pay
3. Each complete year the employee was not in categories 1. or 2.—half a week's pay.

Account is only taken of the last 20 years' service, although any period when an employee is aged under 18 is ignored for all purposes. The Dept. of Employment have published a "Ready Reckoner" (RPL 2 (Rev)) from which redundancy pay entitlement can easily be assessed. Examples of the application of the above formula include the following:

Age	Length of continuous employment	Gross weeks pay	Redundancy pay
28	3	£150	3 × £150 = £450
28	3	£300	3 × £172* = £516
46	10	£150	12.5 × £150 = £1875
46	10	£300	12.5 × £172* = £2149
23	5	£150	3 × £150 = £450
23	5	£200	3 × £172 = £516

* It should be noted that there is a ceiling on a "week's pay," currently at £172. This is uplifted annually with effect from April each year.

Schedule 4 also contains a rule whereby an employee's redundancy pay is reduced by one-twelfth for each complete month he is aged over 64 or she is aged over 59. The Employment Bill 1989 will remove this difference, so that women are put on the same basis as men.

Miscellaneous

It is also possible for an employee to claim statutory redundancy pay after prolonged periods of lay-off or short-time working (see E.P.C.A., ss.87–89). The procedure is particularly complex and is not dealt with in this book. There are also statutory provisions covering the following situations:

1. where employees seek to leave early prior to the expiry of their redundancy notice (E.P.C.A., s.85);
2. where employees are dismissed for striking or gross misconduct within their obligatory notice periods (E.P.C.A., ss.82(2) & 92);
3. employees' entitlement to paid time off during working hours to look for other work (E.P.C.A., s.31).

Unfair dismissal

There is a very substantial body of case law dealing with dismissals other than in the context of a business transfer, which cannot be covered in this book for reasons of space. Therefore the summary of unfair dismissal law below is limited to dismissals arising out of a business transfer.

Entitlement to claim

A person has the right not to be unfairly dismissed only if he is an employee—*i.e.* someone who works under a contract of employment (see E.P.C.A., s.153(1)). He must also satisfy the following conditions:

1. he has two years' continuous employment (in all cases except where the dismissal is concerned with union membership, union activity or non-membership of a union—where there is no qualifying period of employment) (E.P.C.A., s.64(1)(*a*));
2. he ordinarily works inside Great Britain (E.P.C.A., s.141 (2));
3. he is not engaged in one of the occupations excluded from unfair dismissal legislation—*e.g.* certain seafarers, fishermen (paid by a share of the profits) dock workers, etc. (see E.P.C.A., ss.144 & 145);
4. he was not employed under a fixed-term contract of at least one year and he had agreed to waive his rights to claim unfair dismissal on the expiry of that fixed term (E.P.C.A., s.142(1));
5. he has not waived his right to claim unfair dismissal under a settlement agreement conciliated by ACAS (E.P.C.A., s.140(2));
6. he has established that he has been "dismissed" within the scope of E.P.C.A., s.55(2)—*i.e.* either directly dismissed

by his employer with or without notice, or on the expiry of a fixed-term contract without being renewed under the same contract, or constructive dismissal (*i.e.* because of his employer's repudiatory breach of contract);

7. he is not older than (a) the normal (unisex) retirement age for employees of the same description or, (b) where there is no such normal retirement age, 65 years of age (E.P.C.A., s.64(1)(*b*)).

Reasons for dismissal

Unfair dismissal legislation requires an employer to prove that its reason for dismissing the employee in question is one of those permitted under E.P.C.A., s.57(1) and s.57(2). These are: misconduct, redundancy, capability (which includes poor performance, sickness or lack of qualifications), statutory ban (*e.g.* lack of a work permit) and "some other substantial reason of a kind justifying dismissal in the circumstances." This last category is a "catch-all" for those reasons for dismissal which do not quite fit into the first four categories. As such, it is very wide in scope. The onus of proving the reason for the dismissal lies with the employer. To discharge this burden the employer must show, on the balance of probabilities, that the principal reason which activated the decision to dismiss was the one relied on and that it is capable of justifying a dismissal.

Fairness—general principles

Most unfair dismissal cases turn on this issue. Once the employer has established that it has a potentially fair reason for dismissing the employee, the industrial tribunal will then consider whether the employer's decision to dismiss was fair in all the circumstances (taking into account the size and administrative resources of the employer)—see E.P.C.A., s.57 (3). Although, strictly speaking, the burden of proof on this "reasonableness test" is a neutral one, in practice employers are expected to make the running by producing evidence demonstrating that its decision to dismiss was reasonable in all the circumstances.

It is important to note that it is the employer's decision to dismiss that is tested for fairness, not whether or not the employee should feel hard done by. Industrial tribunals recognise that there is a "range of reasonable responses" or a "band of reasonableness" in respect of decisions to dismiss. Lord Denning M.R. put the position concisely in *British Leyland (U.K.) Ltd.* v. *Smith* [1981] I.R.L.R. 91; C.A. as follows:

> "The correct test is: was it reasonable for the employers to dismiss him? If no reasonable employer would have dismissed him, then the dismissal was unfair. But if a reasonable employer might have dismissed him, then the dismissal was fair. It must be remembered that in all these cases there is a band of reasonableness, within which one employer might reasonably take one view and another employer reasonably take another view. One would quite reasonably dismiss the man. The other would quite reasonably keep him on. Both views might be reasonable. If

it was quite reasonable to dismiss him, then the dismissal must be upheld as fair, even though some employers might not have dismissed him."

It is also now established that dismissals can be unfair on purely procedural grounds (*e.g.* for lack of warning or consultation with the employee)—see *Polkey* v. *A.E. Dayton Services Ltd.* [1987] I.R.L.R. 503; H.L. Employers cannot argue that any procedural failings would have made no difference to the decision to dismiss. In effect, this means that industrial tribunals must consider whether any procedural failings in themselves rendered the decision to dismiss unfair (see below).

In the context of a business transfer, dismissals are likely to arise in the following circumstances:

1. redundancies
2. reorganisation of the business
3. changing terms and conditions of employment.

Fairness—redundancy dismissals

It is possible for a dismissal to be unfair even though it is on grounds of redundancy. The unfairness can arise in two ways: redundancy selection and on procedural grounds. It should be noted that genuine redundancy dismissals will not fall foul of the regulation 8 "automatic unfairness" rule (see p. 93 above); although the tribunal will want to be satisfied that the redundancy dismissal was fair in all the circumstances.

Redundancy selection Under E.P.C.A., s.59, it is an automatically unfair dismissal if an employer selects a person for redundancy in either of the following two circumstances:

1. Where the selection is on grounds of a person's membership or non-membership of a trade union, or his participation in the activities of a trade union at an appropriate time (E.P.C.A., s.59(a)). In such a case enhanced levels of unfair dismissal compensation may be payable—*e.g.* up to three years' pay (see p. 176 below). In such a redundancy selection case, the employee must have the normal two years' qualifying service to bring an unfair dismissal claim.
2. Where the redundancy selection is made in contravention of an agreed procedure or customary arrangement dealing with how employees are to be selected (E.P.C.A., s.59(*b*)). The employer can only avoid a finding of automatic unfairness in such circumstances where it can justify the departure from the procedure or arrangement by pointing to "special reasons" for doing so. In practice, tribunals have construed this defence narrowly—*e.g.* to cover situations where an employer needs to retain special skills or experience, etc. There is an evidential onus upon the employer to show that there really were substantial special circumstances which justified its decision to depart from the agreed or customary selection criteria—see *Cross International* v. *Reid & Others* [1985] I.R.L.R. 387; E.A.T.

Both of these rules apply where it is shown that the

redundancy situation applies to one or more other employees in the same undertaking who held positions similar to that held by the complainant of unfair dismissal. For example in *Oxley* v. *Tarmac Roadstone Holdings Ltd.* [1975] I.R.L.R. 100; I.T., the employer owned two factories which were situated relatively near to each other. The two factories were closely linked since they shared a common works manager, bonus scheme, there was a degree of flexibility of labour between the two factories, and some of the employer's same products were manufactured at both factories. When the employer decided to close down one of these factories, it operated its customary "last in, first out" redundancy selection arrangement only for those employees working at the factory to be closed. The tribunal held that, since the two factories were so closely linked with each other, the proper "pool" for selection was both factories, and so the dismissals were automatically unfair.

Even though an employer has avoided the "automatic unfairness" rules under E.P.C.A., s.59, the tribunal will still need to be satisfied of the fairness of the dismissal in general terms under E.P.C.A., s.57(3). This is also the case where there are no existing agreed procedures or customary arrangements for redundancy selections. Of course, if the redundancy selection is automatically unfair under E.P.C.A., s.59, the tribunal cannot go on to consider the question of its fairness in general terms.

Tribunals expect employers to adopt redundancy selection criteria which are themselves fair, and which are fairly and objectively applied (*e.g.* length of service, or requisite skills and experience, etc.). In practice this requires an employer to make itself aware of the facts upon which it is going to apply the selection criteria (*e.g.* reasons for the employee's absence and details relating to an employee's skill and experience, when these are factors taken into account in the redundancy selection process). For example in *Bannister & Others* v. *Brasway Ltd.* [1983] unreported (C.O.I.T. 1377/49) I.T., the vendors of a business were required by the purchasers to make various redundancies. In fact the purchasers made the selections, but based on inaccurate information supplied by the vendors. The dismissals were held to be unfair.

When considering the fairness of redundancy selections, tribunals apply the "band of reasonableness" test—see *N.C. Watling & Co. Ltd.* v. *Richardson* [1978] I.C.R. 1049; E.A.T. However the onus is on the employer to show how, by whom and on what basis the redundancy selections were made—see *Bristol Channel Shiprepairers Ltd.* v. *O'Keefe* [1978] I.C.R. 691; E.A.T. and *Cox* v. *Wildt Mellor Bromley Ltd.* [1978] I.C.R. 736; E.A.T.

Where there is no agreed procedure or customary arrangements for redundancy selections, employers have a fair degree of flexibility in deciding both the criteria to be adopted and the "pool" of employees to whom the criteria are to be applied—see *Thomas & Betts Manufacturing Ltd.* v. *Harding* [1980] I.R.L.R. 25. Where there is a union recognised by the employer in respect of employees to be made redundant, tribunals may take into account whether there has been an attempt by the employer to agree the selection criteria with the union—*Williams* v. *Compair Maxam Ltd.* [1982] I.C.R. 156;

E.A.T. There is no legal obligation on an employer to agree this with a recognised union, although there may be pressing industrial relations reasons for doing so.

Tribunals also seem to have a predisposition towards length of service as a redundancy selection criterion. Although employers are free to adopt other redundancy selection criteria (subject to E.P.C.A., s.59), tribunals will expect employers to explain why those other criteria were chosen. In addition, where on the application of different selection criteria two employees are regarded as equal, tribunals will normally expect employers to retain the employee with the longer service.

"*Procedural unfairness.*" As a general rule, tribunals expect employers to handle their redundancy programmes in a fair way, and in accordance with the CIR's Code of Practice on Industrial Relations. The contents of the Code concerning redundancy dismissals have since been enshrined in case law from which the following "guideline" obligations on employers can be stated:

1. to give employees as much advance warning of impending redundancies as is reasonably practicable in the circumstances—see *Williams* v. *Compair Maxam* [1982] I.C.R. 156; E.A.T.;
2. to consult with employees about the impending redundancies—see *Freud* v. *Bentalls Ltd.* [1982] I.R.L.R. 443; E.A.T.;
3. to consult with trade unions (if recognised for the class of employees to be made redundant)—see the *Williams* v. *Compair Maxam* case [1982] I.C.R. 156; E.A.T.;
4. to offer employees available vacancies within their capabilities—see *Avonmouth Construction Co. Ltd.* v. *Shipway* [1979] I.R.L.R. 14; E.A.T.—in some circumstances, this obligation may extend to looking for vacancies in other companies within the group (especially where those other companies have a close connection with the employer or are located nearby)—see *Vokes Ltd.* v. *Bear* [1973] I.R.L.R. 363; N.I.R.C.

Advance warning. This obligation is obviously tempered by what is reasonable and practicable in the circumstances. In many cases the negotiations over a business transfer may be conducted in secrecy and so make it very difficult for the vendor to give very much by way of advance warning. This will especially be the case where exchange of contracts and completion take place on the same day. The reasonableness test, in effect, requires employers to do the best they can in such circumstances.

Consultations. Employers are expected to consult with individual employees on matters which concern them as individuals, and should not assume that the union has passed on to them details of all discussions with the union—see *Huddersfield Parcels Ltd.* v. *Sykes* [1981] I.R.L.R. 115; E.A.T. It is submitted that it is appropriate to discuss with a recognised union matters such as the reasons for redundancies, the timescale, the selection criteria, the numbers to be made redundant and the level of severance payments, etc. However, it is a matter for consultation with individual employees whether they are interested in other employment in the company or whether the employer has the right facts upon which to apply redundancy selection criteria. Therefore employers are well-advised to conduct the consultation process on these two levels. Where there is no union recognised, the consultation process with the individual employees will cover all the above topics.

Offers of alternative employment. Employers must look not only within their own organisations for available vacancies, but also within other companies within the same group, especially where these have close connections with the employer or are located nearby. It is important that employers are prepared to offer otherwise redundant employees any available job within their expertise or capabilities, even if of a lower status or with a lesser remuneration package. The unfairness in not offering such lesser jobs lies in the denial to the individual concerned of the opportunity in accepting it rather than facing unemployment. Therefore employers should not assume that an otherwise redundant employee would not accept such a lesser job.

Fairness—reorganisation dismissals

It is well-established that a dismissal arising out of a business reorganisation (other than in a redundancy) does constitute some other substantial reason justifying dismissal within the scope of E.P.C.A., s.57(1)(*b*). However, it must be remembered that, if the dismissal is connected with a business transfer, it must satisfy the requirements of regulation 8(2) Transfer Regulations—*i.e.* it must be an "economic, technical or organisational reason entailing changes in the workforce" (see p. 95 above). Most genuine reorganisations will face no difficulty falling within the ambit of those words, since they are aimed to cover exactly such circumstances—*e.g.* where the business reorganisation entails changes in job duties, place of work, hours of work, methods of working or new equipment or processes.

As with redundancy dismissals, a tribunal will still need to be satisfied that a dismissal is fair. When putting forward a business reorganisation as the reason justifying a dismissal, an employer must produce some evidence to demonstrate some business advantage arising from it (*e.g.* greater efficiency or reduction in overheads or an increase in profit margins, etc.)—see *Hollister* v. *N.F.U.* [1979] I.C.R. 452; C.A. However there is no obligation on employers to prove that the reorganisation is necessary. The factors which tribunals take into account on the question of the fairness of a reorganisation dismissal (whether a constructive or a direct dismissal) include the following:

1. whether the employer has the contractual right to make the changes and its reasons for doing so;
2. the employee's reasons for refusing to go along with the changes;
3. advance warning of implementation of the changes;
4. negotiations with recognised trade unions in an attempt to agree the changes;
5. consultation with employees of the changes and an attempt to accommodate any reasonable refusals to go along with them;

6. the timescale of the implementation of the changes;
7. the possibility of offering other jobs to employees who have good grounds for resisting the changes;
8. the practical possibility of allowing the employee to be excluded from the changes where he has good reasons for resisting them;
9. the effect of the changes on employees' earnings (*e.g.* the closure of a nightshift and consequential loss of nightshift premium), and attempt to soften any financial blow.

The fairness of these cases turns very much on their own particular facts; and in many the tribunals end up balancing the employer's reasons for wanting the change against an employee's reasons for resisting them. However it should be noted that a reorganisation dismissal can still be reasonable, even though the employee has good grounds for resisting it—*e.g.* where the employer has no practical alternative but to put it into effect—see *Chubb Fire Security Ltd.* v. *Harper* [1983] I.R.L.R. 311; E.A.T. Whether the employer has the contractual right to make the reorganisation changes to individual employment contracts is a relevant, but by no means the conclusive, factor—see *Redbridge London Borough Council* v. *Fishman* [1978] I.C.R. 509; E.A.T.

Fairness—harmonising terms and conditions

In many cases the purchaser will wish to harmonise the terms and conditions of the employees it has acquired with those of its existing employees. If such a harmonisation programme occurs in connection with a business transfer, then any consequential dismissal will be automatically unfair under regulation 8—*Delabole Slate Ltd.* v. *Berriman* [1985] I.R.L.R. 305; C.A. (see p. 101).

The only way an employer can avoid the effect of regulation 8 is to ensure that its harmonisation programme no longer has any connection with the business transfer. This can be done by either delaying the harmonisation programme until later when the changes can be introduced along with another reorganisation or to finesse such changes with pay increases at the next review date.

Once the connection with the business transfer has been broken, the employer is able to argue that the harmonisation programme is reasonable and was implemented reasonably. Most important, it can take advantage of an argument that the proposed new terms and conditions are broadly equivalent to the employees' existing terms and conditions on a "swings and roundabouts" basis. It should be noted that such an argument is not available to employers where regulation 8 applies.

Remedies for unfair dismissal

An employee must present his complaint within three months of his effective date of termination. Tribunals do have discretion to allow in late complaints if they are satisfied that it was not reasonable for the employee to have presented his claim within the time limit (E.P.C.A., s.67(2)). However this power is exercised sparingly. If an industrial tribunal finds the dismissal to be unfair it has a choice of remedies:

1. to make an order for reinstatement or re-engagement plus an award of compensation representing the employee's lost financial benefits during the period of unemployment (see E.P.C.A., s.69 & s.70); or
2. to award compensation (see E.P.C.A., s.72 to s.75A).

Reinstatement/re-engagement. Industrial tribunals make reinstatement/re-engagement orders in less than 10 per cent. of successful cases. When considering whether to make such an order, the tribunal is required to take into account whether:

1. the employee wants to be reinstated/re-engaged,
2. it is practicable for the employer to comply with such an order, and
3. the employee has contributed to or caused his dismissal by his conduct.

If the tribunal makes such an order, but the employer fails (without good grounds) to comply with it, the tribunal will award compensation (see below) which will include an additional award.

Compensation. Unfair dismissal compensation normally comprises two elements, although further compensation can be awarded where re-employment is sought by the employee. The two usual elements are:

1. *Basic award.* This is calculated on an almost identical basis as statutory redundancy pay (see p. 168) and with only a couple of differences applicable in few cases. There is a minimum basic award where the reason for dismissal is one which could be covered by a special award (see below). The current minimum is £2,520, although this is reviewed annually in April.

2. *Compensatory award.* This award covers lost earnings and other financial benefits caused by the unfair dismissal (*e.g.* salary, bonuses, company car, pension losses, life assurance, BUPA, etc.). It should be noted that the an employee can claim not only losses for remuneration or benefits which formed part of his contract, but also lost non-contractual benefits (*e.g.* discretionary bonuses or *ex gratia* redundancy pay, etc.) which he might reasonably have expected to have received but for his dismissal (E.P.C.A., s.74(2)). The tribunal also applies a "just and equitable" test when assessing the compensatory award. There is a maximum of £8,925 on the compensatory award, although this is reviewed annually in April.

Where the employee has sought reinstatement/re-engagement as his remedy, he may be awarded compensation under either of the following two further awards:

3. *Additional award.* This is only awarded where the special award (see below) is not applicable and the employer has failed to comply with the tribunal's reinstatement/re-engagement order, where compliance was reasonably practicable. Where the reason for the employee's dismissal was race or sex discrimination, the additional award will be in the range £4,472 to £8,944. Where the reason for dismissal is anything else, the

additional award will be in the range £2,236 to £4,472. These figures are normally reviewed annually at about April.

4. *Special award.* This award is only made where the tribunal has found that the reason for the dismissal was the employee's union membership or non-membership of a trade union, or his participation in the activities of a trade union, or his selection for redundancy was on these grounds. If the tribunal rejects the employee's request for reinstatement/re-engagement, he will be awarded two years' pay within the range £12,550 to £25,040. If the tribunal orders reinstatement/re-engagement, but the employer fails to comply with it (where compliance was reasonably practicable), the special award will be three years' pay with a minimum of £18,795 and no maximum. These parameters are reviewed annually in April.

Most of the above awards can be reduced by the tribunal, in its discretion, on grounds of the employee's conduct contributing or causing his dismissal. However such reductions are unlikely to be made in redundancy and reorganisation cases. In addition, a dismissed employee has a duty to mitigate his loss, and so the compensatory award may be limited by any failure by an employee to do so. However it should be noted that the current £8,925 maximum on the compensatory award is applied only after these adjustments have been made.

Miscellaneous

There are a great number of additional provisions dealing with other aspects of unfair dismissal which are not particularly germane to business transfers. These include special provisions dealing with pregnancy, maternity, union membership/non-membership, industrial action, pressure to dismiss, etc. There are also various special rules qualifying the above summary, especially in respect to the provisions on compensation.

Informing and consulting trade unions about redundancies

Under E.P.A. 1975, s.99, an employer has an obligation to inform and consult with any independent trade union which it recognises in respect of any class of employees from whom redundancies are to be made. It does not matter that the proposed redundancy selections also include employees who are not members of the relevant union. The obligation to inform and consult with the trade union arises as soon as the employer proposes to make redundancies. This has been interpreted as meaning that the employer must have decided upon a planned course of action to terminate employment contracts on grounds of redundancy, rather than a mere contemplation that redundancies are a possibility—see *A.P.A.C.* v. *Curvin Ltd.* [1978] I.R.L.R. 318; E.A.T. The reduction of the workforce by the non-replacement of employees who leave for other reasons does not fall within the scope of section 99.

Consultation periods

The obligation to provide specified information and to consult with trade unions arises "at the earliest opportunity" after the proposal to make redundancies has been decided upon (E.P.A., s.99(3)). However the legislation lays down minimum consultation periods, which vary depending on the numbers of employees to be made redundant and the timescale for putting them into effect. These minimum consultation periods are as follows:

90 days – where 100 or more employees at one establishment are to be made redundant in 90 days or less;

30 days – where 10 or more employees are to be made redundant at one establishment in 30 days or less;

Unspecified – in any other case.

These consultation periods are minima, and the primary obligation on employers is to commence the consultation process "at the earliest opportunity," if at all practicable—see *N.U.T.* v. *Avon C.C.* [1978] I.C.R. 626; E.A.T. It should also be noted that the specified consultation periods are calculated back from the date when it is proposed that the first redundant employee leaves his employment, and not by reference to when the redundancies eventually take place—see *T.G.W.U.* v. *R.A. Lister & Co.* This seems to allow for redundancies to brought forward by giving employees their pay in lieu of notice, especially where the union has agreed to such a course of action. However it appears that employers will only be able to do so where both the consultation process has been completed and they had originally intended to put the redundancies into effect at the end of the proper consultation period.

The "unspecified" consultation period will usually apply where less than 10 employees are to be made redundant within a 30-day period. In such circumstances, section 99 does not lay down any fixed minimum consultation period, but employers are advised to adopt a 28-day consultation period, if reasonably practicable.

Meaning of an "establishment"

The appropriate consultation period is ascertained by looking at the number of employees to be made redundant at an "establishment." Unfortunately the legislation does not define this; however tribunals have held that several different sites can constitute a single establishment for the purposes of section 99. Although offices, factories or sites might be geographically separate, they may be regarded as a single establishment if they are closely linked in operational terms. Tribunals have regard to all the circumstances, including whether the sites share a common management, whether they are part of the same collective bargaining unit, the degree of staff interchangeability between sites, the nature of the functions carried out at each site. For example in *Barrett Developments Ltd.* v. *U.C.A.T.T.* [1978] I.C.R. 319; E.A.T., the employers had operations on 14 different building sites, each of which was linked to the employer's head office by a telephone. Each site was co-ordinated by head office staff. The E.A.T. held that the 14 sites were one "establishment" for the purposes of section 99.

Provision of information

The consultation process normally starts with the employer giving the recognised trade union the information prescribed by E.P.A., s.99(5). This information is:

1. the reasons for the redundancy proposals;
2. the numbers and descriptions of employees to be made redundant;
3. the total number of employees of any such description in the establishment in question;
4. the proposed method of redundancy selection;
5. the proposed method of carrying out the redundancies in relation to any agreed procedure and including the timescale in which the redundancies are to take effect.

It is important to note that recognised trade unions also have rights to the disclosure of information to assist them in collective bargaining—E.P.A. 1975, s.17.

What is "consultation"?

Section 99 only requires employers to inform and consult with recognised trade unions. There is no legal obligation to negotiate or agree the redundancy proposals with the union. However, for obvious industrial relations reasons, employers should try to agree their proposals with the union since the consultation process will, in practice, often be transformed into collective bargaining. Section 99(7) of the E.P.A. specifies the minimum requirements of the consultation process as follows:

1. the employer considering any representations made by the union; and
2. the employer responding to those representations, giving reasons why any of the union's representations have been rejected.

Provided meaningful consultation has taken place, there is nothing stopping employers from issuing individual notices of termination of employment to run concurrently with the consultation period, as it runs its course. However employers should beware of issuing such notices at the start of the consultation process, as this could lead a tribunal to conclude that there has been no meaningful consultation at all—see *Green & Sons (Castings) Ltd.* v. *A.S.T.M.S. & A.U.E.W.* [1984] I.R.L.R. 135; E.A.T. To avoid an inference that there has been no meaningful consultation, notices of dismissal should not be issued until at least the employer has responded to the union's representations.

Employer's defence

An employer will not be in breach of section 99 if it can demonstrate that there were "special circumstances which render it not reasonably practicable" for it to comply with its obligations under section 99 *and* the employer has taken all steps towards compliance as is reasonably practicable in the circumstances. In practice, tribunals have construed the scope of this defence narrowly. In *Bakers Union* v. *Clarks of Hove Ltd.* [1978] I.C.R. 1076; C.A., the Court of Appeal said that the term "special circumstances" meant circumstances out of the ordinary. In that case, the court held that the fact of redundancy did not, of itself, constitute a "special circumstance" which rendered union consultation not reasonably practicable. The court suggested that for insolvency to amount to a "special circumstance" it would have had to have come "out of the blue."

However in *Hamish Armour* v. *A.S.T.M.S.* [1979] I.R.L.R. 24; E.A.T., the E.A.T. held where an employer has had to make redundancies to cut costs until the outcome of an application to a bank for extended credit was known, this constituted a special circumstance since such cuts were necessary to keep the company trading solvently. Similarly a sudden withdrawal of credit facilities by a bank could make an insolvency a "special circumstance"—see *U.S.D.A.W.* v. *Leancut Bacon Ltd.* [1981] I.R.L.R. 295; E.A.T. Although there is no case dealing with the issue, it seems likely that tribunals will be wary of treating the need for secrecy over a proposed business transfer as a "special circumstance" which makes compliance with section 99 impracticable. However, if the alternative to such secrecy is that an insolvent business will not be bought, an arguable case might be made out justifying a failure to comply with section 99.

It must be remembered that even if there is a "special circumstances" justifying non-compliance with section 99, the employer must still attempt to comply as far as the "special circumstance" reasonably permits.

The protective award

The right to bring a claim for a breach of section 99 lies with the relevant recognised trade union, not with individual employees—see E.P.A., s.99(9). Applications to a tribunal must be lodged within three months from the date of the dismissal of the first employee in breach of section 99 (E.P.A., s.101(6)). At the tribunal hearing it is for the employer to prove its "special circumstance" defence and that it took all reasonably practicable steps towards compliance in the light of the "special circumstances."

If the tribunal finds the claim well-founded, it makes a declaration to that effect and may make a protective award in favour of those employees proposed to be made redundant. In deciding the amount of the protective award, the tribunal is required to take account of what is "just and equitable in the circumstances having regard to the seriousness of the employer's default in not complying with any requirement of section 99" (see E.P.A., s.101(5)). That subsection also places certain limits on the amount of the protective award as follows:

90 day consultation period –	up to 90 days pay
30 day consultation period –	up to 30 days pay

Unspecified consultation period – up to 28 days pay

In assessing the amount of the protective award, tribunals are required to look at the length of time that consultation took place (if any), the nature of the employer's default, and any steps taken by the employer to deal with the situation—see *Spillers French (Holdings) Ltd.* v. *U.S.D.A.W.* [1979] I.R.L.R. 339; E.A.T. However, the object of the protective award is partly to compensate employees for the adverse effects of the failure to consult or give the specified information, and partly to reflect the seriousness of the employer's default—see *N.U.D.B.T.W.* v. *J. Bradby (Saddleworth) Ltd.* [1982] unreported (E.A.T. 557/80); E.A.T. In particular, tribunals look at the number of days of employment lost by the failure to consult—see *G.K.N. Sankey* v. *N.S.M.M.* [1980] I.C.R. 148; E.A.T. It is sometimes possible for tribunals to find that section 99 has been contravened, but such breach was only technical and the union and its members have not been prejudiced as a result. The protective award is paid gross, not net.

The protective award is, in effect, the right of the employee to receive his normal pay for the relevant protected period. Thus the tribunal will make the protective award in terms of a specified period of time and in respect of a list of named employees. The employer will then have an obligation to give employees their remuneration for that protected period—E.P.A., s.102.

Offsetting. An employer can offset against its liability to pay salary under a protective award, any pay in lieu of notice or any damages for breach of contract in respect of the period falling within the protected period. However an *ex gratia* payment given to an employee cannot be offset against the protective award—see *Vosper Thornycroft (U.K.) Ltd.* v. *T.G.W.U. & G.M.B.A.T.U.* [1988] I.R.L.R. 233; E.A.T.

Non-payment of the protective award

If an employer fails to pay to an employee named by the tribunal, the protective award to which he is entitled, the individual employee can then apply to the tribunal for an order requiring the protective award to be paid. The rights of individuals in respect of a protective award apply equally to union members and non-members.

Notification to the Department of Employment

It should be remembered that employers have an obligation to notify their local Dept. of Employment offices of proposed redundancies on Form HR 1. This advance notification is 90 days (where 100 or more employees are to be made redundant in 90 days or less) or 30 days (where 10 or more employees are to be made redundant in 30 days or less)—see E.P.A. 1975, s.100. Failure to comply will result in either a fine of up to £2,000—E.P.A., s.105.

APPENDIX B

Introduction

This Appendix contains several precedents for warranties, indemnities, and standard letters which may be needed to be used in the context of a business transfer. They cover only employment law matters. It is important to note that there is no "universal" precedent which will always be applicable in all cases. The suggestions which appear below are merely examples which can be amended or modified, depending on the nature of the transaction and the matters which concern the parties.

There may be precedents set out below which are inapplicable or inappropriate to a particular transaction. For example most of the clauses dealing with trade unions will be inapplicable where there is no trade union recognised in respect of the transferring employees. Instead other clauses will be appropriate. It must also be noted that all these warranties and indemnities are drafted on the basis that the relevant transfer of a business takes place at the moment of completion, not on the exchange of contracts. This accords with the current accepted thinking; however different divisions of the E.A.T. have taken different views on this point and definitive guidance from the Court of Appeal is sought.

Warranties

These will be included in the business transfer agreement between the vendor and purchaser. Suitable warranties might include the following, depending on the circumstances of the transaction:

Disclosure of material facts

A. "The Vendor hereby warrants that it has disclosed to the Purchaser in the Disclosure Letter all material facts and matters relating to or concerning the employment of any Transferring Employee (including but not limited to their respective ages, length of service, notice periods, all terms and conditions of employment, employment or benefits policies, any stock option or profit-share entitlements or rights, all other agreements or arrangements or understandings in respect of each of them relating to their employment, any existing or threatened or pending litigation or dispute relating to or concerning all or any of them, all matters which could give rise to any legal claim or right of action whatsoever or other liability in respect of any of them), and that there has been no subsequent change or occurrence in respect of those facts and matters which has arisen since the date of the Disclosure Letter relating to the same or similar facts or matters."

B. "The Vendor hereby warrants that it has disclosed to the Purchaser in the Disclosure Letter all material facts and matters relating to all or any collective agreements, arrangements or other understandings which it has with any trade union, staff association or other body representing employees and all or any threatened, existing or pending litigation or claim relating to or concerning any such trade union or such other body and that there has been no change or occurrence in respect of these facts and matters which has arisen since the date of the Disclosure Letter relating to the same or similar facts or matters."

Commentary. The purpose of both these warranties is to ensure that the vendor has told the purchaser of all material facts relating to employment matters. During the negotiations there is sometimes some argument whether such warranties should be limited to material facts or should be comprehensive. In addition, some vendors may try to insist that their obligation on disclosure should be limited only to matters of which they are aware. However a purchaser may be concerned that a vendor could avoid liability by pleading ignorance of certain facts. A compromise is sometimes reached whereby the vendor's disclosure is limited to: "material facts and matters of which it is aware or reasonably ought to be aware."

Warranty A. above is likely to be fairly standard for most business transfers. In many cases the Disclosure Letter will be accompanied by a vast collection of papers containing all relevant details. Warranty B. is obviously only applicable where there is a union presence in respect of the transferring employees. Where there is no such presence Warranty C.1 will be appropriate (see below).

A list of "Transferring Employees" will normally be contained in a Schedule attached to the Agreement.

Warranty of non-existence of facts

C. "The Vendor hereby warrants that, except as expressly stated in the Disclosure Letter, the following facts or matters set out below are correct on the date hereof: *i.e.* that

1. the Vendor does not recognise (expressly or impliedly) any trade union, staff association or other body representing employees in respect of all or any of the Transferring Employees, and that there are no collective agreements or arrangements or understandings with any such trade unions, staff association or such body representing any of the Transferring Employees;
2. there is no industrial action or dispute threatened or existing or anticipated in respect of or concerning the Transferring Employees;

3. only the Transferring Employees are the Vendor's employees (as defined by reg. 2(1) Transfer Regulations) engaged or working in [the Business] on the date hereof and that no other person has a Contract of Employment or any contract for services with the Vendor on the date hereof;
4. there is no threatened, existing or pending litigation against the Vendor in respect of or concerning [the Business] and no matter which is likely to give rise to any legal claim in respect of [the Business] other than those matters expressly referred to in the Disclosure Letter;
5. the Vendor has not offered a Contract of Employment or a contract for services to any person, company or other business entity other than as disclosed in the Disclosure Letter;
6. the Vendor has not offered, or promised, or agreed for the future any variation in, any Contract of Employment or any contract for services in respect of any person, company or business entity (whether or not Transferring Employees) except as expressly disclosed in the Disclosure Letter;
7. those consultancy contracts listed in Schedule [ ] hereto have been [will be] terminated by the Vendor and that such terminations have taken [will take] effect prior to the date hereof [the Completion Date];
8. there are no persons previously working in [the Business] who are on maternity leave, absent on grounds of disability or other leave of absence and have or may have a statutory or contractual right to return to work in [the Business];
9. the Vendor has paid to the Inland Revenue and any other appropriate authority all taxes, national insurance contributions and other levies in respect of the Transferring Employees in respect of their employment by the Vendor up to the date hereof [Completion Date];
10. there are no Contracts of Employment or contracts for services which cannot be lawfully terminated by three months' notice or less, except as expressly referred to in the Disclosure Letter;
11. there are no inquiries or investigations existing, pending or threatened into the 'Business' by the Equal Opportunities Commission or the Commission for Racial Equality or other similar authority;
12. all notices required to be issued under the Social Security Act 1975 have been duly and properly issued;
13. the Vendor has discharged [will discharge] fully its obligations to pay all salaries, wages, commissions, bonuses, overtime pay, holiday pay, sick pay and other benefits of employment up to the date hereof [Completion Date]."
14. the Vendor has not dismissed any person for a reason connected with this Agreement which is not an "economic, technical or organisational reason entailing changes in the workforce", of either the Vendor or

purchaser, such expression having the meaning ascribed under Regulation 8(2) of the Transfer Regulations.

Commentary. These warranties are, in effect, a list of matters which the vendor promises to be facts as at either the date of the Agreement or on the Completion Date. For ease of reference, the above warranties have been drafted on the basis that the facts represented are correct on the date of the Agreement; and only minor amendment is necessary if there is to be a long gap between exchange of contracts and completion. The suggested wording also contains various expressions which will have been defined in the definitions section of the Agreement. These include:

"Completion date"—*i.e.* the date when the Agreement is to be treated as completed (usually a specified date);

"Transferring employees"—these will be listed in a separate Schedule to the Agreement;

"The Business"—this is a term often used in the Agreement to describe the business or undertaking being transferred to the purchaser;

"Contracts of employment"—the Transfer Regulations have a wider definition of "employee" than either the common law or the E.P.C.A. (see p. 53), therefore the words contract of employment will be defined as "a contract of employment as defined by regulation 2(1) Transfer Regulations" (the Transfer Regulations will also have their full title in the Definitions clause).

The purpose of most of these warranties is self-evident—*i.e.* the purchaser will want to feel secure that there are no potential or contingent problems or liabilities of which he was not aware when he negotiated the Agreement. However some may need some additional explanation.

(a) *Warranty C.3.* This warranty is designed to ensure that the Transfer Regulations transfer into the purchaser's employment only those employees agreed and listed in the Schedule to the Agreement. In effect, it also means that the vendor must take steps to divorce any other employees from "the Business" prior to the transfer date—*e.g.* either by deploying them elsewhere in its own operations or by dismissing them.

(b) *Warranty C.5.* This warranty aims to ensure that the vendor has not made job offers which have been accepted, yet the employee in question will not start work until after the business transfer has taken place. It is a moot point whether a contract of employment (as defined by the Transfer Regulations) is in existence as soon as the potential employee has accepted the job offer. It is submitted that the contract is formed and therefore is capable of being transferred to the purchaser under the Transfer Regulations. The only doubt arises from the regulation 2(1) definition of "employee"; since it refers to a person who "works in" the undertaking (or part) transferred. This word suggests that an employee must be actually working, not due to start work. However, a purchaser needs to be aware of a potential claim in this respect and the costs of successfully defending it.

(c) *Warranty C.6.* Since regulation 5(2) makes the purchaser responsible for all liabilities and acts of the vendor which occurred prior to the business transfer, the purchaser will want to be sure that, even if he is satisfied with the employment costs at the time of the business transfer, the vendor has not given promises to transferring employees to increase their notice periods or pay, etc., with effect from some future date. At the very least, the purchaser will want to have advance notice of these future liabilities.

It will also be noted that this warranty covers consultancies and contracts for services. It should be remembered that, although a particular working relationship may be described as a "contract for services," a court or tribunal may consider it to be a contract of employment and therefore subject to the Transfer Regulations. In a business transfer, the purchaser will want to be aware of that possibility. In a share transfer, the consultancy/contract for services will continue; but the purchaser will want to know what commitments the company has made in this respect.

(d) *Warranty C.7.* This warranty is linked to warranty C.6 above. Normally there will be a general warranty in the Agreement that the vendor has disclosed to the purchaser copies of all contracts and agreements between the "Business" and third parties. The disclosure process will bring to light any consultancy arrangements/contracts for services. In some cases (particularly where the vendor is a small private company) one or more shareholders may have "consultancy contracts" as a means of providing them with an income. The purchaser may want such contracts terminated ahead of the Completion Date (particularly if the transaction is a share transfer).

(e) *Warranty C.8.* In some cases a woman may have the right to return to work following maternity leave, even though her employment has ceased during her maternity leave—see p. 142. The purchaser will want to know which of the vendor's former employees may seek to exercise that right.

Warranty of specified actions taken by the vendor

D. "The Vendor hereby warrants that:

1. it has fully complied with all its obligations under reg. 10 of the Transfer Regulations and s.99 and s.100 Employment Protection Act 1975;
2. it will not, from the date hereof until the Completion Date, in connection with the 'Business,' enter into or offer a Contract of Employment to any person, or change or offer to change any terms and conditions of employment of any Transferring Employee without the prior written consent of the Purchaser;
3. it has not, and will not, make any representations or

statements (whether oral, written or otherwise) to any of its employees in any way connected with or concerning employment with the Purchaser, without the prior written consent of the Purchaser;

4. it will deliver to each of the Transferring Employees a letter in the terms as set out in Schedule [ ] hereto, and to any trade union or staff association recognised by the Vendor in respect of any of the Transferring Employees a letter in the terms as set out in Schedule [ ] hereto, [by] [as soon as reasonably practicable after the date hereof];
5. it will not between the date hereof and the Completion Date do any act, or omit to do any act, the result of which is reasonably likely to result in industrial action by or a dispute with all or any of the Transferring Employees, or in litigation against the Vendor or Purchaser by all or any Transferring Employees or any trade union or staff association representing them, without the prior written consent of the Purchaser;
6. it will terminate all Contracts of Employment between the Vendor and those persons listed in Schedule [ ], such terminations taking effect at least 24 hours prior to the Completion Date;
7. it will by the Completion Date have secured the written and unconditional agreement of at least [per cent.] of the Transferring Employees to those amendments to their terms and conditions of employment as set out in Schedule [ ] hereto;
8. it will procure that Mr. [ ], Mr. [ ] and Mr. [ ] sign their respective new Service Agreements as set out in Schedule [ ] hereto with the purchaser no later than the Completion Date to take effect immediately thereafter;
9. it will procure that Mr. [ ], Mr. [ ] and Mr. [ ] resign as directors of the Vendor no later than 24 hours prior to the Completion Date by each signing and delivering to the Vendor a letter in the terms as set out in Schedule [ ];
10. it will have terminated at its own cost all stock option or similar share acquisition rights of any of its employees (including but not limited to the Transferring Employees) in the issued or unissued share capital of ['the Business']."

Commentary. Not all of these warranties will be needed in all transactions. Much depends on whether it is a business or share transfer and on what action, if any, the purchaser is requiring the vendor to take in respect of its employees. Most of these warranties are of a prohibitive nature—*i.e.* they stop the vendor doing certain things (usually in the period between exchange of contracts and completion) which could increase the purchaser's liability. The same terminology has been used as for the class C. warranties above.

(a) *Warranty D.2.* Where, in the context of a share transfer, the purchaser is concerned about the existence of contracts for services, this warranty may be extended to include these as well.

(b) *Warranty D.3.* This warranty is designed to stop the vendor from making unauthorised representations on behalf of the purchaser to its employees—*e.g.* by telling them that their terms of employment will remain unchanged. For reasons explained on p. 144, there may be circumstances where the vendor can be regarded as acting as the agent of the purchaser. The latter will obviously want to limit and control any purported representations on its behalf made by the vendor (who may have an interest in wanting to put its employees' minds at rest). This control is also important because, under regulation 10, the vendor is required to give to trade unions it recognises for affected employees certain information (including what measures the purchaser proposes to take in respect of them)—see p. 121.

(c) *Warranty D.4.* This warranty is linked to D.3. It requires the vendor to give specimen letters to the Transferring Employees and any trade unions recognised in respect of them. See p. 192 for examples of such letters.

(d) *Warranty D.6.* This warranty will only apply where the purchaser requires the vendor to terminate the employment of specific individuals prior to the Completion Date. The question of who picks up the liability will usually be reflected in the purchase price or an indemnity (see below).

(e) *Warranties D.7 & 8.* These will be applicable where, as part of the transaction, the vendor is required to effect either that a specified percentage of Transferring Employees have agreed to certain changes to their conditions of employment (warranty D.7), or certain key employees, such as directors and certain senior research and development staff, have agreed to new contracts (warranty D.8). The latter may be important where restrictive covenants are to be introduced by the purchaser. Such warranties may be appropriate where a purchaser seeks to effect a harmonisation of terms and conditions of employment in the period between the dates of exchange and completion of contract. In some cases, these warranties are expressed as conditions precedent.

(f) *Warranty D.9.* Especially in cases of share transfers, the purchaser may want the vendor to ensure that certain named persons have resigned their directorships with the vendor (see sample letter on page 193). In addition, in cases of business transfers, director status is also part of an employee's conditions of employment and, if the purchaser does not want one or more named persons to remain as directors after the transaction has been completed, such resignations have to be effected prior to or on completion.

(g) *Warranty D.10.* This warranty is important in cases of share transfers, and desirable for business transfers (see p. 186). A purchaser of all or the controlling interest of the shares in a company does not want to see his control watered down by the exercise of share options by employees. Similarly, if the share option scheme is regarded as part of the employment contract, the obligation to operate one may be transferred to the purchaser, which may be something the purchaser does not want to offer to employees.

Warranties by the purchaser

It is in the nature of both business and share transfers that it will be the purchaser who seeks most of the warranties—since it is taking over the relevant liabilities. However, there are occasions where the vendor might ask for warranties against the purchaser. These are dealt with below.

> E. "The Purchaser hereby warrants that, as at the date hereof, it has no proposals or plans to take any measures in respect of the Transferring Employees, and that it will immediately notify the Vendor in writing if it subsequently decides prior to the Completion Date to take any such measures and of their nature."
> OR "The Purchaser hereby warrants that, as of the date hereof, it proposes to take only those measures in connection with the Transferring Employees as are set out in Schedule [ ] hereto AND that it will immediately notify the Vendor in writing if it subsequently decides prior to the Completion Date to take further or different measures and of their nature."

Commentary. The vendor might seek this warranty to cover itself against a claim by a recognised trade union under regulation 10 (see p. 144) on the grounds that the vendor has incorrectly told it that the purchaser has planned no measures. The alternative version is applicable where the the purchaser proposes certain measures. It should be noted that no purchaser is sensibly going to warrant anything other than its present plans, because to do otherwise will impede future changes it may wish to make.

> F. "The Purchaser warrants that it will not until at least three months after the Completion Date offer employment to any person listed in Schedule [ ] hereto.

Commentary. This warranty will protect the vendor against unfair dismissal claims where it is alleged that the vendor and purchaser conspired to dismiss all the vendor's employees for redundancy, so that the purchaser could have a free choice over whom he wanted to retain but without having to follow the vendor's redundancy selection procedures. The three-month limit relates to the time limit for presenting an unfair dismissal claim to a tribunal (E.P.C.A., s.67). However, in certain exceptional circumstances, tribunals may be prepared to extend this where facts come to light after those three months have expired which indicate that a dismissal is unfair. The warranty will also protect a vendor in the event that the purchaser unwittingly offers a job to a former employee of the vendor who was dismissed whilst taking industrial action. Such an offer can lose the vendor his immunity from unfair dismissal claims from all other persons dismissed in the context of that industrial dispute (see p. 143).

Indemnities

The indemnities set out below are drafted in favour of the purchaser. They can equally be amended so that they are in favour of the vendor, if the nature of what the parties have agreed so dictates.

"1. The Vendor hereby agrees and undertakes to indemnify the Purchaser fully and to hold it wholly harmless at all times from and against all actions, proceedings, claims, damages, demands, fines, penalties, expenses, legal remedies, compensation, court or tribunal orders, awards, costs and all other liabilities whatsoever in any way connected with or arising from or relating to:

1.1 any breach of warranty by the Vendor;

1.2 any claim or other legal recourse by all or any of the Transferring Employees in respect of any fact or matter concerning or arising from employment with the Vendor prior to the Completion Date;

1.3 any claim or other legal recourse by any trade union or staff association recognised by the Vendor in respect of all or any of the Transferring Employees arising from or connected with any failure by the Vendor to comply with its legal obligations to such trade unions or staff associations;

1.4 any claim or other legal recourse by any former or existing or future employee of the Vendor [or any Associated Company] (other than the Transferring Employees) against the Vendor or Purchaser or any Associated Company, or its or their officers, employees, agents or shareholders concerning or relating to any matter whatsoever;

1.5 any claim for redundancy pay, unfair dismissal [basic award], pay in lieu of notice or damages for wrongful dismissal in respect of any Transferring Employee arising from any dismissal (whether by the Purchaser or by way of constructive dismissal) from the employment of the Purchaser PROVIDED THAT:

1.5.1 the Vendor's obligation under this sub-clause 1.5 shall be limited by apportionment by dividing A by B

where 'A' is the period of the relevant employee's continuous employment with the Vendor or any Associated Employer (as computed in accordance with Schedule 13 Employment Protection (Consolidation) Act 1978) up to the date hereof [the Completion Date]; and

'B' is the aggregate of A above and the period of the relevant employee's actual continuous employment with the purchaser;

1.5.2 this indemnity shall only apply for a period of [12] months immediately following the date hereof [the Completion Date] and if the reason for the dismissal is connected with or arises from a redundancy or reorganisation of the Purchaser's business [or the harmonisation of the relevant employee's terms and conditions of employment with those of the Purchaser's existing employees]."

1.6 any claim or fine or other liability arising out of a breach by the Vendor of its obligations under section 100 Employment Protection Act 1975.

Commentary. Not all parts of the above indemnity may be appropriate for all transactions. For example, the vendor may be prepared to give indemnity 1.5 above in return for the purchaser agreeing to take on all of the vendor's employees. The timing of the transaction may give the vendor insufficient time to comply with its obligations to consult properly with trade unions and individual employees, or the vendor may be unwilling to make redundancy selections required by the purchaser. In such circumstances the vendor might be prepared to indemnify the purchaser for the vendor's accumulated liability for redundancy pay, unfair dismissal basic award, and a proportionate part of notice liabilities. Such an indemnity is flexible—*e.g.* for how long it is to last, and the extent of the indemnity.

Although the purchaser does not inherit any liability of the vendor in respect of claims brought by a trade union (see p. 74), indemnity 1.3 is included to cover the purchaser's costs and expenses involved in successfully defending such claims. In the ordinary courts, successful defendants tend to be awarded about 60–70 per cent. of their actual legal costs and in industrial tribunals no costs are awarded unless the applicant's claim is "unreasonable, vexatious or frivolous."

Where a purchaser requires the vendor to dismiss certain employees prior to the transfer date, it may be prepared to grant an indemnity to the vendor in respect of various liabilities arising from the dismissals—*e.g.* redundancy pay, notice pay/damages for wrongful dismissal and, perhaps to an agreed extent, compensation for unfair dismissal. Where the purchaser or vendor does agree to indemnify the other in respect of any part of the unfair dismissal compensatory award, it should ensure that it does not incur liability if the unfairness arises from any act of that other for which it was not to blame (*e.g.* unfair selection, or lack of consultation).

Indemnity for vendor

"1. The Purchaser hereby agrees and undertakes to indemnify the Vendor fully and to hold it wholly harmless at all times from and against all actions, proceedings, claims, damages, demands, fines, penalties, [expenses], legal remedies, compensation, court or tribunal orders, [costs and all other financial losses and liabilities whatsoever] in any way connected with or arising from or relating to:

2.1 any unfair dismissal basic award by an industrial tribunal;
2.2 any statutory redundancy pay awarded by an industrial tribunal;
2.3 any damages for wrongful dismissal or pay in lieu of notice;
2.4 any protective award or liability under sections 99 and 100 Employment Protection Act 1975 (as amended);
2.5 any contract of employment with the Vendor existing on the Completion Date;
2.6 any substantial and detrimental change in the working conditions effected by the Purchaser on or after the Completion Date;
2.7 the change of identity of the employer of those persons listed in Schedule [ ];
2.8 any failure by the Purchaser to provide retirement, or post-retirement, or death in service, benefits for or in respect of any person listed in Schedule [ ] of the same or equivalent level as such persons would have been entitled under the (scheme name) in the Vendor's employment immediately before the Completion Date;

PROVIDED ALWAYS that this indemnity shall only apply in respect of all or any persons listed in Schedule [ ] hereto".

Sample letters

There is no such thing as "the perfect letter." The following are simply examples of the type of letter which might be sent to their recipients in certain circumstances. All business and share transfers differ to some degree, and therefore the contents will differ accordingly.

1. Letter to employees on share transfer—from the company

Dear

I am writing to tell you that with effect from the [controlling] shares in the Company have been [will be] purchased by . This means that the Company is now part of the group of companies.
(The Board feel that this change is in everyone's best interests and should help strengthen the Company's market position and thereby safeguard job security. Now the Company is part of a larger group, this should provide new opportunities for all of us).

This change will not affect in any way your terms and conditions of employment, continuous service, and position within the Company, all of which will remain unchanged. [The only exception to this is the pension scheme. Since the Company is no longer part of the group, you can no longer remain part of that scheme. However arrangements are in hand to provide you with pension entitlements which are broadly similar to your pension benefits prior to this change of ownership.] [All collective bargaining arrangements with recognised trade unions will, of course, continue as before.]

The change in ownership of the Company should not affect your day-to-day duties or working environment. Obviously, since we are now part of the group, no doubt greater contact will be had with other companies in the group and in time we will become more integrated with the group. However, no changes are planned at the moment, and I will obviously let you know if and when there may be changes that affect you.

(It is anticipated that this business of the Company will be transferred to later this year as the final stage of our acquisition by the group. I will let you know when and if this is due to take place.)

I know that I can count on your co-operation to ensure that the Company will play its full part in its new role within the group.

Yours sincerely

[Chairman]

2. Letter to trade unions on a share transfer—from the company

Dear

I am writing to advise you of the [proposed] change of control of the shares of the Company with effect from . From that date, the majority of the Company's shares have been [will be] controlled by .

This change does not in any way affect your members' terms and conditions of employment, continuous service, or job duties. [The only exception is in respect of pensions. As you are aware, whilst the Company was part of the group, its employees were members of the pension scheme; but now we are no longer part of that group, our employees cannot remain members of that scheme. Arrangements are in hand to secure alternative pension arrangements to provide broadly similar pension benefits. I will obviously advise you what these are once the final details have been decided.]

Needless to say all existing collective bargaining arrangements and agreements with your union will continue as before.

Now the Company is part of the group, there will inevitably be close contact with other companies within that group. However there are no plans at present to take any measures in respect of your members. If the situation changes the union will be advised accordingly through the existing consultative machinery. [This change of ownership is the first stage of a proposed transfer of the Company's business to another company within the group later this year. If and when this occurs, the union will be informed accordingly in accordance with our agreed procedures.]

Yours sincerely

[Chairman]

3. Business transfer: letter to transferring employees—from vendor

Dear

I am writing to advise you that with effect from the business of the Company [the Division] has been [will be] transferred to . The reason for this transaction is .

Under the Transfer of Undertakings (Protection of Employment) Regulations 1981 ("Transfer Regulations"), your employment will automatically transfer to along with the business. This means that will be your employer from that date.

[Your terms and conditions of employment (except for pensions) will remain unchanged, you will continue to carry out your existing job duties and you will carry forward your accrued period of continuous employment.]

OR

[Your terms and conditions of employment will be the same as before with the exception of the following:

1. ;
2. ;
3. ;
4. pensions.

Your accrued period of continuous employment with the Company will be carried forward with you to the employment with , and your job will remain unchanged].

Under the Transfer Regulations pension schemes do not automatically transfer to the new owner. [However I understand that are currently examining the feasibility of alternative pension arrangements and they will no doubt advise you accordingly what they propose to do.]

(All existing collective bargaining arrangements and collective agreements with recognised trade unions will continue to be honoured by).

The Board of the Company would like to take this opportunity to thank you for all your past efforts and contribution to the Company and wish you every success in your career with . We feel sure you will find new opportunities with .

Yours sincerely

[Chairman]

4. Business transfer: letter to transferring employees—from the purchaser

Dear

As you are aware, has agreed to transfer its business [Division] to this Company. This transaction was completed on . Under existing employment protection legislation, this means that your employment is automatically transferred to us with effect from that date. I would therefore like to take this opportunity to welcome you to . We are delighted that this transaction has gone ahead and to have you as part of the team. We have no doubt that your joining us will enhance the Company's strength as well as your career opportunities.

[Your terms and conditions of employment will remain unchanged in all respects [apart from pensions], your period of continuous service with will be honoured by us, and you will carry out your existing job duties as before.]

OR

[I would like to offer you revised terms and conditions of employment so that you will enjoy similar benefits as the Company's existing employees. A copy of a new revised contract of employment is attached. Please read it carefully and contact me if you have any queries about it. The main changes from your previous contract are:

1. ;
2. ;
3. ;
4. pensions.]

[I think you will agree that these do represent an overall improvement on your existing terms and conditions]. If you wish to accept this revised contract please sign a copy of the contract and return it to me. If you have any problems with it, please make an appointment with me so that we can discuss it.

[Under existing legislation, the Company is not required to take over your existing pensions scheme. As you no doubt appreciate, pensions are a complex subject, and the Company is currently examining the feasibility of alternative arrangements. I will obviously let you know what the Company intends to do about pensions as soon as a decision has been made.]

[All existing collective bargaining arrangements and collective agreements with recognised trade unions will continue as before.]

If you have any questions about the contents of this letter, please do not hesitate to contact

Yours sincerely

[Personnel Director]

5. Business transfer: letter to existing employees—from the purchaser

Dear

I am writing to let you know that the Company purchased the business of from with effect from .

[This acquisition will be run as a separate division and will not affect your position in the Company. However the Company feels that its acquisition of will materially increase our market presence and therefore enhance job security and career opportunities for all of its employees.]
OR
[This acquisition will initially be run as a separate division, but the Company hopes to gradually integrate it with the rest of its operations over the next year or so. If such integration affects you, you will be advised accordingly in due course. However, the Company considers that its new acquisition will increase its market presence and enhance job security and career opportunities for all of its employees.]
If you have any queries about the contents of this letter please do not hesitate to contact me.

Yours sincerely

[Personnel Director]

6. Business transfers: letter to vendor's remaining employees—from the vendor

Dear

I am writing to inform you that, with effect from , the Company sold its Division [its business] to . The reason for this transaction was because
Although this transaction will obviously have some impact on the Company's remaining business operations, my purpose in writing to you is to assure you that your existing terms and conditions of employment will remain unchanged. The Company will review its operations over the next few months and naturally advise you of what reorganisation measures it intends to take, if any, regarding its remaining business operations.
If you have any questions about the contents of this letter please contact

Yours sincerely

[Personnel Director]

7. Business transfer: letter to trade union—from the vendor

Dear

I am writing to tell you that the Company proposes to sell its business [its Division] [its business] to . It is anticipated that this sale will take place on about . The reason for the proposed sale is .

The effect of this sale means that the Company will no longer operate [its Division] [in the business], but these activities will be taken over by .

[Under existing employment protection legislation, all employees employed in that business as at will automatically transfer into the employment of with their existing terms and conditions of employment and accrued period of employment honoured. The only exception is in respect of pensions, since under the Transfer of Undertakings (Protection of Employment) Regulations 1981, these do not transfer over to . We understand that are currently examining the feasibility of alternative pension arrangements and will advise you accordingly. We also understand that intend to honour all existing collective bargaining arrangements and collective agreements with your union.] [The Company will continue to honour its collective bargaining arrangements and collective agreements with your union in respect of those of your members remaining with the Company.]

The effect of this transaction means that your members will be employed by , which is part of the group of companies.The Company does not envisage any other legal, economic or social implications of the proposed sale [except for].

The Company does not intend to take any measures in respect of any employees affected by the transfer [except for insert details of redundancies or reorganisation or changes in terms and conditions of employment].

The Company has been advised by that it does not intend to take any measures in respect of those employees transferring to it with the business [except for insert any details of redundancies, job changes, reorganisation or harmonisation of terms and conditions of employment, pension arrangements].

If you have any further questions on the contents of this letter, please do not hesitate to contact me.

Yours sincerely

[Personnel Director]

8. Business transfers: letter to trade unions—from the purchaser

Dear

I am writing to advise you that the Company proposes to purchase from , its [Division]

[business]. This purchase is likely to be completed on about . The reason for the purchase is .
We consider that the purchase will benefit our operations because .
The purchase means that the Company will be taking on about of former employees who currently work in that [Division] [business]. These will [continue to work as a separate division] [be gradually integrated into the Company's existing business operations]. Those transferring employees are [not] represented by [a trade union]. The Company sees no need to change its existing collective agreements and bargaining arrangements with your union. Apart from the above, the Company envisages no other legal, economic or social implications arising from the purchase [except for].
The Company currently has no plans to take any measures in respect of your members arising out of the purchase. We intend to review our acquisition over the next few months and will, of course, advise you through our existing consultative procedures of any such measures affecting your members that we propose to take.
[It is anticipated that the transferring employees will be invited to join the Company's pension scheme.]

Yours sincerely

[Personnel Director]

9. Conditional offer of employment—from the purchaser

Dear

As you are probably aware, is negotiating with us for the sale of its [Division] [business] in which you work. It is hoped that these negotiations will be successful and the outstanding matters between and ourselves can be sorted out. Both parties are hopeful that they will be.
My purpose of writing to you is to offer you employment with us on the terms and conditions set out in the enclosed draft contract of employment. However this offer is strictly conditional upon the proposed sale referred to above being completed. If our proposed purchase of 's [business] [Division] is not completed by 19 , then this offer will automatically be treated as withdrawn and as if it had never been made (even if you have in the meantime accepted it). In such circumstances you, of course, will continue in 's employment, as if this offer had never been made. If our proposed purchase of the business is completed, I will write to you telling you so. For the avoidance

of any doubt, the condition of this offer of employment shall conclusively be regarded as not satisfied, unless I write to you telling that it has been completed. I hope this will be in the next weeks.

You will see that the enclosed contract differs from your existing employment terms in the following main respects:

1. ;
2. ;
3. ;
4. ;
5. .

[I think you will agree that the terms and conditions in this contract represent an overall improvement on those you currently enjoy with .]

I would be grateful if you could please carefully read the enclosed conditional contract of employment and, if you are happy to accept its terms, please sign and date in the spaces marked and return the duplicate copy to me to arrive no later than am on 19 . If I have not received your acceptance of the conditional contract by that deadline, the offer will be automatically withdrawn and lapse. I am sorry to put you to deadlines but, as you will obviously appreciate, we need to know ahead of the completion of our proposed purchase who is willing to accept employment with us on the terms offered.

If you have any queries about this letter or the conditional contract, please do not hesitate to contact me on . In addition I will be coming into 's offices on to answer any questions and to collect acceptances to our offers of employment. If you wish to see me on either of these two days, please make arrangements with .

I very much hope that you will accept our conditional offer of employment and that we will be in a position to write to you telling you that the proposed purchase has been completed and to welcome you to the team. [I enclose some literature about the Company and its group for background information.] If all goes according to plan, and you join us on the terms of the attached contract of employment, this will obviously supersede all previous contracts, agreements, arrangements or understandings you have with , (all of which will be treated as terminated by mutual consent). Needless to say, your accrued period of continuous employment with will be honoured by us.

Yours sincerely

[name]—[position]
For and on behalf of Limited

10. Letter of dismissal—from the vendor

By hand

Dear

I write to confirm our conversation earlier today when I advised you that the Company has no alternative but to make you redundant. As I explained during our discussion, the Company is proposing to sell its [business] [Division] to , and have required that we make certain redundancies prior to the proposed sale being completed. Unfortunately, your position is one of those they have required us to make redundant. As we discussed, there is no alternative position for you elsewhere in the Company and I therefore must formally advise you that your employment with this Company will terminate with immediate effect from pm on 19 .

I am aware that, under the terms of your contract of employment, you are entitled to months'[weeks'] notice. Since you will not be receiving your full notice, you will instead receive a payment of £ (less any deductions for tax that the Company is required to make) as compensation for loss of employment. You will also be paid statutory redundancy pay of £ (calculated:), [*ex gratia* redundancy pay of £], and your accrued salary and any outstanding holiday pay still due to you.

I very much regret that it has not been possible to retain you in our employment or to persuade that it needed, after all, someone to undertake the job you performed for us. I would like to take this opportunity to thank you for your contribution to the Company and to wish you success in your future career. If you want a reference, you only have to ask.

Yours sincerely

[name]—[position]

11. Redundancy letter to trade union—from vendor or purchaser

Dear

Further to our meeting earlier this morning, I write to inform you, in accordance with s.99 Employment Protection Act 1975, of the Company's proposal to make redundancies from within its departments. The reasons for the proposed redundancies are

I enclose a copy of form HR 1 for your records. The Company proposes to make the following numbers of people redundant in each of the departments as follows:

Department	Redundancies	Current Staffing
[Paint shop]	[13]	[26]
[Buying Dept]	[9]	[9]
[Personnel & Admin.]	[25]	[28]
[Maintenance]	[8]	[14]

The Company proposes to select those employees to be made redundant on the basis of .

The Company anticipates that the redundancies will take effect on 19 . Employees selected for redundancy will be given reasonable paid time off to look for other work [in accordance with statutory provisions].

The Company proposes making statutory redundancy payments [and *ex gratia* redundancy payments calculated on the following formula].

The Company invites you to make any representations you consider appropriate to these proposals. I propose a meeting at am on at this office when you may wish to respond to these proposals. I would be grateful if you could please confirm that this date is convenient or please contact me to arrange another date.

Yours sincerely

[Personnel Director]

Clauses in employment policies and schemes

On p. 76 above, it was explained that, on a business transfer, there may be some residual liability for the vendor in respect of employment benefits, even though an employee's employment has been transferred to the purchaser under the Transfer Regulations. These may arise in connection with pension and stock option schemes. The following is suggested wording to be incorporated into those schemes to limit or exclude such liability for the vendor. It should be noted that some of the wording may have to be adjusted to fit the terminology of the relevant scheme.

Pensions scheme

> "The [Company] shall have no liability to pay any contributions into the pension scheme in respect of any Member, where that Member leaves the [Company's] employment and enters that of another employer by virtue of a 'relevant transfer' under the Transfer of Undertakings (Protection of Employment) Regulations 1981. The Company's obligation to pay contributions or premiums, in such circumstances, shall cease with immediate effect from the moment of such relevant transfer and notwithstanding that the Employee has received no or insufficient notice of dismissal or of such relevant transfer. In such circumstances, the Member shall have no claim or other legal redress against the [Company] or its officers, employees or the trustees of the [Scheme] for damages for wrongful dismissal, breach of contract or otherwise arising out of such cessation of his membership of the [Scheme]."

Stock option schemes

"The [Employee's] right to exercise his [Options] earlier in accordance with paragraph [ ] above shall not apply where his employment has been transferred to another employer by virtue of the Transfer of Undertakings (Protection of Employment) Regulations 1981. In such event all his [Options] not already validly exercised shall automatically lapse with immediate effect from the moment of the 'relevant transfer' under the aforesaid Regulations and he shall have no claim or other legal redress against [the Company] or its officers or employees in respect of such [Options] which have so lapsed."

Bonus/profit-share schemes

"In the event that the Employee's employment with the Company ceases and is transferred to another employer by virtue of a 'relevant transfer' under the Transfer of Undertakings (Protection of Employment) Regulations 1981 (the 'Transfer Regulations'), the Employee's entitlement to receive any benefit or bonus or profit-share or other remuneration under this Scheme shall cease with immediate effect from the moment that the 'relevant transfer' is completed. In such circumstances, the Employee shall:

1. be paid a *pro rata* bonus/profit-share, calculated by the Company's accountants (who shall act as experts and not as arbitrators) who shall assess his entitlement as if he had resigned his employment with the Company part-way through a financial year (in accordance with paragraph 00 of this Scheme); and
2. have no claim or other legal redress against the Company or his new employer (by virtue of the Transfer Regulations), or their officers or employees arising out of the cessation of his entitlement to participate in the Scheme; and
3. not be entitled to require his said new employer to establish an alternative or other bonus or profit-share scheme in lieu of this Scheme, or to maintain this Scheme."

Clauses in licence/concession/franchise agreement

"1. The [Licensee] undertakes that prior to the termination or cessation or surrender of this [Licence], howsoever arising, he will terminate all contracts of employment (as defined by reg. 2(1) Transfer of Undertakings (Protection of Employment) Regulations 1981) of all persons working at the premises subject to the [Licence]. All such terminations of employment, as aforesaid, shall take effect at least 24 hours before the moment of the termination, cessation or surrender of the [Licence] and shall be at the cost of the

[Licensee]. The [Licensee] shall further fully indemnify and hold the [Licensor] wholly harmless from and against all claims, costs, expenses, damages, compensation, fines, penalties, and other liabilities whatsoever arising from or connected with the termination of such contracts of employment referred to in this clause and the termination thereof."

"2. The [Licensor] shall have the right, in its absolute discretion, to waive the [Licensee's] obligations under clause 1 above in whole or in part and, in such event, the [Licensor] shall inform the [Licensee] in writing of the names of those employees of the [Licensee] in respect of whom the [Licensee] shall be so absolved from dismissing in accordance with clause 1 above."

APPENDIX C: STATUTORY TEXTS

The "Business Transfer" directive (No. 77/187)

Article 1

1. This Directive shall apply to the transfer of an undertaking, business or part of a business to another employer as a result of a legal transfer or merger.

2. This Directive shall apply where and in so far as the undertaking, business or part of the business to be transferred is situated within the territorial scope of the Treaty.

3. This Directive shall not apply to sea-going vessels.

Article 2

For the purposes of this Directive:

(*a*) "transferor" means any natural or legal person who, by reason of a transfer within the meaning of Article 1(1), ceases to be the employer in respect of the undertaking, business or part of the business;

(*b*) "transferee" means any natural or legal person who, by reason of a transfer within the meaning of Article 1(1), becomes the employer in respect of the undertaking, business or part of the business;

(*c*) "representatives of the employees" means the representatives of the employees provided for by the laws or practice of the Member States, with the exception of members of administrative, governing or supervisory bodies of companies who represent employees on such bodies in certain Member States.

Article 3

1. The transferor's rights and obligations arising from a contract of employment or from an employment relationship existing on the date of a transfer within the meaning of Article 1(1) shall, by reason of such transfer, be transferred to the transferee.

Member States may provide that, after the date of transfer within the meaning of Article 1(1) and in addition to the transferee, the transferor shall continue to be liable in respect of obligations which arose from a contract of employment or an employment relationship.

2. Following the transfer within the meaning of Article 1(1), the transferee shall continue to observe the terms and conditions agreed in any collective agreement on the same terms

applicable to the transferor under that agreement, until the date of termination or expiry of the collective agreement or the entry into force or application of another collective agreement.

Member States may limit the period for observing such terms and conditions, with the proviso that it shall not be less than one year.

3. Paragraphs 1 and 2 shall not cover employees' rights to old-age, invalidity or survivors' benefits under supplementary company or inter company pension schemes outside the statutory social security schemes in Member States.

Member States shall adopt the measures necessary to protect the interests of employees and of persons no longer employed in the transferor's business at the time of the transfer within the meaning of Article 1(1) in respect of rights conferring on them immediate or prospective entitlement to old-age benefits, including survivors' benefits, under supplementary schemes referred to in the first subparagraph.

Article 4

1. The transfer of an undertaking, business or part of a business shall not in itself constitute grounds for dismissal by the transferor or the transferee. This provision shall not stand in the way of dismissals that may take place for economic, technical or organizational reasons entailing changes in the work force.

Member States may provide that the first subparagraph shall not apply to certain specific categories of employees who are not covered by the laws or practice of the Member States in respect of protection against dismissal.

2. If the contract of employment or the employment relationship is terminated because the transfer within the meaning of Article 1(1) involves a substantial change in working conditions to the detriment of the employee, the employer shall be regarded as having been responsible for termination of the contract of employment or of the employment relationship.

Article 5

1. If the business preserves its autonomy, the status and function, as laid down by the laws, regulations or administrative provisions of the Member States, of the representatives or of the representation of the employees affected by the transfer within the meaning of Article 1(1) shall be preserved.

The first subparagraph shall not apply if, under the laws, regulations, administrative provisions or practice of the Member States, the conditions necessary for the reappointment of the representatives of the employees or for the reconstruction of the representation of the employees are fulfilled.

2. If the term of office of the representatives of the employees affected by a transfer within the meaning of Article 1(1) expires as a result of the transfer, the representatives shall continue to enjoy the protection provided by the laws, regulations, administrative provisions or practice of the Member States.

Article 6

1. The transferor and the transferee shall be required to inform

the representatives of their respective employees affected by a transfer within the meaning of Article 1(1) of the following:

— the reasons for the transfer,
— the legal, economic and social implications of the transfer for the employees,
— measures envisaged in relation to the employees.

The transferor must give such information to the representatives of his employees in good time before the transfer is carried out.

The transferee must give such information to the representatives of his employees in good time, and in any event before his employees are directly affected by the transfer as regards their conditions of work and employment.

2. If the transferor or the transferee envisages measures in relation to his employees, he shall consult his representatives of the employees in good time on such measures with a view to seeking agreement.

3. Member States whose laws, regulations or administrative provisions provide that representatives of the employees may have recourse to an arbitration board to obtain a decision on the measures to be taken in relation to employees may limit the obligations laid down in paragraphs 1 and 2 to cases where the transfer carried out gives rise to a change in the business likely to entail serious disadvantages for a considerable number of the employees.

The information and consultations shall cover at least the measures envisaged in relation to the employees.

The information must be provided and consultations take place in good time before the change in the business as referred to in the first subparagraph is effected.

4. Member States may limit the obligations laid down in paragraphs 1, 2 and 3 to undertakings or businesses which, in respect of the number of employees, fulfil the conditions for the election or designation of a collegiate body representing the employees.

5. Member States may provide that where there are no representatives of the employees in an undertaking or business, the employees concerned must be informed in advance when a transfer within the meaning of Article 1(1) is about to take place.

Article 7

This Directive shall not affect the right of Member States to apply or introduce laws, regulations or administrative provisions which are more favourable to employees.

Article 8

1. Member States shall bring into force the laws, regulations and administrative provisions needed to comply with this Directive within two years of its notification and shall forthwith inform the Commission thereof.

2. Member States shall communicate to the Commission the texts of the laws, regulations and administrative provisions which they adopt in the field covered by this Directive.

Transfer of undertakings (Protection of Employment) Regulations 1981 [S.I. 1981 No. 1794]

Citation, commencement and extent

1.—(1) These Regulations may be cited as the Transfer of Undertakings (Protection of Employment) Regulations 1981.

(2) These Regulations, except Regulations 4 to 9 and 14, shall come into operation on 1st February 1982 and Regulations 4 to 9 and 14 shall come into operation on 1st May 1982.

(3) These Regulations, except Regulations 11(10) and 13(3) and (4), extend to Northern Ireland.

Interpretation

2.—(1) In these Regulations—

"collective agreement," "employers' association," and "trade union" have the same meanings respectively as in the 1974 Act or, in Northern Ireland, the 1976 Order;

"collective bargaining" has the same meaning as it has in the 1975 Act or, in Northern Ireland, the 1976 Order;

"contract of employment" means any agreement between an employee and his employer determining the terms and conditions of his employment;

"employee" means any individual who works for another person whether under a contract of service or apprenticeship or otherwise but does not include anyone who provides services under a contract for services and references to a person's employer shall be construed accordingly;

"the 1974 Act," "the 1975 Act," "the 1978 Act" and "the 1976 Order" mean, respectively, the Trade Union and Labour Relations Act 1974, the Employment Protection Act 1975, the Employment Protection (Consolidation) Act 1978 and the Industrial Relations (Northern Ireland) Order 1976;

"recognised," in relation to a trade union, means recognised to any extent by an employer, or two or more associated employers, (within the meaning of the 1978 Act, or, in Northern Ireland, the 1976 Order), for the purpose of collective bargaining;

"relevant transfer" means a transfer to which these Regulations apply and "transferor" and "transferee" shall be construed accordingly; and

"undertaking" includes any trade or business but does not include any undertaking or part of an undertaking which is not in the nature of a commercial venture.

(2) References in these Regulations to the transfer of part of an undertaking are references to a transfer of a part which is being transferred as a business and, accordingly, do not include references to a transfer of a ship without more.

(3) For the purposes of these Regulations the representative of a trade union recognised by an employer is an official or other person authorised to carry on collective bargaining with that employer by that union.

A relevant transfer

3.—(1) Subject to the provisions of these Regulations, these Regulations apply to a transfer from one person to another of an undertaking situated immediately before the transfer in the United Kingdom or a part of one which is so situated.

(2) Subject as aforesaid, these Regulations so apply whether the transfer is effected by sale or by some other disposition or by operation of law.

(3) Subject as aforesaid, these Regulations so apply notwithstanding—

(*a*) that the transfer is governed or effected by the law of a country or territory outside the United Kingdom;
(*b*) that persons employed in the undertaking or part transferred ordinarily work outside the United Kingdom;
(*c*) that the employment of any of those persons is governed by any such law.

(4) It is hereby declared that a transfer of an undertaking or part of one may be effected by a series of two or more transactions between the same parties, but in determining whether or not such a series constitutes a single transfer regard shall be had to the extent to which the undertaking or part was controlled by the transferor and transferee respectively before the last transaction, to the lapse of time between each of the transactions, to the intention of the parties and to all the other circumstances.

(5) Where, in consequence (whether directly or indirectly) of the transfer of an undertaking or part of one which was situated immediately before the transfer in the United Kingdom, a ship within the meaning of the Merchant Shipping Act 1894 registered in the United Kingdom ceases to be so registered, these Regulations shall not affect the right conferred by section 5 of the Merchant Shipping Act 1970 (right of seamen to be discharged when ship ceases to be registered in the United Kingdom) on a seaman employed in the ship.

Transfers by receivers and liquidators

4.—(1) Where the receiver of the property or part of the property of a company [or the administrator of a company appointed under Part II of the Insolvency Act 1986] or, in the case of a creditors' voluntary winding up, the liquidator of a company transfers the company's undertaking, or part of the company's undertaking (the "relevant undertaking") to a wholly owned subsidiary of the company, the transfer shall for the purposes of these Regulations be deemed not to have been effected until immediately before—

(*a*) the transferee company ceases (otherwise than by reason of its being wound up) to be a wholly owned subsidiary of the transferor company; or
(*b*) the relevant undertaking is transferred by the transferee company to another person;

whichever first occurs, and, for the purpose of these Regulations, the transfer of the relevant undertaking shall be taken to have been effected immediately before that date by one transaction only.

(2) In this Regulation—

"creditors' voluntary winding up" has the same meaning as in the Companies Act 1948 or, in Northern Ireland, the Companies Act (Northern Ireland) 1960; and

"wholly owned subsidiary" has the same meaning as it has for the purposes of section 150 of the Companies Act 1948 and section 144 of the Companies Act (Northern Ireland) 1960.

Effect of relevant transfer on contracts of employment

5.—(1) A relevant transfer shall not operate so as to terminate the contract of employment of any person employed by the transferor in the undertaking or part transferred but any such contract which would otherwise have been terminated by the transfer shall have effect after the transfer as if originally made between the person so employed and the transferee.

(2) Without prejudice to paragraph (1) above, on the completion of a relevant transfer—

(*a*) all the transferor's rights, powers, duties and liabilities under or in connection with any such contract, shall be transferred by virtue of this Regulation to the transferee; and

(*b*) anything done before the transfer is completed by or in relation to the transferor in respect of that contract or a person employed in that undertaking or part shall be deemed to have been done by or in relation to the transferee.

(3) Any reference in paragraph (1) or (2) above to a person employed in an undertaking or part of one transferred by a relevant transfer is a reference to a person so employed immediately before the transfer, including, where the transfer is effected by a series of two or more transactions, a person so employed immediately before any of those transactions.

(4) Paragraph (2) above shall not transfer or otherwise affect the liability of any person to be prosecuted for, convicted of and sentenced for any offence.

(5) Paragraph (1) above is without prejudice to any right of an employee arising apart from these Regulations to terminate his contract of employment without notice if a substantial change is made in his working conditions to his detriment; but no such right shall arise by reason only that, under that paragraph, the identity of his employer changes unless the employee shows that, in all the circumstances, the change is a significant change and is to his detriment.

Effect of relevant transfer on collective agreements

6. Where at the time of a relevant transfer there exists a collective agreement made by or on behalf of the transferor with a trade union recognised by the transferor in respect of any employee whose contract of employment is preserved by Regulation 5(1) above, then—

(*a*) without prejudice to section 18 of the 1974 Act or Article

63 of the 1976 Order (collective agreements presumed to be unenforceable in specified circumstances) that agreement, in its application in relation to the employee, shall, after the transfer, have effect as if made by or on behalf of the transferee with that trade union, and accordingly anything done under or in connection with it, in its application as aforesaid, by or in relation to the transferor before the transfer, shall, after the transfer, be deemed to have been done by or in relation to the transferee; and

(*b*) any order made in respect of that agreement, in its application in relation to the employee, shall, after the transfer, have effect as if the transferee were a party to the agreement.

Exclusion of occupational pensions schemes

7. Regulations 5 and 6 above shall not apply—

(*a*) to so much of a contract of employment or collective agreement as relates to an occupational pension scheme within the meaning of the Social Security Pensions Act 1975 or the Social Security Pensions (Northern Ireland) Order 1975; or

(*b*) to any rights, powers, duties or liabilities under or in connection with any such contract or subsisting by virtue of any such agreement and relating to such a scheme or otherwise arising in connection with that person's employment and relating to such a scheme.

Dismissal of employee because of relevant transfer

8.—(1) Where either before or after a relevant transfer, any employee of the transferor or transferee is dismissed, that employee shall be treated for the purposes of Part V of the 1978 Act and Articles 20 to 41 of the 1976 Order (unfair dismissal) as unfairly dismissed if the transfer or a reason connected with it is the reason or principal reason for his dismissal.

(2) Where an economic, technical or organisational reason entailing changes in the workforce of either the transferor or the transferee before or after a relevant transfer is the reason or principal reason for dismissing an employee—

(*a*) paragraph (1) above shall not apply to his dismissal; but

(*b*) without prejudice to the application of section 57(3) of the 1978 Act or Article 22(10) of the 1976 Order (test of fair dismissal), the dismissal shall for the purposes of section 57(1)(*b*) of that Act and Article 22(1)(*b*) of that Order (substantial reason for dismissal) be regarded as having been for a substantial reason of a kind such as to justify the dismissal of an employee holding the position which that employee held.

(3) The provisions of this Regulation apply whether or not the employee in question is employed in the undertaking or part of the undertaking transferred or to be transferred.

(4) Paragraph (1) above shall not apply in relation to the dismissal of any employee which was required by reason of the

application of section 5 of the Aliens Restriction (Amendment) Act 1919 to his employment.

Effect of relevant transfer on trade union recognition

9.—(1) This Regulation applies where after a relevant transfer the undertaking or part of the undertaking transferred maintains an identity distinct from the remainder of the transferee's undertaking.

(2) Where before such a transfer an independent trade union is recognised to any extent by the transferor in respect of employees of any description who in consequence of the transfer become employees of the transferee, then, after the transfer—

(*a*) the union shall be deemed to have been recognised by the transferee to the same extent in respect of employees of that description so employed; and
(*b*) any agreement for recognition may be varied or rescinded accordingly.

Duty to inform and consult trade union representatives

10.—(1) In this Regulation and Regulation 11 below "an affected employee" means, in relation to a relevant transfer, any employee of the transferor or the transferee (whether or not employed in the undertaking or the part of the undertaking to be transferred) who may be affected by the transfer or may be affected by measures taken in connection with it; and references to the employer shall be construed accordingly.

(2) Long enough before a relevant transfer to enable consultations to take place between the employer of any affected employees of a description in respect of which an independent trade union is recognised by him and that union's representatives, the employer shall inform those representatives of—

(*a*) the fact that the relevant transfer is to take place, when, approximately, it is to take place and the reasons for it; and
(*b*) the legal, economic and social implications of the transfer for the affected employees; and
(*c*) the measures which he envisages he will, in connection with the transfer, take in relation to those employees or, if he envisages that no measures will be so taken, that fact; and
(*d*) if the employer is the transferor, the measures which the transferee envisages he will, in connection with the transfer, take in relation to such of those employees as, by virtue of Regulation 5 above, become employees of the transferee after the transfer or, if he envisages that no measures will be so taken, that fact.

(3) The transferee shall give the transferor such information at such a time as will enable the transferor to perform the duty imposed on him by virtue of paragraph (2)(*d*) above.

(4) The information which is to be given to the representatives of a trade union under this Regulation shall be

delivered to them, or sent by post to an address notified by them to the employer, or sent by post to the union at the address of its head or main office.

(5) Where an employer of any affected employees envisages that he will, in connection with the transfer, be taking measures in relation to any such employees of a description in respect of which an independent trade union is recognised by him, he shall enter into consultations with the representatives of that union.

(6) In the course of those consultations the employer shall—

(*a*) consider any representations made by the trade union representatives; and
(*b*) reply to those representations and, if he rejects any of those representations, state his reasons.

(7) If in any case there are special circumstances which render it not reasonably practicable for an employer to perform a duty imposed on him by any of the foregoing paragraphs, he shall take all steps towards performing that duty as are reasonably practicable in the circumstances.

Failure to inform or consult

11.—(1) A complaint that an employer has failed to inform or consult a representative of a trade union in accordance with Regulation 10 above may be presented to an industrial tribunal by that union.

(2) If on a complaint under paragraph (1) above a question arises whether or not it was reasonably practicable for an employer to perform a particular duty or what steps he took towards performing it, it shall be for him to show—

(*a*) that there were special circumstances which rendered it not reasonably practicable for him to perform the duty; and
(*b*) that he took all such steps towards its performance as were reasonably practicable in those circumstances.

(3) On any such complaint against a transferor that he had failed to perform the duty imposed upon him by virtue of paragraph (2)(*d*) or, so far as relating thereto, paragraph (7) of Regulation 10 above, he may not show that it was not reasonably practicable for him to perform the duty in question for the reason that the transferee had failed to give him the requisite information at the requisite time in accordance with Regulation 10(3) above unless he gives the transferee notice of his intention to show that fact; and the giving of the notice shall make the transferee a party to the proceedings.

(4) Where the tribunal finds a complaint under paragraph (1) above well-founded it shall make a declaration to that effect and may—

(*a*) order the employer to pay appropriate compensation to such descriptions of affected employees as may be specified in the award; or
(*b*) if the complaint is that the transferor did not perform the duty mentioned in paragraph (3) above and the transferor (after giving due notice) shows the facts so mentioned, order the transferee to pay appropriate compensation to

such descriptions of affected employees as may be specified in the award.

(5) An employee may present a complaint to an industrial tribunal on the ground that he is an employee of a description to which an order under paragraph (4) above relates and that the transferor or the transferee has failed, wholly or in part, to pay him compensation in pursuance of the order.

(6) Where the tribunal finds a complaint under paragraph (5) above well-founded it shall order the employer to pay the complainant the amount of compensation which it finds is due to him.

(7) Where an employer, in failing to perform a duty under Regulation 10 above, also fails to comply with the requirements of section 99 of the 1975 Act or Article 49 of the 1976 Order (duty of employer to consult trade union representatives on redundancy)—

(*a*) any compensation awarded to an employee under this Regulation shall go to reduce the amount of remuneration payable to him under a protective award subsequently made under Part IV of that Act or Part IV of that Order and shall also go towards discharging any liability of the employer under, or in respect of a breach of, the contract of employment in respect of a period falling within the protective period under that award; and

(*b*) conversely any remuneration so payable and any payment made to the employee by the employer under, or by way of damages for breach of, that contract in respect of a period falling within the protected period shall go to reduce the amount of any compensation which may be subsequently awarded under this Regulation;

but this paragraph shall be without prejudice to section 102(3) of that Act and Article 52(3) of that Order (avoidance of duplication of contractual payments and remuneration under protective awards).

(8) An industrial tribunal shall not consider a complaint under paragraph (1) or (5) above unless it is presented to the tribunal before the end of the period of three months beginning with—

(*a*) the date on which the relevant transfer is completed, in the case of a complaint under paragraph (1);

(*b*) the date of the tribunal's order under paragraph (4) above, in the case of a complaint under paragraph (5);

or within such further period as the tribunal considers reasonable in a case where it is satisfied that it was not reasonably practicable for the complaint to be presented before the end of the period of three months.

(9) Section 129 of the 1978 Act (complaint to be sole remedy for breach of relevant rights) and section 133 of that Act (functions of conciliation officer) and Articles 58(2) and 62 of the 1976 Order (which make corresponding provision for Northern Ireland) shall apply to the rights conferred by this Regulation and to proceedings under this Regulation as they apply to rights conferred by that Act or that Order and the industrial tribunal proceedings mentioned therein.

(10) An appeal shall lie and shall lie only to the Employment Appeal Tribunal on a question of law arising from any decision of, or arising in any proceedings before, an industrial tribunal under or by virtue of these Regulations; and section 13(1) of the Tribunals and Inquiries Act 1971 (appeal from certain tribunals to the High Court) shall not apply in relation to any such proceedings.

(11) In this Regulation "appropriate compensation" means such sum not exceeding two weeks' pay for the employee in question as the tribunal considers just and equitable having regard to the seriousness of the failure of the employer to comply with his duty.

(12) Schedule 14 to the 1978 Act or, in Northern Ireland, Schedule 2 to the 1976 Order shall apply for calculating the amount of a week's pay for any employee for the purposes of paragraph (11) above; and, for the purposes of that calculation, the calculation date shall be—

(*a*) in the case of an employee who is dismissed by reason of redundancy (within the meaning of section 81 of the 1978 Act or, in Northern Ireland, section 11 of the Contracts of Employment and Redundancy Payments Act (Northern Ireland) 1965) the date which is the calculation date for the purposes of any entitlement of his to a redundancy payment (within the meaning of that section) or which would be that calculation date if he were so entitled;

(*b*) in the case of an employee who is dismissed for any other reason, the effective date of termination (within the meaning of section 55 of the 1978 Act or, in Northern Ireland, Article 21 of the 1976 Order) of his contract of employment;

(*c*) in any other case, the date of the transfer in question.

Restriction on contracting out

12. Any provision of any agreement (whether a contract of employment or not) shall be void in so far as it purports to exclude or limit the operation of Regulation 5, 8 or 10 above or to preclude any person from presenting a complaint to an industrial tribunal under Regulation 11 above.

Exclusion of employment abroad or as dock worker

13.—(1) Regulations 8, 10 and 11 of these Regulations do not apply to employment where under his contract of employment the employee ordinarily works outside the United Kingdom.

(2) For the purposes of this Regulation a person employed to work on board a ship registered in the United Kingdom shall, unless—

(*a*) the employment is wholly outside the United Kingdom, or

(*b*) he is not ordinarily resident in the United Kingdom,

be regarded as a person who under his contract ordinarily works in the United Kingdom.

(3) Nothing in these Regulations applies in relation to any person employed as a registered dock worker unless he is wholly or mainly engaged in work which is not dock work.

(4) Paragraph (3) above shall be construed as if it were contained in section 145 of the 1978 Act.

Section 94 Employment Protection (Consolidation) Act 1978

(1) The provisions of this section shall have effect where—

(*a*) a change occurs (whether by virtue of a sale or other disposition or by operation of law) in the ownership of a business for the purposes of which a person is employed, or of a part of such a business, and

(*b*) in connection with that change the person by whom the employee is employed immediately before the change occurs (in this section referred to as "the previous owner") terminates the employee's contract of employment, whether by notice or without notice.

(2) If, by agreement with the employee, the person who immediately after the change occurs is the owner of the business, or of the part of the business in question, as the case may be (in this section referred to as "the new owner"), renews the employee's contract of employment (with the substitution of the new owner for the previous owner) or re-engages him under a new contract of employment, sections 84 and 90 shall have effect as if the renewal or re-engagement has been a renewal or re-engagement by the previous owner (without any substitution of the new owner for the previous owner).

(3) If the new owner offers to renew the employee's contract of employment (with the substitution of the new owner for the previous owner) or to re-engage him under a new contract of employment, subsections (3) to (6) of section 82 shall have effect, subject to subsection (4), in relation to that offer as they would have had effect in relation to the like offer made by the previous owner.

(4) For the purposes of the operation, in accordance with subsection (3), of subsections (3) to (6) of section 82 in relation to an offer made by the new owner—

(*a*) the offer shall not be treated as one whereby the provisions of the contract as renewed, or of the new contract, as the case may be, would differ from the corresponding provisions of the contract as in force immediately before the dismissal by reason only that the new owner would be substituted for the previous owner as the employer, and

(*b*) no account shall be taken of that substitution in determining whether the refusal of the offer was unreasonable or, as the case may be, whether the employee acted reasonably in terminating the renewed, or new, employment during the trial period referred to in section 84.

(5) The preceding provisions of this section shall have effect (subject to the necessary modifications) in relation to a case where—

(*a*) the person by whom a business, or part of a business, is owned immediately before a change is one of the persons by whom (whether as partners, trustees or otherwise) it is owned immediately after the change, or (*b*) the person by whom a business, or part of a business, is owned immediately before a change (whether as partners, trustees or otherwise) include the person by whom, or include one or more of the persons by whom, it is owned immediately after the change,

as those provisions have effect where the previous owner and the new owner are wholly different persons.

(6) Sections 82(7) and 84(7) shall not apply in any case to which this section applies.

(7) Nothing in this section shall be construed as requiring any variation of a contract of employment by agreement between the parties to be treated as constituting a termination of the contract.

Paragraphs 17 & 18 Schedule 13 Employment Protection (Consolidation) Act 1978

17.—(1) Subject to this paragraph and [paragraphs 18 and 18A], the foregoing provisions of this Schedule relate only to employment by the one employer.

(2) If a trade or business or an undertaking (whether or not it be an undertaking established by or under an Act of Parliament) is transferred from one person to another, the period of employment of an employee in the trade or business or undertaking at the time of the transfer shall count as a period of employment with the transferee, and the transfer shall not break the continuity of the period of employment.

(3) If by or under an Act of Parliament, whether public or local and whether passed before or after this Act, a contract of employment between any body corporate and an employee is modified and some other body corporate is substituted as the employer, the employee's period of employment at the time when the modification takes effect shall count as a period of employment with the second-mentioned body corporate, and the change of employer shall not break the continuity of the period of employment.

(4) If on the death of an employer the employee is taken into the employment of the personal representatives or trustees of the deceased, the employee's period of employment at the time of the death shall count as a period of employment with the employer's personal representatives or trustees, and the death shall not break the continuity of the period of employment.

(5) If there is a change in the partners, personal representatives or trustees who employ any person, the employee's period of employment at the time of the change shall count as a period of employment with the partners, personal representatives or trustees after the change, and the change shall not break the continuity of the period of employment.

18. If an employee of an employer is taken into the employment of another employer who, at the time when the employee enters his employment is an associated employer of the first-mentioned employer, the employee's period of employment

at that time shall count as a period of employment with the second-mentioned employer and the change of employer shall not break the continuity of the period of employment.

Section 45(1) Employment Protection (Consolidation) Act 1978

(1) The right to work of an employee who has been absent from work wholly or partly because of pregnancy or confinement is, subject to the following provisions of this Act, a right to return to work with her original employer, or, where appropriate, his successor, at any time before the end of the period of twenty-nine weeks beginning with the week in which the date of confinement falls, in the job in which she was employed under the original contract of employment and on terms and conditions not less favourable than those which would have been applicable to her if she had not been so absent.

Section 30(3) and (4) Trade Union and Labour Relations Act 1974

(3) Subject to subsection (4) below, in this Act "successor," in relation to the employer of an employee, means a person who, in consequence of a change occurring (whether by virtue of a sale or other disposition or by operation of law) in the ownership of the undertaking or of part of the undertaking for the purposes of which the employee was employed, has become the owner of that undertaking or of that part of it, as the case may be.
(4) Subsection (3) above shall have effect (subject to the necessary modifications) in relation to a case where—

(*a*) the person by whom an undertaking or part of an undertaking is owned immediately before a change is one of the persons by whom (whether as partners, trustees or otherwise) it is owned immediately after the change, or
(*b*) the persons by whom an undertaking or part of an undertaking is owned immediately before a change (whether as partners, trustees or otherwise) include the persons by whom, or include one or more of the persons by whom, it is owned immediately after the change,

as that subsection has effect where the previous owner and the new owner are wholly different persons; and any reference in this Act to a successor of an employer shall be construed accordingly.

Index